300 Missions
Over Vietnam

300 Missions Over Vietnam

An F-100 Pilot's Account with Letters Home

STEWART CRANSTON

VOICES IN AMERICAN MILITARY AVIATION

McFarland & Company, Inc., Publishers
Jefferson, North Carolina

ISBN (print) 978-1-4766-9777-2
ISBN (ebook) 978-1-4766-5592-5

Library of Congress cataloging data are available

Library of Congress Control Number 2025027543

© 2025 Stewart Cranston. All rights reserved

No part of this book may be reproduced or transmitted in any form or by any means, electronic or mechanical, including photocopying or recording, or by any information storage and retrieval system, without permission in writing from the publisher.

Front cover image: author by his F-100D, suited up, ready to climb into the cockpit (author's collection).

Printed in the United States of America

*McFarland & Company, Inc., Publishers
Box 611, Jefferson, North Carolina 28640
www.mcfarlandpub.com*

To all those left at Home in a time of war
who sustain the connection to the Real World
and, all too often, must bear the loss.

Acknowledgments

I would like to thank Margaret Cranston for her invaluable help in completing this project. She is my collaborator and chief critic. She has an incredible eye for detail coupled with a mastery of syntax, grammar and punctuation. She was relentless in searching out errors, large and small, in my manuscript. She is a talented artist in a number of mediums and lent an artist's touch to my visuals. And she is an accomplished writer in her own right, having just published her second book, *Home in All Seasons*.

I'd also like to thank Dr. David Vaughan, the senior editor for McFarland's Voices in American Military Aviation series, for his help and encouragement with this project. From the moment I contacted him about the book idea, he was enthusiastic and encouraging. He was a patient critic in straightening out my introductory material and in correcting spelling of Vietnamese place names. In all of this he gently pushed me forward with the project.

Table of Contents

Acknowledgments	vi
Preface	1
Introduction	5
One—Beginning	9
Two—Troops in Contact	36
Three—Settling In	43
Four—Bullpup Training	50
Five—Attacked	60
Six—Just a Routine Combat Sky Spot Mission	84
Seven—Bombing Halt (or "Who the hell is Richard?")	95
Eight—Anticipation	120
Nine—Hawaii	128
Ten—Battle Damage	132
Eleven—Ho Chi Minh Trail	141
Twelve—Times Are Changing	152
Thirteen—Loss	161
Fourteen—Looking Ahead (or Slipping Away?)	165
Fifteen—George	175
Sixteen—Fini and Home	188
Epilogue	197
Military History of Stewart E. Cranston	199
Bibliography	203
Index	205

Map of South East Asia showing the location of Tuy Hoa, as well as other principal air bases in South Vietnam (Air Force Office of History).

Preface

In the fall of 2022, I came across a packet of letters in an old trunk that I had stored away many years ago. The letters, 130 of them, were my correspondence with people back home while I was stationed in Vietnam as an F-100 pilot in 1968/69.

In April 2024, I became aware of McFarland's series, Voices in American Military Aviation. The letters I hold provide a contemporary record of the life of a young fighter pilot in the peak year of the Vietnam War, and I believed they would contribute a unique aspect to McFarland's series. They contain an authentic view of the life and experiences of a single pilot in a year of near daily combat flying in Vietnam. In general, the letters contain vivid descriptions of combat operations including briefings and flight protocols as well as descriptions of targets, tactics, weather, and terrain. They tell of the lifestyles and dangers faced by pilots in that conflict; and they speak richly of the beauty and fury of Nature in that distant land.

Importantly, the letters reveal that war is a human endeavor. It is more than just troop formations, maneuvers, equipment and combat actions. It is a realm of intense human response, of exhilaration and despair; of barely contained excitement, and deep melancholy. I believe this aspect remains relevant today and is important to understanding military combat aviation from the human perspective.

The letters also provide insight into the frustration of our troops in not being able to communicate in a timely manner with friends and family back home. Letters were the only way of communicating in those days and mail service was erratic at best—there was no option to call home from Vietnam. Warfighters could not find reassurance from their loved ones in the event of the loss of a friend or a particularly harrowing experience. The delayed communication could have a significant impact on moods and morale. At the least, it heightened the sense of being alone at times of great stress. While today's military members may be more readily connected to home, it is important to recognize that they are still alone at critical times. They are still left to cope on their own with their uncertain future. These human responses are still relevant today. The letters tell that human story.

This book is built on the 75 letters for which I am the original author. In addition, excerpts from the 55 letters written by my principal correspondent, Jean Tuomy, are included where needed to understand the context of my letters to her. The letters are presented in chronological order. As I explored this concept for this book, I realized that the letters, by themselves, did not tell the full story for modern readers. Letters, by their very nature, have a limited focus. Accordingly, I have written supplementary commentaries interspersed with the letters to provide additional background information.

In developing this book, I have relied on the letters and my memory. Except for verifying dates of external events and specific facts, I have avoided further confirmation in other works. There are many books on Vietnam that provide such information. I believe it is important that the letters be left to speak for themselves without further elaboration. Similarly, my comments on the state of the war are my interpretation alone based on my experiences. Within their narrow scope, the letters are historically accurate and, in that respect, they provide a unique first-person view of those times. I believe future researchers may benefit from the contemporary view provided by the letters.

❖ ❖ ❖

Note that much of the personal information has been edited out of the letters to focus on the war-related aspects. These deletions are indicated by ellipses. In addition, I have added comments to explain terms and technical details not familiar to modern readers. These comments are italicized and set off by brackets. All misspellings, minor grammar and typographical errors in the letters have been silently corrected.

Jean Tuomy's authorship is cited in introductory notes to her text. The material written by her is italicized. The introductory notes are prefaced by the word "Note" followed by a colon.

A final note: In 2023 I transcribed the letters, including those of my principal correspondent, Jean Tuomy, and compiled them into a book titled *Is Love Enough? Letters from Vietnam*. That book was published through Amazon KDP in June 2023 to preserve the letters for personal use. (*Is Love Enough?* is no longer in print.) In this book, *300 Missions Over Vietnam. A Pilot's Account with Letters Home*, the narratives in

Chapter Nine and Chapter Sixteen and some of the commentaries are adapted from *Is Love Enough? Letters from Vietnam*, as are the excerpts from Jean Tuomy's letters. Her authorship is clearly identified in the text of this book as noted above.

Also note the story in Chapter Six, "Just a Routine Combat Sky Spot Mission," was previously published in the *Friends Journal* of the Air Force Museum Foundation, Fall 2022, Vol 45, No. 4, page 10–16, 39.

—SEC

Introduction

The Vietnam War was born in the turmoil of the aftermath of World War II. Part of that turmoil involved the breakup of long-standing European colonial empires. French Indo China was one of those empires. In 1954, an international treaty, the Geneva Accord, created two countries out of the ashes of French Indo China in traditional Vietnam: the Democratic Republic of Vietnam, or North Vietnam, in the northern part; and the Republic of South Vietnam, or simply South Vietnam, in the southern part. The line between the two countries was set at the 17th parallel. The Communist Party under Ho Chi Minh claimed control of North Vietnam while the government of South Vietnam was democratically elected. The Geneva Accord envisioned that the two Vietnams would ultimately be united through a democratic election process. North Vietnam, however, was determined to unite the countries under a communist government. To this end, it continued its support of an indigenous communist insurgency in South Vietnam. As an ally of South Vietnam, the United States provided support against this insurgency through advisers and surplus military equipment.

The conflict between North and South Vietnam continued in this state until an incident involving warships of the United States and patrol boats of North Vietnam occurred in the neighboring waters of the Gulf of Tonkin in August 1964. This was the catalyst for a significant buildup of regular military forces of the United States that would peak in early 1969 at over 500,000 personnel. This book is about the experiences of an F-100 pilot in a part of that war during the period from May 1968 to May 1969.

Tet is an important religious holiday in the Vietnamese culture. During Tet 1968 the insurgents in South Vietnam, the Viet Cong, launched a major offensive across the breadth and depth of the country. This was a crucial turning point in the war. While Tet '68 was a tactical shock to the U.S. forces in-country, it was a strategic failure for the South Vietnamese communist insurgents. Gone was their hope of a popular, unstoppable uprising of the people across the breadth of the country that would sweep away the American intruders. Pockets of the Tet offensive gains, such as in the Hue Citadel, would hold out into the early spring, but the VC would no longer play the lead role in the major combat operations in South Vietnam. Instead, the North Vietnamese Army, or NVA as they were known to U.S. forces, would become the main opposition force for the conflict in the South.

While the NVA would be directed and supplied by the North, they did not operate as a typical invading army, at least not yet. Instead they depended on small unit actions—up to regimental size—operating from sanctuaries within South Vietnam and in the adjacent countries of Cambodia and Laos. There were no decisive battles to be fought by the technically superior American and South Vietnamese forces. Rather, it was a shadow war across the entire breadth of the country. The dense jungle that covered much of South Vietnam helped conceal movements of the NVA/VC forces.

The U.S. air forces, honed in the large unit conflicts of World War II and Korea, were left to adapt to this small unit, running gun battle. Direct support of U.S. forces in contact with the NVA/VC was an important aspect of the air war, to be sure, but much of the air effort was directed at searching out and destroying hidden pockets of NVA supplies within the South and interdicting the flow of these supplies coming down the infamous Ho Chi Minh Trail in Laos.

※ ※ ※

This was my war. I was a young F-100 pilot, fresh from nearly two years of training in the United States. The cockpit of the F-100D, *Jeannie*, was my office. The North American F-100 was designed as an air superiority fighter to replace the F-86 of the Korean War era. But as the threat of war with the Soviet Union emerged in the 1950s, the F-100 was adapted to the fighter-bomber role with the capability to carry nuclear weapons as well as the full range of conventional air-delivered weapons. It was in this role that the F-100 was deployed to Southeast Asia as the Vietnam War heated up following the Gulf of Tonkin incident. The F-100 would come to bear the brunt of tactical air support in South Vietnam.

I was assigned to the 31st Tactical Fighter Wing (TFW), Tuy Hoa Air Base, Republic of South Vietnam. Four wings of F-100s were deployed to South Vietnam between 1964 and 1966. The 308th Tactical Fighter Squadron, a unit of the 31st TFW, was first deployed to an existing base, Bien Hoa, just north of Saigon in December 1965. The 31st

Introduction

My F-100D loaded for combat with 4 Mk 82 500 lb. bombs. My helmet and parachute are at the base of the ladder, waiting to be placed in the cockpit (author's collection).

Wing, now joined by its remaining two squadrons, the 306th and the 309th, redeployed from Bien Hoa to Tuy Hoa in December 1966. Later, in June 1968, two Air National Guard (ANG) squadrons were activated and deployed to join the 31st TFW at Tuy Hoa. These were the 136th TFS, New York ANG, Buffalo, New York, and the 188th TFS, New Mexico ANG, Albuquerque, New Mexico. These two ANG units would return to the United States in June 1969.*

Bien Hoa would remain an active F-100 base until 1971. The bases to house and support the other three wings were carved out of rural land in the country side. This was the case for Tuy Hoa Air Base. It was built on a remote river delta populated only by a small fishing village. To its east lay the South China Sea; to the north and west, there was hilly terrain covered by dense foliage. To the south about 20 miles, a rocky mountain rose abruptly to several thousand feet. Located mid-way between the border with North Vietnam and the vast stretches of the Mekong River delta, Tuy Hoa was ideally situated to prosecute the war across the entire country of South Vietnam.

Tuy Hoa would be my home from May 1968 to May 1969. During that year, I flew 300 combat missions comprising 514 combat hours. These missions and other experiences, addressed in the following pages, are recorded in 72 of the original letters which I wrote. Fifty-nine of my letters were to my girlfriend, Jean Tuomy; thirteen of the letters were to my parents. (The three letters not included are redundant.) My story is

---

*F-100 Super Sabre Units of the Vietnam War.

told through these letters, supplemented by excerpts from Jean's letters to me.

I met Jean at a party in July 1966. She had completed her freshman year at Mount St. Mary's College and I had graduated in June from the University of Southern California. We were immediately attracted to each other. We dated through the summer. But then I left California to begin Air Force pilot training in Laredo, Texas, 1,500 miles away. We kept in touch through letters and my trip home at Christmas. In September 1967, I was transferred to F-100 training at Luke Air Force Base, Phoenix, Arizona. There we were much closer to each other, and during this interlude, we dated at every opportunity when I could be home. Our relationship became very close during this time.

Then I was off to Vietnam. Jean would be my primary connection to the real world for that coming year. She and I exchanged more than 114 letters during that 12 months. In a sense, my year in Vietnam revolved around my two *Jeannies*—my F-100 in Vietnam and my girl back home. "Could I keep them both through this uncertain year? Will I expose the one to too much danger or the other to too little understanding? Will I lose one—or the other?" As the letters reveal, there would be moments of doubt on both counts. The following pages tell that story—the tale of a young F-100 fighter pilot in the depths of the Vietnam War in the late 1960s.

One

Beginning

May 8, 1968. Los Angeles International Airport. I said goodbye to my mother and father, kissed Jean one last time and boarded a plane for San Francisco, en route to Travis AFB [*Air Force Base*] and the War.

As I settled back on the short flight to San Francisco, I reflected on the two years of intensive training that had gotten me to this point. First came Air Force Undergraduate Pilot Training (UPT) at Laredo AFB, Texas. I already had my private pilot's license, but UPT was a challenge. It started with a brief period in the T-41, a military version of the Cessna 172, where basic aptitude for flying was evaluated. Then on to the first jet trainer, the T-37, a fully aerobatic airplane where the full range of piloting skills were taught—instruments, aerobatics, formation, flight planning and navigation. Flying in this phase was paced with academics that covered the practical knowledge behind the flight skills. Next came the T-38, a supersonic airplane with flight characteristics similar to operational fighter aircraft. In this phase, I watched as classmates "washed out" of pilot training because they couldn't adapt to the demanding handling qualities of the T-38. In this phase, class standing became all important because your follow-on aircraft depended on your class standing. I wanted to be an F-100 fighter pilot, so my class standing had to be high. Fortunately, it was.

Next came six months of training in the F-100 in Phoenix, Arizona, to learn the operational skills required of a fighter pilot, including aerial combat, air-to-ground weapons delivery and low-level navigation. This phase was demanding, but fun—little chance of "washing out." That would come in Vietnam for one of my classmates—in a fatal way.

Finally, there were the survival schools, land and POW [*Prisoner of War*] survival training in the mountains of eastern Washington, and sea survival in Miami, Florida. In land survival we were introduced to the torture techniques of the North Vietnamese.

As we landed in San Francisco, I came out of my reverie. Sara picked me up at the airport. She was a friend from college in a master's program at Stanford; had been my colleague and supporter in the ROTC program at Southern Cal. I was the Cadet Corps Commander of the ROTC unit my last semester in 1966; Sara was a member of Angel Flight, the women's auxiliary that supported the all-male cadet corps. She was pretty and outgoing, and we had kept in touch with each other through occasional letters during my two years of training. It was not romance with Sara—just a close, caring friendship.

Sara and I did San Francisco that afternoon—rode the cable cars, climbed Telegraph Hill, visited Coit Tower, had cocktails at the top of the Fairmont, dinner at Fisherman's Wharf. Late in the evening, we headed for Travis. On the way, Sara said, "I'll be going back to Manila as soon as school is out. I'll spend the summer there with my parents as I usually do. I hope you can meet me there sometime this summer."

Her father was an executive in a Philippine company. They lived in a gated community in Manila, had been there for a number of years.

I squeezed her hand, "I don't know, Sara, I have no idea whether they let the inmates out once they have you in-country. I'll write and let you know."

"Well, just in case, here's my parents' phone number and address in Manila," Sara replied.

"Thanks, Sara, I'll try. It would be wonderful to see you."

At Travis, we hugged, said I'll see you, good luck at school, take care of yourself. Neither one of us knew what lay ahead.

I turned and walked into the Travis terminal, into my new life.

✢ ✢ ✢

May 20, 1968

My Darling Jean,

Here I am—finally arrived in the combat zone after nearly two weeks, no, nearly two years, of anticipation. I got into Tuy Hoa yesterday about 1:00 o'clock and while they didn't hand me an M-16 when I got off the plane, they did issue us flak vests and steel helmets today to underscore the fact that there is a war going on.

Let me start from the beginning and relate to you my adventures enroute to the Orient. It started on an unhappy note when I had to take that last long, fond look at you and bid you goodbye. That was one of the saddest moments of my life. I got to Travis without incident Wednesday night and our aircraft left on schedule bright and early Thursday morning. It was a chartered flight from TIA ("Travel in Agony") and had to be one of the most miserable flights of my life. It took five hours to get to Honolulu where we stopped for 1½ hours and just enough time for a drink. From there we took eight hours to get to Guam with another 1½-hour layover. And finally, it took another four hours to get to Clark Air Base in the Philippines. On that leg we crossed the International Dateline of course, so we got to Clark on Friday afternoon.

The Philippines contain that strange tropical admixture of the white man's affluence and the native squalor. For the white man living is languid, easy and luxuriant (to a point). The average Filipino lives in squalor beyond belief. We had two days to while away prior to starting jungle survival training on Monday. Friday and a good bit of Saturday I simply slept, having been exhausted by the long trip and the hot climate. I discovered an old friend from pilot training stationed at Clark and I spent much of the weekend with him.

On Monday we began jungle survival school with a day long series of lectures of the usual variety. They tell you how to get blood from a turnip, how to do open heart surgery on yourself and how to swing through the trees in order to evade the enemy. These lectures tend to lose contact with reality.

On Tuesday they loaded us into trucks for our three-day Boy Scout camp—nature hike adventure. This was interesting and afforded me with an opportunity to see a unique part of the Philippines. An hour and a half truck ride took us to the veritable edge of the civilized world (and that edge wasn't very civilized). From there a seven-minute helicopter ride (that saved six and a half hours of walking) placed us in the middle of a jungle clearing from which we began to hike halfway up a mountain to our base camp. It was somewhat like you might imagine except that we didn't have to cut our way through the jungle—paths had long since been made by previous survival school classes. The only indigenous people to the area are Negritos, an aboriginal race that feature loincloths and bows and arrows as their chief clothing. The area is also quite mountainous, much more so than one commonly conceives of the jungle.

At the base camp we built the usual parachute shelters (these actually worked, oddly enough) and learned the usual assortment of woodlore. We had a Negrito guide with us who was exceptionally adept at living in this environment, and much of what he had to show us was fascinating as well as informative. For instance, our entire source of water for two days was a water tree which is tapped, and which provided an overabundance of water for 12 people. As usual, food was at a premium during this time and we ate such things as mangos, papaya, wild bananas, heart of palm, etc. Actually, those two days were kind of a restful stay in the woods.

On the third day we proceeded by foot and helicopter back to the truck area where we played with helicopter pickups and rescue radios. About two in the afternoon, we began our little game of hide and go seek which comprised the final portion of our training. In this exercise we were given four hours to escape into a designated area and hide. At six in the evening, a band of Negrito warriors were dispatched to find us. They were given a pound of rice for every escapee they found. The game went on all night until we, the students, were rescued by helicopter about seven in the morning. It was all somewhat akin to hiding in someone's backyard with the kids of the house watching your every move, so undetected escape was nearly impossible. I only got caught once, which wasn't too bad. About all I learned was that if you hide in the brush in a jungle, you will be devoured by ants, mosquitoes, and rats; that if it rains (it did for four hours) you will get wet—but by damn you can survive. I did live through it all with nothing worse than a massive cold.

Saturday, I began trying to find a flight into Tuy Hoa. Jack and I were lucky enough to find a C-130 rescue bird coming directly into here and thus avoiding Tan Son Nhut in the Saigon area. Unfortunately, our 130 aborted on Saturday, but we were able to get out of Clark on Sunday. I understand Saigon is a real mess to get through because of the mass exchange of people coming in and out. And besides the VC are shooting at people down there.

The base isn't bad at all for either facilities or security. They have never been attacked except for a few harmless mortars a couple of weeks ago. The base is protected by Republic of Korea troops, and they are pretty tough. The VC doesn't mess with them very much. The facilities on the base are primitive but adequate. My quarters consist of a trailer like building which I share with two other guys. It is small but fully air conditioned—which is a real blessing in this climate. The beach is about 150 yards away and the officers' club bar about the same, so I'm in good shape.

May 21

The war started for me here about 9:00 last night and I had to go watch a bit. All it amounted to was some distant artillery fire—all outgoing, fortunately. I don't even know what they were shelling.

I think that I have just about completed my narrative of a journey to Vietnam. Since I got here on Sunday, I have done little except go through the standard procedures of checking into the base. Today we were engaged in various intelligence and weapons briefings, and I finally got all of my flying gear in order. I have my first mission early tomorrow morning, so I should find out what it's all about then. Actually, I will just be riding in the back seat with a highly experienced pilot to see how a mission goes. They have a pretty extensive checkout program here.

I have been carefully avoiding the subject of telling you how much I miss you.... I can only hope that we will not be strangers to each other when we meet again at the end of this year.

I hope that you were able to make up the damage I did to your academic pursuits. Say hello to your parents when you see them.

Be good now—

Love, Stu

✤ ✤ ✤

Checking In

Tuy Hoa Air Base
Republic of South Vietnam
May 1968

Young Sports: A group of fifteen of us young pilots arrived at Tuy Hoa over several days in mid–May, straight from our two year "pipeline" training courses. We were all 1st Lieutenants and we were immediately dubbed the "Young Sports." Previous and current F-100 pilots in the Wing had extensive experience in the F-100, typically over 1,000 hours in Europe. We, the young sports, had accumulated just 120 hours in F-100 upgrade training at Luke or Cannon [*Air Force bases*]. As with most rookies in any endeavor, we were subjected to a certain amount of good-natured ribbing. But there was a war to be fought and we were thrown into the mix without further ado. There were checkout flights, of course, and some prudent supervision—that was just the Air Force's way. Soon we would prove our mettle on combat missions. By late fall, we were leading flights and giving introductory briefings to senior captains and majors just arriving at Tuy Hoa. We were still "young sports," but we had earned our place in the squadrons.

Hooches: The pilot quarters at Tuy Hoa consisted of small transportable units much like a recreational vehicle without wheels. They were about 8 × 24 feet, separated into two living/sleeping areas and a central bathroom. Approximately 10 of these units were clustered on a central concrete pad for each squadron for a total of about 30 "trailers," as they were known. This was adequate to house the aircrews of the three fighter squadrons of the 31st Tactical Fighter Wing when it redeployed from Bien Hoa to Tuy Hoa in 1966. Each cluster of trailers housed approximately 24 pilots.

Urban legend had it that the trailers originally housed the management and engineering personnel of the company that constructed Tuy Hoa Air Base. Their contract allegedly called for removal of the trailers when the construction of the base was completed. However, the arriving pilots of the Wing quickly saw the advantages of these air conditioned, sound proof trailers. It wasn't hard to see the utility of them as quarters for combat aircrew with their requirement for 24-hour operations in the hot, humid climate of South Vietnam. The arriving pilots prevailed on the construction contractor (at gun point, it was said) to leave the "trailers," and one of them became my home for the year.

Junior pilots were assigned two to a living/sleeping area. There was a double bunk bed on one side of the approximately 8 × 10 foot area, with lockers on either end. A small desk was on the opposite side with two small chairs. The center area of the trailer had a shower, toilet and sink. Field grade officers had their own, single end of a trailer.

Although small, the trailers were perfect for squadron pilots—they were air conditioned and soundproofed, and previous tenants had long since covered the small windows with foil so outside light was totally eliminated—no problem sleeping when coming off a 12-hour night alert shift. I had the upper bunk on my side, and I well remember coming off of several successive days on night alert and sleeping for 12 hours without interruption.

Each 10-trailer cluster was identified with a particular squadron. I was assigned to the 308th Tactical Fighter Squadron, nicknamed the "Emerald Knights," radio call sign, "Saber."

Each of the three

Image 308th Tactical Fighter Squadron emblem. The 308th were known as the "Emerald Knights," call sign "Saber" (author's collection).

active squadrons had converted the area immediately in front of their trailers into a patio area with tables, various types of lounging chairs, and a bar (of sorts). The squadrons also had "make do" work-out equipment (e.g., concrete barbells and a chin up bar). These common areas were a primary gathering place for off duty pilots. All meals were taken in a common Wing Officer's Mess [*Dining Hall*].

Personal Flight Equipment: A critical part of checking in was gathering all the personal gear necessary for flying the F-100 in combat. Some of it had been brought with me while most was issued by the squadron. Our basic uniform was a cotton flight suit [*coveralls*] worn over cotton underwear. Fire retardant material, while commonly used in many automobile racing circuits at the time, was not introduced into Air Force flight gear until the mid–'70s.

The flight suit had only a name tape and rank insignia in black lettering; all unit identifying badges and patches were removed. Footgear consisted of "jungle boots," a combat style boot that had a hard rubber sole with heavy canvas uppers. Unique to these boots was a steel plate in the sole intended to deflect "punji sticks," sharpened bamboo sticks put in on trails by the VC, sharp end up, to wound foot traffic.

Over the flight suit was an anti–G suit (called simply a "G-suit") and a survival vest. "G's" refers to the apparent force of gravity caused by the turning of an aircraft. The G-suit consisted of a broad waist band covering the lower abdomen, and leggings. Both the waist band and the leggings could be adjusted to an individual pilot by lacings. The waist band and the thigh leggings contained rubber bladders that inflated under G loading to help the pilot resist G forces. The bladders were inflated by air bled from the engine compressor through a short flexible tube that attached to the G suit. Part of preflight included attaching that hose to the aircraft. I carried a water bottle in a lower leg pocket of the G suit.

The survival vest was a mesh vest with pockets for various survival items including first aid supplies, condensed rations, flares (illumination/colored smoke), a knife and a survival radio. The radio was by far the most important survival item. It was a hand-held FM radio used to communicate with search and rescue forces. It was critical to the recovery of hundreds of downed airmen throughout the South East Asia combat zone.

The vest also contained a tree lowering device developed specifically for the triple canopy trees that made up the jungle that covered much of South Vietnam. In the unfortunate event you had to eject over this jungle, the parachute would likely get entangled high up in these trees, 200 feet or so above the ground. The tree lowering device would get you down safely it was said. I never heard of anyone who tried it.

The next piece of personal gear was the flight helmet and oxygen mask. The helmet was a white plastic shell with internal webbings that semi-custom fit the helmet to a specific individual. The helmet was white, per Air Force regulation, to ward off cosmic radiation at high altitude. It would be the mid–'70s before a more suitable olive drab or gray helmet was permitted. The helmet contained ear phones, and an oxygen mask connected to it with quick release clips and a communications (comm) cord. The oxygen mask was a plastic and rubber mask covering the nose and mouth. The mask contained a microphone for the aircraft mounted radio. A breathing tube and comm cord connected the mask to the aircraft. Supplemental oxygen was fed to the mask automatically when the aircraft was above 10,000 feet. Contrary to the movies, the mask was almost never unclipped in flight, primarily because it was the means of communicating. And yes, it was hot in the tropics at low level.

The final piece of personal equipment was the personal weapon, the Colt Combat Masterpiece, a .38 caliber pistol. It was heavy but reliable. I carried mine in a holster and gun belt complete with spare ammunition a la Wyatt Earp. In the cockpit, the gun rested along my right thigh. I qualified with the pistol in training, but I never heard of anyone, including myself, that actually fired it in combat.

The personal flight gear was rounded out by gloves. These were close fitting fine leather gloves. They were great gloves, flexible enough for delicate controls, yet protective.

In the F-100, the parachute was carried to the aircraft for each flight. It was a back style parachute with a standard harness assembly that was fitted to the individual pilot. Thus fitted, that parachute became essentially "his" parachute. The parachute assembly included an oxygen canister connected to the oxygen mask through a separate quick disconnect fitting. This canister was intended to provide oxygen to the pilot in case of high-altitude bailout.

※ ※ ※

May 28, 1968

My Darling,

My first week of war has slipped quietly by with no mishaps. I have been flying combat missions daily and have yet to see any ground fire. In fact, most of the time we merely seem to be bombing trees.

Sunday, I got back in the D model (the single seat F-100) for the first time. It really felt good to be in an airplane that was all mine again. That mission took us down to the Saigon area where we had hit some suspected bunkers just north of Bien Hoa. There were little puffy clouds all over the place to make it interesting. It was very difficult to keep the FAC (Forward Air Controller) or the target in sight, and all of our bomb deliveries required diving through the cloud layer on the final run in. The trip down and back was really beautiful. Part of the time we were skimming through the tops of clouds. To the West near the Cambodian border there were huge thunderstorm buildups that towered above us and looked very dark and foreboding. (By the way when I say "we," I'm referring to the flight. All of our missions are flown in two or three ship flights for mutual support and protection.)

Yesterday, I had the dawn patrol which seems to be my fate. On that one we literally hit a clump of trees about eight miles northwest of Phu Cat, one of the new F-100 bases, about 80 miles north of Tuy Hoa. The FAC in that area was trying to uncover some VC activity, I guess.

Just got word that I have to brief for a mission in about half an hour. Guess I'll have to finish this later.

Later—

That turned out to be an unusually good mission. First, we hit a bunker area west of Saigon about 10 miles from the Cambodian border. We managed to knock several of those out with our bombs. Then we picked up a strafe target about two miles due north of Tan Son Nhut, Saigon's civilian airport. Friendly troops along the east bank of a canal were receiving automatic weapons fire from some bad guys on the west bank. The friendlies had some wounded they were trying to get out and we were asked to strafe the bad guys and suppress their fire. This required us to fire within 50 yards of the friendlies which is getting pretty close. (Note: Normal Rules of Engagement prohibited air strikes within 100 meters of friendly forces. In this case, the ground commander said if you don't get the VC, they're going to get us, so go ahead.) Everyone in the flight had really good passes and we hope that we helped our troops out. We don't often get a mission with troops in contact with the enemy and it does make you feel good to help the guys on the ground out. By the time we had fired out, we were getting low on fuel and had 200 miles to go to get home, so we didn't get to see much results from our handiwork.

You will be pleased to know that this is a very sterile environment here. It is a seven day a week war and most of those days are long. The base is completely devoid of women and Tuy Hoa city is only on limits from one to four in the afternoon. The base itself is very secure but there is continual shelling and light enemy contact in the surrounding area. Occasionally we have a fighter mission put in just outside the perimeter fence.

Other than flying, I can't say that I am doing very much except missing you.... It occurs to me that this is going to be a cruelly long year. Have fun—but be good.

Love, Stu

✢ ✢ ✢

June 1, 1968

My Darling Jean,

I got your letter (of the 7th) yesterday. It was so very good to hear from you.... Your comment that I'm rather strange brings to mind the thought that there are some vital aspects of my being which you don't understand either. But enough of this. We can discuss that matter later.

Today was a day like all days in Southeast Asia—hot, stifling hot; electric with the ever-present scent of danger underscored by the distant rumble of artillery shells. Unheeding, I took my fighter to the very doorstep of the enemy and methodically chopped 2,000 cases of toothpicks from the forest. It was another tree cutting mission. It was made a little interesting by the fact that I was dropping napalm into the side of a hill, and it was a little close clearing the top.

Coming back from the mission we got an emergency call to RESCAP [*provide cover for a rescue operation*] for an F-4 that got shot down about 20 miles south of Tuy Hoa. We orbited overhead, our guns ready in case the rescue helicopters started receiving any ground fire. Fortunately, they didn't, and our services were unneeded. After about 45 minutes of effort the choppers managed to pick up both pilots. The aircraft commander apparently had a streamer chute [*parachute failed to open*] and was killed during the bailout. The GIB (guy in back) landed in some nasty rocks and had a broken arm and leg as well as other injuries. He's going to be all right, however.

A couple of guys in the squadron took .50 caliber machine gun hits today. This is very unusual, and they were quite excited. No harm was done to either one of them.

Tomorrow will be a day like all days. One day seems to blend into another so that it is very difficult to remember precisely what day it is. I have a fairly late brief tomorrow (8:30 a.m.), so I'll get to sleep in for my Sunday. You will please note that this is Saturday night, and I am writing you a letter, so I am not out catting around either.

I think that it was very nice that you called my mother. You will be happy to hear that I wrote her a very nice letter shortly after I wrote to you. (There is an order of priority for such matters you know.) But anyway, thank you for your thoughtfulness. You're wonderful.

You should be nearly into finals by the time you receive this. I hope that school is going well, and that you are studying diligently.

Be good now—

Love, Stu

P.S. Jack says, "Hi!"

✤ ✤ ✤

June 6, 1968

My Dearest Jean,

Looks like the mail service between us isn't too good, is it? I've finally gotten four of your letters, but they seem to take a long time getting here. But maybe that just reflects my great desire to get your letters. Any word of you or from you is my only source of happiness.

Thank you for the picture you sent along. It is a tremendous picture of you, I think. I'm afraid that I look terribly grubby. In fact, I look like I've literally come down out of the hills. You should have seen me after

Author and Jean after a hike at her parents' mountain cabin. Spring 1968 (author's collection).

I got back from jungle school. I was really grubby then (and you talk about a beard!).

In reply to your query, a FAC is a Forward Air Controller. He is a person, usually an Air Force pilot, who controls air strikes such as the F-100 makes, to ensure that the ordnance is delivered on the proper target and that no friendly forces are endangered. He normally flies over the target area in a little light airplane, such as the one we went flying in, and marks the target with smoke rockets. In our jet fighters we are moving much too fast to effectively seek out concealed enemy targets. The FAC does this for us.

But let me describe to you the sequence of events during a normal mission. The mission actually starts as much as 48 hours before the strike when ground forces discover the need for air support. (Air cover can be there within minutes also if the situation warrants.) The requirement for an air strike is passed through command-and-control channels until it arrives at the fighter squadron in the form of a fragmentary order or frag. The frag normally comes out in the late evening for a morning strike and includes such information as the target location, general description, the FAC that will be working the strike. and the ordnance load.

For us, the mission begins two hours before the scheduled takeoff time with a mission briefing. This includes a detailed intelligence, weather, and situation briefing and then a discussion by the flight lead on how he wants the mission conducted.

An hour before takeoff we don our flying gear, check survival radios, pistols, parachutes, etcetera and proceed to the aircraft. You wouldn't believe the equipment we have to wear on these flights—90% to be used only if we get shot down.

Once at the airplane, I do a thorough preflight of the aircraft and the ordnance to ensure that it is properly loaded and ready to go. Then comes the chore of strapping in. With all the junk I have on, there is barely room in the cockpit for me. Normally, I plan to start engines 30 minutes prior to takeoff. This provides a little extra time in case something is found amiss with the airplane after the engine is started. There are also numerous post start checks that need to be done by me and the crew chief.

About 20 minutes prior to takeoff, we taxi to the end of the runway where the arming area is located. Here, safely away from everything, the safety pins are pulled from the bombs and our guns are made "hot" or ready to fire.

Then the big moment arrives and we roar down the runway. Because takeoff is so critical with the bombs and the heavy weight of the airplane, we don't make formation takeoffs. However, we do join up shortly after takeoff, checking over each other's airplane for possible hits during takeoff. Charlie does occasionally shoot at airplanes on takeoff and landing when they are low and slow and most vulnerable.

After the damage check, the formation is loosened up to combat formation and the flight proceeds to the target area. Most of the navigation is done by Lead with radio aids or radar from ground stations. For me there is little to do on the way to the target but stay with Lead, look for other airplanes and enjoy the ride. It gets a little wild when we fly through thunderstorms, but that's about it.

Once at our rendezvous in the target area, Lead will contact the FAC and get a visual sighting on him. Lead will then give the FAC some specific details including our mission number, number of aircraft in the flight, ordnance and loiter or "play" time. This all goes something like this:

Lead, "Cutie 32, Cutie 32 (FAC's call sign), this is Saber 61." (Saber is the 308th's call sign.)

FAC, "Roger, Saber 61, Cutie 32 and I have a tally." (I see you.) "I'm at your 9 o'clock (off you left wing), about 3,000 feet."

[*The word "Roger" was a term used to acknowledge receipt of a radio transmission. It is still used today in military aviation.*]

Lead, "Saber 61, Roger, tally. Are you ready for the line-up?"

FAC, "Rog 61, ready to copy."

Lead, "OK Cutie 32, this is Saber 61 flight with two Foxtrot 100s, mission number 5512. We've got eight mark 117's (750 lb. bombs) and 20 mike mike" (20-millimeter cannon ammunition. We each carry 800 rounds of this). "And we've got 20 minutes of play time."

FAC, "Roger 61, copy."

The FAC in turn will then give us a detailed target briefing including the exact location and type of target, recommended attack direction, position of nearest friendlies, and some technical data such as wind, target elevation and barometer pressure which we need to bomb accurately.

When all of this information has been transmitted to everyone's satisfaction, the FAC will mark the target by firing a smoke rocket at it. This produces a puff of white smoke on or near the target which we can readily see. If there are friendlies nearby, say within 500 yards, they will mark their position with colored smoke.

We will not drop without a proper mark and FAC clearance because of the danger of hitting friendly troops. Often, the target is buried or concealed, and we have nothing to aim at but the smoke marking the target. Once we are satisfied with the mark, we arm up our ordnance and the fun begins.

It normally takes three passes apiece to drop our heavy ordnance (bombs, napalm, etcetera) and three or four passes to use up the 20 millimeter. The FAC will direct the fire, moving the bombs around as the target is opened up. Normally, we like to save some of the 20-millimeter ammunition to cover the FAC when he goes in to check the target. He does that after the strike is over to assess the effectiveness of the strike. We merely circle overhead, ready to cover him if he receives ground fire.

Once the FAC is clear of the target area, he gives us the bomb damage assessment or BDA, which reflects the effectiveness of the strike, and we head for home. If we have some play time left and haven't strafed, we may try to get another target from one of the controlling agencies. Play time depends on our fuel supply and how far we have to go to get home.

After leaving the target area, we again join up to check each other over for possible hits or battle damage. Quite often you don't even know when you are being shot at or even when you have been hit. Back at Tuy Hoa it's a normal landing, or a radar-controlled approach if the weather is bad, then through de-arming where the guns are made safe and back to the parking area.

Once the airplane is safely parked we have the debriefings to contend with. First maintenance must be debriefed on any aircraft problems. Then intelligence must be given the BDA and information on the target. And finally, the weather people want a report on the actual weather conditions. And then the mission is finished. All the ground time together takes 2½ to 3 hours which, for a normal 1½ hours of flying time makes the entire thing about four to 4½ hours. Add to the one or two missions a day the additional duties everyone has (I'm on the junior officer council and am a pay officer for the squadron) and you have a pretty full day.

I just got back from a mission up in the Hue area. We tried to hit a target in the A Shau valley [*located west of Hue in the northern part of South Vietnam*], but the weather was really down. Instead, we got diverted to a target near Hue. The A Shau valley has been the scene of very intense fighting. I couldn't believe the number of shell craters it contained. That was a pretty good mission for a change.

Now that I've taken up pages telling you all of that, let me get to the heart of this message in a few short words.... It is very lonely without you. Because of this I'm glad of the long and continuous working days. That still doesn't keep me from missing you terribly.

I guess I had better close this while it will still fit in a single envelope. I wish you luck with finals. You have my deepest sympathy for all of the hardships you are suffering (school, lack of dates, etcetera).

I'm especially glad you're being good.

Love, Stu

※ ※ ※

Tools of Our Trade

The North American F-100 was the primary tactical fighter of the U.S. Air Force in the mid–1950s and '60s. Designed in the early '50s, first flown in 1953, it was the Air Force's first supersonic capable aircraft. It was a single engine aircraft (J57-P-21A turbo jet, 10,200 lbs. of thrust at 100 percent [military] power; 16,000 lbs. in afterburner). Empty weight was 20,638 lbs.; design maximum takeoff weight, was over 38,000 lbs. The F-100 measured 47'5" in length with a wing span of 38'9". There were three external stores stations on each wing. Three models of the F-100 were used to equip Air Force units in Vietnam—C and D models (single seat) and F model (two seat).*

Like all fighters, the F-100 was very responsive to the pilot. Slight movements of stick or rudder would send powerful hydraulic forces to the control surfaces that would deflect them as needed even at high speed or high G loads. Like most fighters of its era, the F-100 was designed to withstand 7.33 G's in normal operation.

The controls of the F-100 were sensitive of course, but that was to be expected. The original "A" model's vertical tail had been too small and it tended to depart controlled flight at high angles of attack. But that was corrected in the later models. One flight characteristic that you had to keep in mind was the ability to pull the airplane into too high an angle of attack (a too high nose attitude) where the airflow over the wings separated from the wing surface and stopped developing lift. This resulted in a high-speed stall. The airplane would then stop turning, would simply "mush" even though its nose was held high. This characteristic was a crowd pleaser at airshows but was potentially deadly on bomb deliveries into rising terrain.

A unique feature of the F-100 design was aerodynamically deployed slats on the leading edge of the wings. These were intended to increase lift at higher angles of attack and thereby to lower the landing speed. The pilot had no control over the slats; they were automatically deployed

---

*National Museum of the U.S. Air Force Air and Space Museum.

F-100D cockpit. A complex array of gauges and controls (Ty Greenlees, National Museum of the United States Air Force).

by the airflow over the wings. But if the slats deployed unevenly, or only on one wing, they would impart a strong rolling force on the airplane. This was controllable at landing speeds, but at combat speeds—such as pullout from a dive bomb pass—it could be violent. My instructor in pilot training, a former F-100 pilot, had warned me of this and I witnessed it once in my wingman on a low-level bomb delivery. I was always careful on preflight to check that I could press on the outboard end of the slats and see them retract evenly and smoothly.

The F-100 cockpit was small and purposeful. No frills here. The control stick between my legs and the throttle by my left thigh fell readily to hand. The cockpit was dominated by the central instrument panel in front of my knees. The panel was filled with nearly 30 gauges and dials arranged like everyday coffee cups in a kitchen cabinet—the most used ones were in the center, up front. The rest just seemed to be where they would fit. The critical flight instruments, attitude indicator, airspeed, altitude, heading were centered just below eye level. Various switches and controls for less frequently used equipment were arrayed along consoles by my left and right thighs. The radio and weapons controls were on the left console just behind and outboard of the throttle. Like a cluttered office desk, with familiarity, everything was readily accessible when needed.

The F-100 was certified to carry both nuclear weapons and most of the conventional weapons of that era. A typical weapons load in South Vietnam was four Mk 117 750-pound bombs and 800 rounds of 20-millimeter cannon ammunition. Other weapons certified for carriage on the F-100 included Mk-82, 500 lb. bombs, Mk-82 Snake Eye bombs (500 lb. bombs fitted with deploying fins that rapidly slowed the bomb, allowing the dropping aircraft to escape the bomb fragmentation pattern at low altitude), BLU-27, 750 lb. napalm canisters, cluster bombs (small anti-personnel bomblets carried in a canister that spun-up after release, then opened up to distribute the bomblets), 2.75-inch rocket pods, and various specialized munitions. Up to six weapons could be carried by the F-100, but the center station on each wing was normally reserved for a 270-gallon external fuel tank. A usual combat load (weapons and external fuel) raised the takeoff gross weight of the F-100 to nearly 39,000 lbs. On a hot summer day in Vietnam this meant a takeoff roll of more than 8,000 feet on the 10,000-foot runways typically found on fighter bases in South Vietnam. I often felt the departure end barrier cable bump under my wheels on takeoff roll.

The barrier, or arresting gear, consisted of a heavy cable stretched across the runway, 1,500 feet from the departure end. The cable was attached to large energy absorption devices on both sides of the runway. Its purpose was to rapidly slow an aircraft in case of a high-speed aborted takeoff. It was engaged by a hook on the aircraft that was lowered by the pilot in the aborting aircraft.

None of the weapons we carried were precision guided weapons.

Rather the weapons followed a predicted ballistic flight path once released from the carrying aircraft. The pilot's job was to get the bombs to the point in space where the weapon's ballistic profile would intersect with the target. This was achieved by the use of an aiming reticle (commonly called a pipper) projected on the airplane's windscreen. The aiming reticle offset the release point to account for the shorter flight path of the weapons as opposed to the flight path of the airplane. The aiming reticle could be adjusted to account for the ballistic characteristics of the different weapons and dive angles. In essence, the pipper on the wind screen showed the specific amount of offset required to hit the target. Left-right errors were basically negligible with the relatively low altitude of the release point and short time of flight of the bombs. If necessary, such as in high wind conditions, the left-right drift was accounted for by offsetting the pipper upwind. In practice, achieving the right off sets depended on the pilot's sense of the airplane's movement relative to the target. An experienced pilot could achieve a circular error of about 25 feet with typical high explosive bombs. This was about the size of the crater created by a 500 lb. bomb.

Fighter missions in South Vietnam were always conducted under the control of a Forward Air Controller, or FAC. Combat missions were always flown in a "flight" with at least two aircraft for mutual support. There could be up to four aircraft in a flight. Typical tactics in the target area involved circling the target at 10,000 to 12,000 feet altitude, with the strike aircraft equally spaced around the circle, or orbit as it was called. The aircraft would then sequentially dive at the target at a 20 to 30-degree dive angle, releasing their weapons at 3,000 feet above the ground and pulling off with a 4G [*four times the force of gravity*] recovery. This gave ground clearance of 1,500 feet above the target, safely clear of the bomb fragmentation pattern. For aircraft stability reasons, the out-board weapons were always released in pairs, while the inboard stations were normally released separately. Thus a typical mission involved three weapon delivery passes by each aircraft plus any cannon fire passes that were required.

Enemy defensive fire in South Vietnam consisted mostly of heavy machine guns (up to 14.75mm) and small arms. In Laos, anti-aircraft batteries up to 23mm (and 37mm in northern Laos) were increasingly encountered as the war progressed during my year. There were no enemy fighters or surface to air missiles in South Vietnam, although unguided rockets were occasionally encountered. The ever-changing tropical weather and jagged, mountainous terrain, especially in Laos, added to the complexity—and danger—of air operations.

※ ※ ※

One—Beginning

June 12, 1968

Dear Mom & Dad,

    I'm slowly building up my combat time as the war drags endlessly on. I now have 20 whole missions which hardly makes me a seasoned veteran. I do fly nearly every day, seven days a week. There is little respite from the daily regimen of briefing, flying and debriefing—except the ever-present hope that you will get a good mission. Most of our missions are simply tree busters in which we bomb suspected enemy positions, roads, etcetera. The only visible result is a few less trees than there were before.

    Today, I had a better-than-average mission. We were on a road cut near the Special Forces camp of Kham Duc near the Laotian border. The road cut was normal and we expended our 750 lb. bombs on that. Afterwards we ventured over to Kham Duc, which as you probably know was overrun two weeks ago and now is in VC hands. We strafed [*fired 20-millimeter cannons at*] the airfield and adjacent camp. It is the first time since I've been here that I've really had a target to shoot at. Charlie has abandoned the camp as it seemed pretty deserted and we received no ground fire. We were primarily trying to destroy the remaining U.S. supplies and buildings left in the camp so that the VC couldn't use them. I ought to get some good film out of it.

    So far I've flown over just about the entire country from the A Shau valley and Hue down to the delta area south of Saigon. And so far I've neither seen any of the enemy nor been shot at. I've had a couple of missions in direct support of ground forces who were receiving fire or were pinned down. Even then, no one shot at us that I know of, but then at 500 knots it's hard to tell.

    Yesterday, I managed to create a bit of excitement with a graceful trick. While post-flighting my war plane after a strenuous mission (eight scant miles from Tuy Hoa is where the target was), I very cleverly walked into the refueling probe on the airplane and cut my head. It started bleeding quite profusely and before I could be whisked to the hospital, I had blood streaming down my face, and the rag held to my head was quite blood soaked. The bleeding had stopped by the time I got to the hospital, but the stage was set. There I was, attired in full battle dress including pistol, G suit, survival vest, etcetera, and somewhat blood and sweat soaked. The reception I got when I entered the hospital was outstanding. They never see any blood on this base and they thought they had a real war victim on their hands … people stared; the corridors were cleared for me. It was really quite amusing. The single stitch it took to close the wound was almost a letdown.

I was happy to hear that George got his F-100. I think that he will be quite happy with it, especially if he goes to Luke. I'll have to see if I can get him assigned to Tuy Hoa. That would serve him right.

That's about all the news I have for you. Sorry it can't be more exciting, but maybe that is well.

Say hello to everyone for me.

Love, Stu

✣ ✣ ✣

June 14, 1968

Dearest Jean,

I'm sure you are much relieved that school is out and that you are free to live a life of leisure for the summer. I'm sorry to hear that you've elected to work for your father again this summer. I think you should kindly tell your parents you aren't interested and to strike out on your own for the summer. The experience would do you a lot of good and besides, you'd have a hell of a lot more fun. Indeed your parents would be wise to push you out on your own in some way.

Life isn't too exciting here on the shimmering coast of the South China Sea. I have had a few good missions of late, but most of them are routine. I hope that my vivid description of a typical mission made some sense to you. As you can tell, I really don't work too hard.

I had an outstanding day on the baseball diamond the other day. The base has a softball league and like any good fighter squadron, the 308th fields a team and we play about three times a week. We had kind of a slump for a while, but last Thursday we really exploded and beat the opposition 17–6. I got a triple and two singles—batted .750 for the game. It was really tremendous.

The days really seem to blend into one another around here. With a seven-day work week there is nothing to delineate one day from another. Indeed, it really gets difficult to remember what day it is. (I almost missed TGIF [*Thank God It's Friday*] today because I forgot it was Friday.) ... I miss you very much. I'm afraid that I can't help but despair when I look to the future and can see nothing for a year except these endless days and nights without you.

I hope that you have fun this summer. Consider the infinite wisdom of my advice. Like most things which I can say I know, I learned the wisdom of that through bitter experience. You know, we are very much alike, you and me. I wonder why we disagree so much.

Be good now—

Love, Stu

One—Beginning

June 18, 1968

My Darling Jean,

You aroused my deepest sympathies with your tale of woe in your last letter. I do hope that you got all of your papers completed and finals passed. I'm really not being facetious. Nobody works harder or suffers more mental anguish than a college student during the last few weeks of the semester. I would rather fly a flak suppression mission [*attack an anti-aircraft gun battery*] than to suffer that. I trust that you are now safely beyond all of that and are presented with the luxury of an entire summer spread before you.

I'm really sorry that I haven't been writing to you more often. In answer to your query, I must plead that there is nothing but the war to keep me busy—and it has been keeping me busy enough of late. I've flown nine missions in the last four days. Tomorrow I'll get my 30th mission and will then be qualified to pull alert. That means 12 hours of sitting around the alert shack, ready to launch in response to a target request. We're supposed to be airborne 15 minutes after the klaxon sounds (actually it's a telephone). That means we have to wear all of our flying gear all day long (or all night long). The alert flights usually do get the best missions so there is some good in it.

Right now, I'm just very, very tired from something. You wouldn't think that just riding around in an airplane all day would be very tiresome, would you?

Yesterday I had a bit of diversion for a change. We had to hold over the target area for so long that I was very low on fuel when we began the strike. I was somewhat less than minimum fuel coming off the target and as we were streaking for home, Tuy Hoa announced that they had just been visited by a thunderstorm and that landing there was out of the question. To make a long story short, we diverted to Phu Cat, an air base about 80 miles north of here. It was interesting to see another base for a change. I haven't been out of Tuy Hoa since I got here (at least not on the ground).

I've had some fairly good missions lately. Most of them have been around Dak Pek and Kham Duc in the Tri border area [*where Laos, Cambodia and South Vietnam meet*]. That is a pretty hot area, and it appears that the VC are mounting an attack against Dak Pek. We have been cutting their roads, bombing bridges, etcetera. Today I got a rocket position that they had been using against Dak Pek.

Things have been pretty quiet around here lately, except that a FAC who flew out of here was shot down and killed about 40 miles northwest of Tuy Hoa last Saturday.

Note: Before we parted in May, Jean and I had decided to use our letters in the separation to get to know each other at a deeper level. This meant sharing our most private thoughts on life and hopes, fears and dreams. The rest of this letter is my first attempt at this self-reflection.

I think that I put myself out on a limb when I offered to discuss my mystifying being at some later time. You will give me no rest till I do.... Just for openers, let's consider the subject of flying because it is very dear to me and offers many avenues for exploration.

I gather that you view flying, and my participation in it, as being more or less just a job, albeit an enjoyable thing, but nonetheless, essentially, just a way to make a buck. But you see, to me it is much more than either of these. It is fun and it is an enjoyable way to make a living, but it is also much more than that. And here is where I get into trouble because to try to make you understand the many facets of this "thing" would be to attempt the invariably futile exercise of describing an emotion and all its underlying causes. What is the fascination of flying? It is many fold. First, flying is a highly technical and precise skill (in high performance aircraft), a skill that has been mastered by only a few. Secondly, the act of flying involves a totality of sensory experiences that has few equals in the world. Thirdly, but certainly not least, flying a combat aircraft is dangerous. All of these things combined produce a problem for the pilot that is all but overwhelming.

Consider that the mere mechanical skill of flying a high-performance jet requires a great deal of finesse in the manual manipulation of controls, coupled with the continual processing of data inputs to the brain, to be combined with a rather complex store of technical knowledge and thereby to make the correct decisions on how to manipulate the controls. This all requires nearly complete concentration for the duration of the flight. But of course, there are other things that require even greater knowledge and skill.

Now consider the rush of sensory inputs that boggle the mind and strive to overwhelm the vital and precise decision-making process mentioned above. From the first surge of acceleration at brake release to the jolt of the drag chute deploying at the end of the flight, the pilot is assailed by a variety of sensory stimulus including the ever-present roar of the engine, the crushing weight of G forces that won't even permit you to raise your hand, the radio that must be deciphered, the instruments—all demanding immediate attention. And of course, there is always the awesome beauty of the world stretched out below you, of massive clouds that tower and tumble about you, of sparkling seas or lush green forest all stretching out in an endless expanse of a many-colored tapestry. And at low altitude there is the mystifying attraction of tremendous speed when things tend to blur together in a stream of flashing shapes and colors. The totality of the sensual experience is, in a word, thrilling. It has few equals in the world.

And now we come to the part that gives the whole thing substance, and which, I think you are the least able to understand. And that of course is the danger. It is this that makes the "thing" more than an interesting exercise in the brain's ability to interpret and coordinate a certain amount of data inputs. It is this that makes it more than skilled labor; it is this that takes flying out of the realm of the amusement park ride. As they used to say in pilot training, "If you don't hack it, you die." This fact must always lurk in the back of men's minds to thrust itself forward with the icy, paralyzing grip of fear at the most critical moments. In the cockpit of a fighter, you're very much alone. Indeed, it is one of the few places in our society where you are really alone in a time of stress. If the pilot is to survive the situation, then he must be master of himself as well as his machine. The first solo flight is a major challenge because once the aircraft lifts off the runway, success or failure rests entirely with the pilot. And the price of failure is not a scolding word or a slapped wrist.

The crux of the matter then is not whether you, the pilot, are sufficiently skillful and knowledgeable to fly the aircraft. Rather the question is whether or not you master yourself enough to overcome the fear and put the skill and knowledge to work. The sensations serve to overwhelm the mind and enhance the fear.

I'm sure that now you must be asking yourself why in God's name would anybody thrive on or enjoy danger. That is, I think, a question that has puzzled women for ages. To answer it would be to attempt to explain the nebulous quality that is "man"—that is, the male of the species. Just as a bullfighter or a mountain climber is attempting to prove his own mettle against the power of nature, then I too am pitting my skill and knowledge against the forces and laws of nature. And the stakes being ultimate, the game itself becomes ultimately fulfilling. This is not a death wish or an attempt to prove anything to anybody. It is a deeply personal thing involving mastery of self. The human frailties and failings are the greatest danger because they are the unknown elements. It is fear that paralyzes the mind and muscles and enables nature to claim her victim. And it is this that is challenged.

In reading back over this, it all seems rather sketchy and vague. I don't think I have explained it at all well. Suffice it to say that just as I have a tremendous need for intellectual exploration and stimulus (a thing we have discussed and understand), just as I have a need for emotional fulfillment (for which I lean very heavily on you), so too, do I have a need for physical experience and adventure. Thus, I love to ski where the wind and cold and speed and fatigue all battle against you; thus, I love to climb hills and cliffs and mountains to battle against the steady pull of gravity. All of these things provide psychological stimulus of which you apparently are not aware.

Thus, the subject is breached. I think that I have opened it rather poorly, but perhaps you may begin to fathom that side of me that is so alien to you. And don't misunderstand me—flying is not a terrifying experience—far from it. Perhaps I emphasize the danger too much; it is the totality of the stimulation that makes it what it is.

I shall eagerly await your reaction to the foregoing.

Be good now—

Love, Stu

⁕ ⁕ ⁕

June 24, 1968

My Darling Jeannie,

Thank you for the card. I enjoyed it very much—although it did suffer a little from the mail service.

As for my baseball career, that is but one of my additional duties. A fighter pilot has an obligation to support the squadron in all ways. I only mentioned it because I knew that you know nothing about it.... (By the way, I got a double which just missed clearing the fence—and a single last game.)

This has been a week of firsts for me. Last Thursday (the 20th) I spent my first day on alert. That was quite exciting. I sat around the alert shack, pistol strapped to my hip, waiting for the message to scramble. About eleven o'clock it did, and I did. I raced out to my waiting aircraft jumped in, started it up and roared out of the revetments while I was still strapping in. In true Hollywood fashion, we lit the afterburners and roared off down the runway and into the air. We climbed in afterburner to altitude and streaked to the target area, only to hold for 45 minutes. I was a little less hasty on the next scramble.

On Friday I had my first day off since I've gotten here. I took a busman's holiday of sorts and went flying in a C-130 (that's a big four engine transport). I have a good friend here who flies them, and he had invited me to go along sometime and see how the other half lives. So, I got up at six in the morning (that was the hardest part) and took him up on it. We flew all over the southern part of Vietnam including Nha Trang,

One—Beginning

Phan Thiet, Tan Son Nhut, Binh Thuy (down in the Delta), Vung Tao and Qui Nhon. It was interesting to see some of these places from up close. Phan Thiet for instance is just a little outpost with less than 3,000 feet of runway (Tuy Hoa has 9,500 feet). The people there literally live in sandbagged tents and bunkers. The place is surrounded by rolls of barbed wire, and machine gun nests are placed strategically around the runway and dining area. The soil there is a red clay much like Georgia. The entire camp looks like a raw open wound on the green countryside. Of course, everything around the camp has been cut down to prevent possible infiltration. Vang Tao is much the same way. Binh Thuy is a fairly large camp on the Mekong River. The land there is absolutely flat, much of it is flooded and the rest is crisscrossed with a maze of canals and waterways. The Mekong and its many branches wander aimlessly, forming many broad serpentine bands across the face of the earth there. Binh Thuy is built of Quonset huts and prefabricated buildings. It got hit last night.

It turned out to be a very interesting day. I got to fly the 130 including a landing at Tan Son Nhut. That has to be one of the busiest airports in the world. In addition to the airplanes in the landing pattern, you have to dodge the air strikes which seem to always be going on around there.

I got back from that flight about 6:30 in the evening, just in time to eat and have a drink (I'm not becoming an alcoholic) and go brief for my mission that day (night). We ended up having our takeoff time slip and didn't get airborne until 2:10 in the morning Saturday. It was blacker than the hole of Calcutta and I was really having to struggle to stay on the wing (or to stay awake). As luck would have it, we were up for two hours and five minutes. By that time, I had been up nearly 22 hours and was lucky to even find the runway.

Saturday night I had a wild time. I knew it was going to be a great night when I had to abort the takeoff on the runway when my afterburner refused to light. Lead had already taken off and was circling the field as I raced back to the parking area to get a spare. Half an hour later (that is about too fast) I was finally airborne but was faced with the problem of finding Lead in the utter blackness above. Well, that worked out pretty well, but we had no sooner joined up when we flew into a thunderstorm. We were on a radar ground control bomb run called a "Sky Spot." In this we play B-17, fly along at 20,000 feet taking directions from a ground station. At the right point in space, the ground controller says, "Hack," and we drop our bombs. This procedure is normally looked at askance by any good fighter pilot, because it is not very sporting. But combined with a little night weather formation and it becomes very gamey indeed, if not downright terrifying.

Yesterday I didn't fly, so I spent the afternoon lounging on the beach. Need I say more? The beach here is really quite nice. It is wide and sandy, steep like the California beaches, but the South China Sea is warm and clear and often very placid like a lake early in the morning. The sand is coarse, almost gravelly in places, and seems to stretch off forever in both directions.

As I was lounging there on that magnificent beach, I was thinking how much you would like it. I was also thinking how wonderful it would be for you to be here to share it with me, indeed, to share the whole beauty of this strangely primitive country.

You may be interested to know that I have already considered the prospect of going to Hawaii for R&R. Heretofore, I hadn't hoped to think perhaps you could meet me in Hawaii. We will have to discuss it later. I'm afraid it would prove to be frightfully expensive.

When I think of the year and the miles that separate us, I wonder if we will survive the year separation. But instead of withering it seems to be growing by leaps and bounds.

I think with that observation, I will close this letter.

Work hard this summer.—

Love, Stu

✤ ✤ ✤

June 28, 1968

Dear Mom and Dad,

I just got your letter from Colorado. It sounds like you all are leading a pretty exciting life. I was glad to hear that all went well with George's graduation [*from Air Force pilot training*]. I wish that I could have been there to see Dad pin George's wings on. That will make a good story for the *Air Force Times*. No doubt George is ready for a little vacation now, prior to having at the "Hun" [*F-100*].

My life is beginning to take on the monotony of any routine—although it is occasionally brightened by moments of stark terror. I am maintaining an average of a little over one mission a day. In fact, I now have 40 missions to my credit. I sat alert for the first time last week. This is a 15-minute alert to provide a quick response to any troops that get themselves in trouble. Something like SAC [*Strategic Air Command*] except that we do get scrambled. That is quite exciting. Normally the alert flights get the best missions due to the urgency of the situation. The first time we got scrambled, I raced madly about, was taxiing out of the revetment while I was still strapping in. We raced for the runway and thundered into the air with only the briefest run-up. Then we streaked for the target area in afterburner—only to hold over the rendezvous for 30 minutes while two other flights scattered there ordnance about. After that I began taking the scrambles with a grain of salt.

Last Friday I had a bit of an interesting diversion. I flew your favorite airplane, Dad—a C-130.... I was amazed at some of the fields they take those 130s into. I was also surprised at the way the 130 flew. I flew two of the legs, including a takeoff and two landings. It was quite a bit of fun to fly a big airplane like that. I didn't expect it to be as responsive as it is. (I still like the "Hun" better, however.)

That's been about the sum total of my adventures recently. The rest of my missions of late have been pretty routine. A week and a half ago we were going to the Dak To, tri border area nearly every mission. Now I seem to either go up near Phu Cat or down in the Bien Hoa, Saigon area. We had a mission with troops in contact near Song Bay (50 miles north of Saigon) this afternoon. It was a divert [*change from the assigned target to a higher priority target*]. The ceiling was low (about 2,000 feet); we stayed around the target a little too long and all three of us were minimum fuel. Then Lead lost his radio and had a drag chute failure on landing and taxied into the barrier. I landed with 800 lbs. [*of fuel*]. (600 lbs. is considered to be an emergency situation.) When it rains it pours.

I hope that this letter finds you all well and happy.

Take care now—

Love, Stewart

Two

Troops in Contact

The narrative below describes an alert mission that occurred shortly after I was qualified to "pull" alert. It was typical of the type of urgent missions that were assigned to the alert crew. The dialogue in this story has been reconstructed to give the reader a sense of being in the cockpit with me.

31st Tactical Fighter Wing
Tuy Hoa AB, Republic of Vietnam
June 26, 1968

I was on alert today with Jim, one of the senior captains in the squadron. This was only my third time on alert. I was still finding it kind of exciting. We arrived at the alert shack about 0730 to set up the airplanes. This entailed doing all of our preflight walk around and cockpit checks up to engine start. Parachutes were placed in the seat and helmets placed on the cockpit rail with oxygen mask and comm cord hooked up, ready to go. Then it was suit-up in full flight gear—G suit, survival vest, pistol belt—and wait. Wait for the phone to ring and send us scrambling to our aircrafts.

The alert aircraft provided a rapid, close air support capability for urgent, unplanned contingencies. Often this involved troops in contact with enemy forces. Consequently, our weapons load was typically anti-personnel munitions. Today, Jim, as the Flight Lead, had four high-drag 500 lb. bombs with fuse extenders. Fuse extenders are 36-inch pipes that put the fuse well in front of the bomb. This causes the bomb to explode while it is slightly above ground level, resulting in a wider spread of bomb fragments and greater damage to soft targets. My airplane was loaded with four 750 lb. napalm canisters. We each had 800 rounds of 20mm cannon ammunition. With the aircraft cocked and ready to go, we could be airborne in less than 15 minutes.

Two—Troops in Contact

We relieved the previous alert crew at 0800 and waited for the phone to ring. As we were suiting up, Jim had said, "The weather is basically clear here and along the coast, so, on takeoff, take minimum spacing and get joined up as quickly as you can. I'll stay VFR (visual flight rules) until you're aboard. Then you're cleared to spread formation after the clean and dry check." This check was made to insure there were no loose panels or holes in the aircraft, and no leaking fluids. Hence the name.

Generally, we could expect at least two scrambles in a 12-hour alert shift, sometimes three. Today seemed quiet and the minutes began to drag into hours. Finally, the phone rang about 11:15.

Jim picked up the phone and quickly jotted down the critical information on his mission card.

He put down the phone and turned to me. "We have troops in contact. Rendezvous is 185 (degrees) for 32 (miles) off of Ch 50 with FAC Helix 1 2. His freq [*radio frequency*] is 386.7."

With that, we both raced to our airplanes parked in revetments about 30 yards from the alert shack.

At the airplane, I bounded up the ladder and into the cockpit with my crew chief, right behind me. He helped me into my parachute harness, and as I pulled on my helmet, he threw the seat shoulder straps over my shoulders, jumped down and pulled the ladder away. I threw on the electrical master switch, looked to see if he was clear and pushed the button for the engine start cartridge. Smoke bellowed from the starter exhaust vent and the engine began to wind up with its characteristic whine. At 10 percent rpm, I pushed the throttle to idle and heard the slight whump as the fuel that was sprayed into the turbine section ignited. The engine began its usual acceleration to idle power. I watched the engine instruments settle to their normal readings and gave the chocks out signal to the crew chief.

Momentarily, the radio crackled, "Tuy Ground, Litter Zero One, scramble two," Jim said. [*"Litter" was the call sign for all 31st Wing alert aircraft.*]

I called, "Two's on."

Ground replied, "Roger, Zero One, Runway 21, wind 060 at 8, altimeter 29.96."

We both advanced power and I swung out of the revetment in trail behind Lead.

As we taxied to the active runway, I continued to strap in, fastening my lap belt and doublechecking my G suit was connected. We paused briefly at the threshold to the runway while the arming crew pulled the weapon pylons' safety pins and made a quick check for leaks. A thumbs up and we were set to go.

Lead called, "Zero One, channel three, go." Then momentarily, "Tower, Litter Zero One, ready for takeoff, check."

I had switched radio channels and replied, "Two."

Tower said, "Litter Zero One, cleared for immediate takeoff."

We taxied into position on the runway, pushing up power as soon as the brakes were set. With a quick glance at me, Lead gave an abbreviated salute and released brakes. Five seconds later, I released brakes. We were airborne at 11:27.

Once airborne, it was about a twenty-minute flight north to our rendezvous point 32 miles south of Chu Lai. We stayed along the coast as we climbed to 15,000 feet. The weather along the coast was clear, but inland, over the coastal mountains, the typical summer cumulus clouds, "puffs" we called them, had begun to form at about 3,000 feet. The puffs were scattered to broken and went up to 5,000 feet or so.

As we approached the rendezvous, Lead called, "Litter, go manual."

I switched my radio to the mission frequency, 386.7. We generally tried to avoid stating the working frequency in an effort to prevent the VC (Viet Cong) from monitoring our conversations in the target area.

In South Vietnam, FACs carried FM radios to be able to talk to troops on the ground, as well as UHF radios to communicate with us. In a troops in contact situation like we had here, the FAC coordinated continuously with the friendly forces to ensure we did not inadvertently endanger them with our bombs. FACs were assigned to specific geographic areas which they flew over daily and knew like the back of their hand. They were armed only with white phosphorous rockets, called Willy Pete, for marking targets.

We arrived at the rendezvous at about 12:00. Lead called, "Helix One Two, Litter Zero One, at the rendezvous, your frequency."

After some delay, Helix came up on the frequency. He had been coordinating with the ground party that was under attack on his separate FM radio.

He said on our initial contact, "Okay buddy, we got something besides a tree buster for you this morning."

"Roger," Lead called, "are you ready to copy our lineup?"

"Roger," Helix replied, "standing by."

Lead said, "OK, Helix, Litter Zero One, two fox one hundreds, Lead has four MK 82 snake eyes with daisy cutters [*fuse extenders*]. Two has four BLU-27 napalm. We each have 800 rounds of 20 mike mike."

"Perfect," Helix said. "I need you to come inland about twenty miles. I'll be orbiting over a river bend just south of a small mountain at 1,500 feet."

As we turned west, Helix continued with the mission briefing, "We have a LRP (Long Range Patrol), about platoon size, that stumbled into a company of VC maybe 70 to 100 strong. The LRP is pinned down but is in a relatively good defensive position on a ridge up slope from the VC. The VC are in a tree line along a stream that flows through a ravine south west of the LRP position. The ravine as you will see runs generally south to north up to the ridge line west of the LRP position. The LRP has held off Charlie so far, but they're running low on ammo. We need to suppress the VC, so the LRP can be extracted."

As we progressed inbound to the target, I reflected on what a marine lieutenant, who had led long range patrols, told me about their tactics. Their basic mission was to recce [*reconnoiter*] areas where the VC or NVA were suspected to be operating and to set up ambushes for small enemy units. They carried 80 lb. packs, mostly ammo and water, and just enough concentrated rations to last three days. If they happened on a superior force, their tactic was to lay down heavy fire, consolidate to a defensive position and call for help. It looked like this was the situation we had here. Litter Zero One was the help.

In a few minutes we arrived in the target area, and took up a left orbit at 3,000 feet, just under the clouds. That put us about 1,500 feet above the ridge line. As we circled, we could see the river and the ravine and the general terrain layout, but the position of the target was not yet clear. The FAC would mark the exact area we were to hit with a Willy Pete rocket. But what was clear was that the terrain would force our run-in line to be up the ravine into the rising terrain. The crest of the mountain rose sharply hundreds of feet above and behind the target area. This was going to be dicey even without ground fire since both Lead and I had munitions that required low level delivery.

As we orbited, we got a visual on the FAC. Helix was in an orbit at 1,500 feet, south of the target area. He was safely outside small arms range from the VC but positioned such that he could monitor our strikes.

Lead called, "Helix, we have you in sight. Two, go trail."

I reduced power and took up spacing in trail of Lead. With a two ship, we generally tried to space ourselves on opposite sides of the orbit so one of us was continuously in position to threaten the target.

Helix called, "Litter, I have you in sight, stand by for my mark."

As we continued around our orbit Lead called, "Set 'em up hot."

The FAC then fired a Willy Pete rocket into the target area. The white phosphorus smoke was slow filtering up through the trees and Lead was out of position when it became visible.

I was far enough behind Lead at this point to be able to start an attack. I called, "Two's base, I have the target."

Helix replied, "Roger, Two, I have you and you are cleared. Hit my smoke."

I pulled the airplane around hard to get on the run-in line and dropped down towards the jungle floor. As I rolled out I checked my airspeed, 350 knots, and dive angle, five degrees. A little slow I thought. Better plug in the afterburner. It lit with a small thump and whine. The pipper, my aiming reticule on the cockpit wind screen, drifted towards the tree line as the aircraft accelerated. At 400 knots, I pulled the power back to min afterburner.

By now I was below the crest of the mountains. This was going to be close.

Napalm is most effectively delivered in near level flight as low as you dared get. "Scrape 'em off on the trees" was the standard description. This enabled the tumbling napalm canisters to maintain a nearly horizontal flight path, so that when they hit and ruptured the jellied gas spread out forward along the attacking path. This was especially important in jungle terrain. A more standard 20 or 30-degree dive bomb profile would cause the canisters to enter the trees nearly vertically and significantly limit the coverage of the jellied gas. With troops in contact, we wanted as much coverage as possible.

As I sped towards the target, I saw a number of flashes from the tree line ahead. Charley knew how we had to run in and had us bracketed. It was too late to jink [*make sudden defensive maneuvers*] now. I'm almost there, I thought, and besides, I have to clear that mountain ridge on the recovery.

I concentrated completely on the pipper as it advanced towards the target.

Easy now, I thought. Wait ... Wait.

More flashes from the tree line.

Steady. Don't be early. The pipper is almost there.

My thumb caressed the pickle button.

Ready.... Ready.... NOW! Pickle and Pull.

Instantaneously, the explosive cartridges on the outboard bomb racks fired, and 1,500 lbs. of ordnance were kicked free of the airplane.

I felt the jolt, but now my focus shifted fully to the rising terrain in front of me. Damn, that hill really goes up. All I could see was green foliage. I applied back stick as smoothly and precisely as I could. The key was to get maximum turning performance from the airplane as quickly as possible. Too little or too slow with the stick and you won't clear the ridge. Too abrupt and you can force the airplane into a high-speed stall and mush into the mountain side. You have to feel the airplane; feel what she's telling you.

There, that's about all she'll take, I thought, as the rapidly increasing G's pushed me down into the seat. Now it's just a matter of waiting and watching. Patience, I said to myself, don't screw this up. Time seemed frozen. The airplane buffeted from the G Load, but in a moment blue sky appeared in the wind screen. The airplane skimmed across the trees as it arched into the sky.

Somehow, I had cleared the ridge. I'm not sure how 'til I checked the G meter. A cool seven G's, I noted.

The FAC yelled, "Beautiful, Two, right in there. Now Lead, put your bombs a little long and right of two's smoke."

I let my breath out. I was into the clouds on the recovery and had to dive back down to reacquire the target. With satisfaction, I saw the black plume from the nape rising from the edge of the woods where the flashes had been.

Helix made a small adjustment to our aim points. "Two, put your next nape just past Lead's bombs."

On the second pass, I was more cautious of the ridge. Still to get to the target, it was a constant and real danger, only a split second away from the release point.

I saw no flashes on the second pass, but the FAC asked me if I heard ground fire. I chuckled at that. In our little cocoon in the cockpit, you can't hear anything but the radio and the sounds of the airplane itself.

Helix confirmed his own question, "The Army guys say you're taking pretty heavy ground fire."

Then, "Lead, move your next pass about 20 meters up the tree line from Two's nape."

The third pass was more of the same.

After expending our ordnance, we turned the bomb switches to safe and set the guns up hot. We made one strafe pass, and Helix went in to look things over. As he approached the target area, he got ground fire from another set of trees.

He called, "Litter, I'm getting fire from a clump of trees about 50 meters south of the target area."

Lead replied, "Roger, I'm in on that target." He pumped a good burst into those trees. That seemed to finish off Charlie, and I didn't see muzzle flashes on my subsequent strafe pass.

Helix moved in again to look things over. You got to hand it to these guys. Here they are in a tiny airplane with max speed of maybe 120 knots, barely above the ground and no way to protect themselves. A guy could get hurt doing that!

After a few orbits over the target area, Helix said, "Beautiful work

Litter, great bombing, 100% of your ordnance was on target. The army says all is quiet and they are moving out to their extraction point."

There was satisfaction in that. Helping the guys on the ground was what it was all about as far as we were concerned. That made everything worth it.

I joined up with Lead and looked over his aircraft on both sides for battle damage. I didn't see any obvious holes or streaming fluids and called, "Lead, you're clean and dry."

Jim gave me the lead and looked my airplane over. "Two, you're clean and dry," he said.

It was a pleasant flight back along the coast to Tuy Hoa. The tension of the mission had drained away. It was just a perfect day for flying. The blue green water of the South China Sea sparkled as it lapped at the sugary beaches of Vietnam. It's so beautiful, I thought. Maybe someday we will be building resort hotels here, rather than dropping bombs.

Soon we were back on the ground, and the airplanes were being refueled and re-armed for the next mission.

As we walked to debriefing, Jim said, "That was a gratifying mission. Poor Army guys have a tough war tramping around the jungle, while we get to sit in our 'air-conditioned' cockpits." Jim continued, "That terrain was certainly challenging. Looked like you got pretty close on that first pass."

"Yes, Sir," I replied. "It was pretty tense there for a moment."

I took a deep breath, reflecting. I almost pushed *Jeannie* too far, exposed her to the fatal danger of the rapidly rising terrain. I need to learn to give her a little more margin, I thought.

Three

Settling In

After being in Vietnam for a month and a half, things began to settle into a routine as they always do. By this time I had seen the entire country of South Vietnam and had experienced most of the types of missions that would make up my experiences here. But the reality of being in a war zone would also come near as friends and acquaintances would be killed in action. These events reflected the capricious nature of life and death.

On June 29, I would experience a malfunction in the nose gear steering of my aircraft. This malfunction caused the airplane to partially depart the runway for about 4,000 feet before I was able to get the airplane back. I thought I'd made a great save and was dismayed that the Wing leadership assumed the incident was just the result of poor piloting and made no effort to understand the true cause. I was most bitter at having my skill as a pilot disparaged by the Wing authorities over this runway incident. My pride was deeply wounded as described in the following letter.

My letters to Jean also settled into a routine pattern during this period. She did decide not to work for her father this summer and instead she got a summer job in a hardware store. She tells me she isn't dating, and that she thinks I've lost my mind for my attitude towards flying and its dangers.

My July 4 letter begins to reveal the frustration of delayed connections through the letters. We simply couldn't carry on a coherent conversation with the three-week turnaround between a letter sent and a reply received. This would become a serious issue in the coming months.

⚜ ⚜ ⚜

June 28, 1968

My Darling Jean,

Another day has passed in the endless stream of nameless, expressionless days. Today holds the same hot, blistering sun, the oppressive heavy heat of the mid-morning, the massive thunderheads in the afternoon, the not quite balmy evening. I literally have to consult a calendar (Playboy type) to know what day, indeed what month it is. The days and nights blend together in a never-ceasing routine of briefings and flying. I think without some diversion I shall go quite mad. I've even grown tired of drinking. (By the way, judging from your last letter I should say you are the one in danger of becoming an alcoholic.)

Do you remember Bob Scott and his wife from your brief sojourn at Luke [*Air Force Base*]? I shouldn't imagine you do. He is quite tall and slender. They were at our party as well as graduation. Well, at any rate, he bought the farm [*crashed*] up at Qui Nhon last Tuesday. He had been stationed at Phu Cat—hadn't been there more than two weeks. Apparently, he was pressing a little delivering high drag bombs into the side of a hill. Anyway, he couldn't make the pull out and impacted about 15 feet below the crest of the hill.

It is strange how one never expects this sort of thing to happen to a friend. It is somehow unreal to think of him as the victim of so tragic a mishap. It is much more real to think of him as I knew him in pilot training and at Luke. And of course, I feel very sorry for his wife. It must have been a terrible shock to her, especially since it happened so soon after he got here. I already have altogether too long a list of friends that have fallen victim to this interminable war.

Hearing from you gives me something to turn to when the world turns black.

June 30

Today is Sunday, the proverbial day of rest. I only had to get up at 5:30 this morning to go fly; then my airplane broke, and I didn't go after all.

Yesterday I had a bit of a harrowing experience. Apparently, I had a malfunction in the nose wheel steering of the aircraft and the nose wheel got cocked about 45 degrees to the right. [*It was standard procedure in the F-100 to engage the nose wheel steering system immediately after touchdown.*] Anyway, when I touched down on landing and engaged the nose wheel steering, the airplane headed for the side of the runway. All of my efforts to prevent it from going off the runway were ineffective, and I taxied off the side going about 130 mph. As you may imagine, a 30,000-pound airplane doesn't taxi too well in the sand. I was certain that the right gear would dig in and it would flip when it left the runway. But luck was with me, and it didn't. In fact, I managed to get it under control and back on the runway, although it left deep ruts along the side of the runway for about 4,000 feet and wiped out some runway lights. The aircraft was not damaged except for a badly cut and beat up tire. It was quite a ride, but as I was to find out, that was nothing compared to the maelstrom that was engendered by the powers that be around here over the incident. My ability as a pilot immediately became suspect as they just naturally assumed that I had just let the airplane motor off the runway. As far as I'm concerned, they can all go straight to hell. God himself couldn't have kept that airplane on the runway. They are lucky the son of a bitch didn't roll up in a pile of junk.

I think that I had better close this letter and get it mailed. I feel terrible today. I was so pissed off about my misadventure yesterday, or more accurately their reaction to it, that I stayed in the bar too long last night.

Be good now—

Love, Stu

※ ※ ※

July 4, 1968

My Dearest Jean,

Happy 4th of July! I even had the day off today. Actually, the war didn't stop for the holiday. I just didn't happen to be scheduled to fly today. A friend and I celebrated the festive occasion with a bottle of champagne on the patio. Everyone else around thought we were crazy, but it seemed only appropriate to do something for the holiday. We decided to forego the fireworks. We see enough of that in our daily routine.

You have no idea of the impact of a day off around here. After I awoke, which was blessedly quite late.... I found I would be happy for the distraction of a combat mission. The time passes more quickly then, and the emptiness seems a little shorter.

Tragedy struck Tuy Hoa a few days ago. One of the pilots in the 306th squadron bought it on a napalm attack. He had just gotten here—in fact, he was on his first solo combat mission. They don't know whether he took a hit or not. It seems he simply didn't pull out after dropping his napalm cans. I didn't know him too well, but I happened to have breakfast with him that morning. He took off shortly before I did that day. It's strange. He simply never came back.

I'm glad that you enjoyed my soliloquy several weeks ago. You know it's hard to maintain the chain of thought when it takes at least three weeks for a reply to be formulated and sent. I had hoped that you would have some probing questions to prod me on.

I don't think I've told you yet, but I think my parents are about to move away from Los Angeles. As you know my father has been somewhat dissatisfied with North American. At any rate he got an offer for a vice presidency of a firm back in Washington DC. (I don't even know the name of the company.) My mother has hinted that they will be moving sometime during July. I haven't heard any firm plans from them yet. They just returned from a trip back to Texas for Georgia's graduation. (He got F-100s to Cannon Air Force Base, New Mexico.)

I trust that you are enjoying your summer. Don't work too hard now. I hate to think of you slaving away at the drudgery of manual labor. I was glad that you didn't decide to work for your father, however.

Be good now—

Love, Stu

✢ ✢ ✢

July 9, 1968

My Darling Jean,

The days are slipping quietly by in an almost unnoticed procession. To say that life here is routine and tedious is not quite the truth. It does have its moments of excitement and grim entertainment.

Tonight, it looks like I get a bit of that greater danger I was talking about previously. I take off at 1:30 in the morning, but for where I cannot say. Night missions are generally regarded as something akin to the plague here. I rather enjoy them myself as long as they don't involve bad weather. It is too easy to blunder into a thunderstorm at night. But if there is a moon out (which there is tonight) it is intensely beautiful to fly at night. The earth below takes on an eerie, ethereal existence. Lakes and mountains blend together until they are indistinguishable. The ocean is detected by its nonexistence for it appears as a completely empty void except where it may reflect the moon. Over here the lights on the ground are few and scattered and are far outnumbered by the stars so that the world becomes topsy-turvy, and you begin to mistake the stars for the ground. A solipsist could will himself into nonexistence under this stimulus.

I can't say that I've done anything exciting lately. I've taken to reading cheap novels in my spare time. I'm presently enmeshed in the *Green Berets*, *Islands* by Huxley and Koestler's *Darkness at Noon*, all simultaneously. Unfortunately, it's impossible to obtain any books of a more stimulating nature over here. Something by Hesse would be very kindly received.

Three—Settling In

I was glad to hear that you were enjoying your summer job so much. Just think of the vast knowledge of the hardware business you are gaining—and a candid insight into a male preoccupation (as you noted by the male and female descriptions for plumbing fittings). Console yourself with the thought that no knowledge, however extraneous, is wasted and that all money is inherently good.

I hope you are well and happy and that you are enjoying the summer. But don't forget to be good—

Love, Stu

P.S. Say hello to your mother and father and Julie for me.

❉ ❉ ❉

July 16, 1968

My Darling Jean,

If you could see me now you would think that I was on a vacation rather than fighting a war. I have been flying at night lately, so I have nothing to do during the day but lie about in the sun. I'm getting to have a beautiful tan by now. Of course, I deserve some compensation for braving the dark and scary night. Last night we went up by the DMZ [*Demilitarized Zone that separates North and South Vietnam*]. It was blacker than pitch with thunderstorms and lightning all around. Then we had to hold in the weather so long that we had to drop our bombs in order to have enough gas to get home. I wasn't sure I was going to make it until I touched down here at Tuy Hoa.

Note: There follows a rambling discourse on the meaning of life and death. Or the lack of meaning. In retrospect, I believe I wrote this for myself, now caught up in the reality of daily combat. This kind of thinking precedes the descent into fatalism which is the final coping mechanism for many people in a continuing environment of lethal danger. Jean was merely my sounding board for my own reflections.

I should like to comment for a moment on a portion of your last letter (of the 8th where she says she doesn't share my lust for life). In it you disavow any lust for life but at the same time you evidence a definite shrinking from death. There is, I think, a contradiction implied in that. You are attracted by neither life nor death. Indeed, it would seem that you are repulsed by both, but are driven, as it were, to life by an even greater fear of death which is altogether abhorrent to you.

The curious thing is that this approach to the state of being must ultimately lead to the most abject clinging to life which is, in itself, repugnant. An interesting paradox perhaps. But is there then nothing in the world which would make the fact of being alive, of being a conscious being, worthwhile and meaningful to you? And is there nothing in life itself that is important enough to you for you to risk the very fact of life in order to retain it?

Forgive me. I don't mean to be cruel. But you have restricted your interrelationship with life to a pseudo-rational one. And this can only lead to the intellectual cynicism which you now evidence. You have searched for a causal relationship in life, but in doing so you have falsely assumed that life operates on this basis of Justice and Reason. Subconsciously you expect life to adhere to your Judeo-Christian ethic, to reward the Good and punish the Evil. But life was not bound by your concept of morality, was it, and life's capriciousness seemed both incomprehensible and grossly unjust. (Note the untimely and senseless death of your friend.)

But how does the rationalist react to the evidenced apathy and stupid capriciousness of life? What logic can the intellectual apply to a thing that appears basically senseless? The average (and not too courageous) intellectual reacts with despair ("Why am I cursed amongst men?"), self-pity ("Intelligence is a curse of man.") and bitterness (as evidenced by the rejection of one's moral or religious heritage). The synthesis of this reaction is usually a bitter cynicism of all of life.

Instead of accepting life for what it is, you now bitterly persevere under the burden that is life. The many small blows of fate become fuel for your self-pity and scars for your self-imposed martyrdom of life. Indeed, the stupid may be the blessed of the earth for they accept life. You cannot, for you have questioned life and are now tortured by its senselessness, by its refusal to answer to or be bound by your questioning.

Well do I know the path of this self damnation. You ask how I developed this lust for life. It came from the slow realization that life was not to be categorized, that life demands to be experienced in order to be placed in its proper context. By the same token death must be approached to remove its horror. You ask what aspect of life was more important to me. I confess to favor the intellect. But as an intellectual I am a cynic. It is only relatively recently that I have begun to recognize the intrinsic value of the physical and emotional parts of life. However abhorrent the idea may be, we are both physical and emotional beings. This side of us cannot be denied. I might add that the experience of knowing you has done much to make me recognize this side of my being.... I cannot claim to accept life now. But at least I no longer feel that I have been viciously cheated by life. I can now accept that life is neither cruel nor kind; it is merely apathetic. Life is meaningful only as far as I make it meaningful.

Well, I seem to be lecturing you, and for that I am sorry. I'm merely trying to persuade you to let yourself live. Have confidence in your own abilities and worth. Stop reviling against the treacheries and deceit of fate. Stop reviling Life and become a part of it. Open your heart and mind to the lessons of Life.

Love, Stu

Four

Bullpup Training

Sid and I had just suited up for our morning mission and were heading out the door for the step van and the short trip to the flight line. As we walked down the hall, the Ops Officer came out of his office, and seeing us, held up his hand for us to stop. He approached and said, "Stu, we're sending you to Clark for Bullpup training next week." Without further elaboration, he continued down the hall to the ops counter.

Sid and I boarded the step van and put our helmet bags on the floor. "What was that all about?" I asked him.

He laughed. He was an "old head" [*was nearly complete with his yearlong assignment*] here at Tuy Hoa. He had done a tour in Europe before coming to Vietnam and was due to rotate in a couple of months. "You know what a Bullpup is from your training at Luke?" he asked.

"Yes," I said, "it's that missile that we're supposed to guide from the cockpit of our diving airplane by putting the flare on the back of the missile over the target and holding it there. I've never actually seen one, let alone tried to guide one."

Sid laughed again. "Well, neither have I," he said, "and there aren't any here at Tuy Hoa. In fact, I don't think there are even any in the whole of Vietnam. But there is a training simulator at Clark."

"So...?" I asked.

Sid smiled. "You young guys don't catch on very fast, do you? Bullpup training is just an excuse to get you out of country for a while. Our leadership understands that constant combat missions tend to build up a recklessness in us pilots, so they try to get us away from here every couple of months to break the tension. So you get TDY [*temporary duty*] orders to Clark and you can do what you want for a week. Nobody expects you to actually use the Bullpup simulator."

"Oh," ... I said. "You mean I don't even have to stay at Clark?"

"Whatever you want," he replied.

I immediately thought of Sara and her family in Manila. As soon as

Four—Bullpup Training

I got back to my hooch, I fired off a letter, telling her I'd be in the Philippines on the 19th and would try to come down to Manila.

The next Friday, I caught a ride to Clark in the back seat of an "F" model that was being ferried to Taiwan for heavy maintenance. I called Sara as soon as we landed. She was excited about me coming to Manila. "There's a daily Embassy courier flight that runs between Clark and Manila," she told me. "You might try to get on it tomorrow. I'll pick you up at the airport—as usual," she laughed. "You can stay with us."

"Great," I said. "I'll see you tomorrow."

I was in Base Ops, still dressed in my flight suit, when I called Sara. After we hung up, I went to the main ops counter to see about the flight to Manila. Sure enough it was there on the flight schedule board—Embassy Courier, 1300, daily except Sunday.

I stepped up to the counter and said to the sergeant there, "I'd like to get on the courier flight to Manila tomorrow."

He looked up from the papers he was sorting. "OK," he said, matter-of-factly. "Let me see your orders."

He took the orders, scanned them, and pushed them back to me. "I can't put you on the courier flight, it's official business only."

"What do you mean," I protested. "I'm here on TDY orders from Vietnam. What's more official than that?"

He shrugged indifferently, "You're here TDY to Clark, not to Manila, Lieutenant."

"What difference does that make?" I asked.

Now he looked at me, shook his head, "You young guys, don't they teach you anything in basic, anymore?"

Now I was beginning to panic. How the Hell will I get to Manila, I thought? This had all seemed so easy with the courier flight. Now what?

With a sigh, the sergeant said, "Let me see your orders, again."

I passed them over. He looked quickly at the orders, put his thumb on a particular spot and said, "Look, Lieutenant, see this box here that says, 'Variations in Itinerary Authorized'?" It's not checked. "You're TDY to Clark, not authorized to go to Manila."

"But...." I said.

"You guys from Vietnam think you can do anything you want. But here rules are rules," he said and turned away.

I walked away from the counter, dazed. One little X not in a box and my plans are blown up. Who knew?

As I walked through the waiting room towards the exit, thinking "one little X," I noticed an administrative section at the rear of the operations area. The door to this area opened and shut as people came and went. Through the open door, I saw women sitting at desks, typing.

One little X. I went into the admin area, saw a nice looking, middle-aged woman several desks back along the aisle. She was just completing typing something. She looked friendly, might be willing to help. I walked up to her, gave her my best smile, and said, "Can I use your typewriter for a minute?"

She looked at me quizzically for a moment, then smiled and said, "Sure, Lieutenant. What do you need? Maybe I can do it for you."

I said, "Thanks, but you probably don't want to do that. I'll just be a minute."

She stood up and indicated her seat. I sat down, put my orders in the roller and started to line up the variations box.

She saw what I was doing and said a little conspiratorially, "A little to the left and down a bit. Here, let me adjust it." She did and nodded.

I hit the X key. It was perfect.

I rolled the orders out of the typewriter, stood up and said, "Thanks."

She looked at me with a wry smile, nodded at my flight suit. A trace of melancholy showed in her eyes. "Our son is there," she said. "Good luck." She sat back down.

Later, I presented my orders at the Ops Counter and was dutifully placed on the manifest for tomorrow's flight. One little X. I called Sara.

✢ ✢ ✢

The courier flight arrived in Manila about 1:30 on Saturday. It was a short flight from Clark.

Sara was waiting for me as promised. She was in a cluster of Filipino women, easy to spot as she was a head taller than the others. We hugged. One of the Filipino women nearby kept asking, "But where is your 'Priend'?"

I looked quizzically at Sara. She said, "It's not proper here in the Philippines for a young woman like me to meet a man without an escort. She's been watching me for 15 minutes. She's scandalized." We both laughed. "Is that all you have?" Sara asked indicating my small travel bag.

"Yes," I replied. "I just brought a couple of changes of clothes."

"I hope you brought a swim suit," Sara teased. "Otherwise...."

"Otherwise what?" I asked.

"Well, tomorrow we're going to Pagsanjan Falls and otherwise you'd have to go native." She grinned.

"I'll let you find out tomorrow," I teased back.

Four—Bullpup Training

We walked through the sparse terminal and out to the curb. Her father's driver was waiting for us. We climbed in the back seat, and Sara said to the driver, "Drop us at the Colonial Club. Then don't worry about us. We'll take a Jeepney to the house around six."

"Yes ma'am," he said. "Have fun."

The Colonial Club was situated right on Manila Bay. We had a delightful late lunch on the veranda. It was hot, of course, but there was a nice breeze off the Bay and the ceiling fans kept the air stirred when the breeze faltered. After lunch, we toured the downtown shops, lots of silver jewelry, exquisite fabrics, and beautiful wood carvings. Although I wasn't yet in the reckless spending mode—that would come in a while—I bought a lovely Patadiong [*soft, fine cotton*] table linen set for Sara's mother, a pin for Sara and a barong Tagalog, the famous Manila dress shirt, for myself.

Five o'clock found us back at the veranda of the Colonial Club.

"A beautiful girl, a perfect gin and tonic, and a wonderful view of the Bay," I said. "I could learn to love this. It sure beats the Hell out of Vietnam."

Sara smiled tightly, "Be careful over there. We don't want to lose you."

"So what's Pagsanjan Falls?" I asked to lighten the mood.

"Oh, it's fun," Sara said. "It's a river that runs down from the volcano. You take dugout canoes up the river about five kilometers from the small town of Pagsanjan to a pool at the base of the falls. There you get to swim—suit or not."

"You mean I have to paddle for a couple of miles upstream just to swim?"

"Oh no," Sara said. "The Filipino boys do the paddling. All you have to do is sit back and relax. Alice, one of my friends here who is also in school in the States, will be going with us. So you'll have two girls to look after you. You should be OK."

We both laughed.

The Jeepney dropped us at the gate to San Lorenzo Village, an upscale private neighborhood in Manila. We walked the short distance to Sara's parents' house.

"My parents are anxious to meet you," Sara said as we walked. "Especially my Dad. He wants to share war stories, I think."

Her parents were delightful, and her father and I did spend hours telling war stories, much to the chagrin of Sara and her mother.

On Sunday mid-morning we drove to Pagsanjan, a small town where the canoe trip up the river originated. The dugout canoes were smaller than I had imagined, just two paddlers and two riders.

Her parents declined the canoe ride, rather they stayed in Pagsanjan and enjoyed a relaxing lunch and a stroll around the town. Sara, as I expected, insisted that Alice and I take one canoe while she rode alone in the other. That was so typical of Sara. She always seemed to defer to someone else; never asserted herself to do what she wanted.

The trip up the river was fun; the paddlers fought to get the canoe through the various rapids; the placid stretches were quiet and serene. The passenger space in the canoe was small, and Alice had no choice but to lean back against me. Sara in the other canoe tried not to look unhappy.

At the falls, we swam, enjoyed lunch, and Mai Tai. The water was cool and refreshing, the day tropical but pleasant.

"Too bad about the swim suit," Sara chided.

When it was time to leave the falls, Sara started for the single canoe. I grabbed her hand, shook my head. "Ride with me," I said. She started to protest, then squeezed my hand. The ride back down the river was very pleasant; the rapids were exhilarating. I held her tight as the dugout dipped and surged. In the quiet stretches, Sara relaxed against me. It felt good to both of us.

After dinner back at Sara's house, her parents discreetly left us alone in the living room. Sara and I sat on the living room couch. We talked about things—our day in San Francisco three months ago, her graduation from her master's program, her new teaching job, the war.

"There seem to be growing protests against the war back in the States, especially on college campuses," Sara said. "You remember all the guys that joined ROTC at USC your last semester?"

"Yeah," I said. "Most were there just to get out of the draft for a while, hoping the war would end."

Sara nodded. "You're there now, in the thick of it. What do you think of it?"

"I don't know," I replied. "You have to feel for the families of the guys that don't come back. I had a friend from pilot training who was killed a couple of weeks ago. I feel so sorry for his wife. And the Army guys that are maimed for life, it's hard to comprehend their suffering."

I paused, reflecting, then said, "I guess I'm lucky in that regard. In my business the outcome is usually binary—you either survive or you don't."

Sara was quiet for a while. "So what do you think about it now?" she asked. "Is any of it worth it? Does the risk you take every day mean anything? Are the protesters right?"

I didn't answer at first as I gathered my thoughts. "Yes," I said. "It is worth it in the long run. I think the protesters, maybe much of the

Four—Bullpup Training

country, has been seduced by an ideal that doesn't exist. They think a war 'of the people' is a good thing. And they sure don't know much about history, about the communists. They talk about 'the people,' but communism has never been about the people, not in reality. It's always been more about the tyranny of the few over the many."

"The march of communism has not been pretty," I continued. "Russia 50 years ago, North Korea in 1948, China in '49, North Vietnam five years later—how did all that work out? How many millions perished under Stalin's benevolent rule, or Mao's great leap forward? Who wants to live under Kim Il Sung's nice dictatorship? And North Vietnam—what do you suppose the communists there have in mind for the people in the south?"

Sara touched my shoulder. I took her hand and continued, "So yeah, I think what the United States is doing, what I'm doing, is right. I know some people scoff at it, but stemming the march of communism is important, important for the ordinary people of South Vietnam, important for my maid, just a simple peasant girl, but a nice person who just wants a quiet life with her family. But war is an ugly business and many people have to suffer, pay the price to get to the right end." I shook my head. "I know it's tough in many ways, a lot of sacrifice and loss; but I think we will prevail if only we have the will, the courage as a Nation to see this through."

"Just don't you be one that pays the price," Sara said. She snuggled close to me, and I put my arm around her shoulders. I sensed she wanted to be more than just friends, at least for this evening. She needed to be held, to hold me safe for a little while. We kissed and stroked each other.

The next day, Monday, we continued to explore Manila and its rich culture. In the afternoon, we went to the Manila American Cemetery and Memorial. It memorializes the American and Filipino soldiers that were killed in the fight against Japan in World War II. There, spread out in solemn relief, are over 17,000 white crosses, row upon row of crosses on a vast green expanse. Both American and Philippine flags soar over the carefully manicured setting. Each cross represents one who did pay the ultimate price. None wanted to do so, I'm sure, but each was willing if need be, to arrest the march of tyranny. We surely can do no less, I thought.

On Tuesday, I caught the Embassy courier back to Clark, and on Wednesday returned to the War.

✦ ✦ ✦

Back at Tuy Hoa

July 25, 1968

Darling Jean,

I'm so sorry that I haven't written more faithfully lately ... but the days just seem to slip away. I'm afraid that my recent attempts at baring my "true inner self" have not turned out for the best.... I fear that I've given you a distorted view in my attempt to emphasize the areas of my personality that you (and I) seem to understand least. Look on it as a caricature. I should hope that in reality I am more balanced.

Last Friday I went to Clark Air Base in the Philippines. I was supposed to be helping to ferry an airplane to Taiwan for maintenance overhaul. Well, the airplane broke down at Clark and they didn't get it fixed until last Wednesday. The guy I was with went ahead and took the airplane to Taiwan and I came on back to Tuy Hoa to get on with the war. While I was in the Philippines, I went down to Manila for a few days. It was really nice to be able to walk the streets and shop and dine in comfort and to be away from the war zone. I had a very nice time while I was there. The Philippines are not a particularly good place for great buys, so I didn't buy much. Now I'm anxious to get to Hong Kong or Tokyo so that I can spend hundreds of dollars on stereo equipment, a camera, etc. I'll probably go broke saving money on the bargains over here.

Letters from the various members of my family indicate that they are spread to the far corners of the country. My father left California for Virginia last Sunday (the 14th). On the way he deposited Ronnie in Kansas. George has gone back to Reese on his way to Miami and the survival school circuit. My mother and Janet are still in California. Janet will be staying out there to go to school at UCSB, but mother will be heading east as soon as she can sell the house. They all seem excited and happy about the change. I was glad that my Dad did decide to take the job. I hope that it turns out well.

Not having flown any combat for a week, I have kind of lost contact with the war. It seems to be going about the same, although the weather has been very bad. We lost another plane and pilot from the Wing today.

I hope that you are having a beautiful summer. You sound as if you are enjoying your job a bit more now. I hope so. I hate to think of you being unhappy.

Be good now—

Love, Stu

Four—Bullpup Training

July 25, 1968

Dear Dad,

I imagine that you are already immersed in your new endeavor. I certainly hope that everything works out well for you with this job. Personally, I was glad to see you make the change. You seemed to be so completely dissatisfied with your job in Los Angeles.

I must say that I shall look forward to the prospect of coming home to the Farm. I suppose that it is as much a home to me as any of the places we have lived. At any rate, I know that you will find it nice to have a little room to move about in.

Today was my first mission since I got back from my little trip. It was routine except that the weather has turned rotten around here of late. We are now blessed with low stratus ceilings combined with driving rain and blowing sand. There was a sandstorm in progress when we landed. It was blowing so hard that the tower couldn't see us on landing roll out and had to ask us to call clear of the active [runway]. They still were calling the visibility a mile and a half, however. The wind made bombing interesting too.

I now have 60 combat missions, and about 85 combat hours. I have yet to take a hit or have anything very serious go wrong—save for my little excursion off the runway. I'm still incensed at the aftermath of that little episode. The command structure from the squadron commander on up seemed to immediately assume that I had permitted the aircraft to taxi off the runway, either through carelessness, ignorance or inexperience. This opinion was reached before any of the physical evidence or the details of the incident had been reviewed. Since the aircraft was not damaged, they seemed more than willing to ascribe the whole thing to pilot ineptitude and drop the entire matter right there. I have since found out that the whole thing was the result of a malfunction in the nose wheel steering system, but this was found through a routine maintenance inspection of the aircraft, and not the result of any investigation. And therefore it is an unofficial finding.

At any rate, the whole affair has left me dismayed, a trifle embittered and certainly gravely dubious of the value of risking my life for this sort of an organization. There is, I'm afraid, certain truth to the saying amongst the junior officers that the only thing you have to look forward to in Air Force flying is an FEB [*Flying Evaluation Board*].

Well, I didn't mean to cry on your shoulder. Things have been going well enough of late. We have lost two pilots and four airplanes since I've gotten here so I guess I shouldn't complain about my petty problems.

I got a letter from George a few days ago. He seems to be quite enthusiastic about his assignment. As he understands it, he may well go to Europe for his first tour in the F-100. That would be a good opportunity for him to see Europe.

Well, I guess I had better close for now. Good luck to you with your new work. I hope you are able to get the farm fixed up the way you want it.

Love, Stewart

※ ※ ※

Note: In retrospect, I can see the way the Wing leadership handled my runway incident was the right way. I was not hurt and the airplane was not damaged except for a cut tire. A check ride with an IP [*instructor pilot*] and I was back on the flying schedule. No lingering discussion or official reports. The squadron ops officer did confirm from tire marks on the runway that the nose wheel steering had gone hard over every time the squat switch on the nose gear strut engaged it. And a follow-up maintenance inspection of the nose wheel steering system found an intermittent fault in the system. A more experienced pilot would probably have diagnosed the problem in the instant and simply turned off the system. Mostly, it was my pride that was wounded.

※ ※ ※

Note: On July 24, Jean wrote her riposte to my letter of July 16. I received her letter about the 28th or 29th after I got back from Manila. This letter provides a remarkable insight into her being. It was the first time she really opened herself up to me—not all life-shaping events come in combat. I had been too self-absorbed to understand her struggles. She wrote:

I finally came to a conclusion about your last letter. You wouldn't believe how many letters of protest I've written that I haven't sent.... This answer has been so long coming because your letter was quite a blow to my pride.

You are also wondering if I will ever, as you put it "let myself live." I have concluded that this is very important to you.... I can't give you a concrete answer. I can't tell you what kind of person I will be next month or next year.

What you failed to understand is my relationship to my Judeo-Christian ethic.... There is a reason for my constant gravitation towards that ethic. But my constant desire to return to what I have known is much more than just force of habit. There is a love in your life which can be replaced by no known human being, one of which is very unique for you because of its impact on your being. Consider your reaction if you could never fly again. There used to exist for me an idea of Beauty, Goodness and Truth. This idea gave me something to die for, and more importantly something to live for. It was the object of all the love I could not give to anyone else, least of all myself.... It died a more agonized death than you have ever guessed at. I know this idea exists only in my mind, but this doesn't mean that I suddenly stop loving it after all this time.

Yes, I still search for what was lost, never to be regained. Stewart, I don't think you realize the difficulty of what you ask. Your outlook is desirable. But a person is <u>their</u> reaction towards life. That's all we are. I admit I'm changing but I can't say if I'm changing into the person you seem to desire. But that's the way it's always been, hasn't it?

I'm sure you can understand now why this has been a difficult letter to write. Maybe I've said one of those things which never should be voiced between a couple, but it's hard to know sometimes what should be said and what should be left unsaid.*

---

*Jean Tuomy, *Is Love Enough? Letters from Vietnam* (Amazon KDP, 2023), 73.

Five

Attacked

Tuy Hoa was bordered on the south by Phu Hiep, an Army base. A South Korean army division was garrisoned at Phu Hiep which accounted for the security of Tuy Hoa in no small measure. The South Koreans were very tough and gave little quarter to the VC/NVA.

As I have mentioned previously, Tuy Hoa had never been attacked or seriously mortared. That changed the night of July 29, when a VC sapper team [*A sapper team is a small combat team equipped with explosive packages and automatic weapons.*] got through the perimeter defenses and blew up two C-130s with satchel charges and damaged several other aircraft. Interestingly, they chose to attack these transport aircraft rather than the F-100 fighter bombers that harassed them. Perhaps that was because the C-130s were more exposed in their parked position on the tarmac. The F-100s were all parked in 10-foot-tall revetments made of thick walls: two outer layers of corrugated steel planks with the space between filled with sand. The revetments were mainly intended to prevent an explosion in one aircraft (such as from a mortar round) spreading to adjacent aircraft. With the revetments, the F-100s were pretty well protected. Not so much the C-130s.

My letter of July 31 speaks to the reaction of the pilots during this attack. It was pretty nonchalant to what could have been a very serious situation. It reflected a cavalier attitude not appropriate given the danger to the base security forces and other personnel.

※ ※ ※

July 31, 1968

Darling Jeannie,

I owe you an apology. It was only when I read your last letter (of the 24th) that I realized how careless of your feelings I had been.... I of course had no right to instruct you on the matters of your being.

Five—Attacked

I guess that we both realized when we launched upon this road of frank self-revelation that it might prove treacherous.... Let us hope that the understanding it has brought outstrips the grief.

Now, let me tell you all the excitement around Tuy Hoa. Last Monday (the 29th) I was awakened about 1:30 in the morning by artillery explosions that seemed to be altogether too close. A quick look outside verified that indeed there were incoming rounds which were exploding in gay profusion all over the ramp where the airplanes are parked. The ramp is located about ¼ of a mile from the hooch where I live. So-o-o, in order to gain a better perspective of the action, I climbed atop the bunker where I joined a clutch of the other pilots in the squadron. Soon parts of the parking area were engulfed in flames as one of the C-130s caught fire. As one of the guys then explained, "By damn, we are under attack, somebody get me a Scotch and water." Some of the other guys opted for their cameras in lieu of a drink. But there we stood, clustered on the top of the bunker clad in shorts or some such, drinks or cameras in hand and watching the fireworks.

Shortly afterwards the shelling stopped and sometime after that the base warning sound blew telling us an attack was imminent. I had already put on my steel helmet (for a lark) but escalated to my flak jacket (primarily because I was cold) when they blew the siren.

As we watched the airplanes burn and speculated on the wonder of the whole thing, the squadron commander called and allowed as how he thought maybe we ought to report to the squadron. The squadron building is located right next to the ramp and would seem to offer a better vantage point, so we all piled into a truck and sped down there. There we all strapped on our pistols and stood about for an hour or so. Meanwhile, we learned that most of the damage was done by VC sappers with satchel charges. Small arms still rattled in the distance and helicopter gunships were working over something, but the great attack was essentially over. About 3:30 we all went home and went back to bed.

Fortunately, no friendlies were killed in the attack although a few were wounded. Two airplanes were destroyed, so it wasn't a bad night's work for Charlie. He shook up some of the complacency here abouts anyway. Our security is terrible.

I can't say that I have had any particularly exciting missions lately. Things got pretty hot while I was TDY and several of the guys got shot up pretty badly. Then last Thursday one of the National Guard troops got shot down near Chu Lai. He didn't have a successful ejection apparently because he was dead when they picked him up. July has been a bad month for F-100s. But don't worry, my luck is still good. I haven't been hit yet.

Speaking of luck, it occurs to me again how lucky I am to have you.

Stewart

✤ ✤ ✤

August 4, 1968

Dearest Jean,

I received your letter of the 29th today and the books a few days earlier. Thank you for the books. I enjoyed the *Cartoon History*, but as yet I have not had the courage to delve into *The Idiot*. I can't help but wonder if there isn't some subtle message in that title. (Indeed, I must be an idiot for ever leaving you and delving into this madness.) At the present time, I am deeply engrossed (between flights and other duties) in Velikovsky's *Worlds in Collision*. It contains a truly fascinating theory of early cosmological history, and it is very thought provoking.

August 5

It is Sunday today (or so my Playboy calendar tells me). The sky is dark and foreboding with clouds hanging like a black curtain to the South. I was up earlier today flying around in that tumultuous darkness. It was quite exciting. We were supposed to go into the infamous A Shau valley today but got diverted at the last minute for some reason. It has been a pretty hot area lately. In fact, the Wing lost another airplane up there two days ago. The pilot ejected successfully and was picked up uninjured a short time later.

I was bemused by your remarks concerning our losses over here. It would seem that for some reason the people back in the States refuse to face the fact that we are fighting a war over here. Perhaps it is because the war is so removed and does not touch them. But it is the nature of war to kill people. We are lucky that our loss rate hasn't been higher. Up until the end of June this year, Tuy Hoa had only had one combat loss in the past year and the pilot escaped from that one uninjured. Now for some reason we have lost four airplanes and two pilots in the last five weeks. It would appear that the VC are better armed and supplied than previously. Could there indeed be truth to the militaristic view that the bombing pause in the North is costing American lives in the South? [*President Johnson had imposed a bombing pause in North Vietnam north of the 20th parallel on March 31, 1968.*] But then the noble pacifist will tell us that any step towards peace (if indeed this is) is worth the price, any price—as long as someone else is paying it. But forgive me if I must seem a trifle bitter. You needn't worry about me. I have too much to live for to let myself get shot down.

Tonight, we are about to have a party. One of the guys in the squadron is due to go back to the States in a week, so we are having a going away party for him. He flew his last mission today and will soon be homeward bound. We will all be sorry to see him go because he is both a great pilot and a great guy. But on the other hand, it would be worse to not see him go. It brings us all a little closer to our own rotation date.

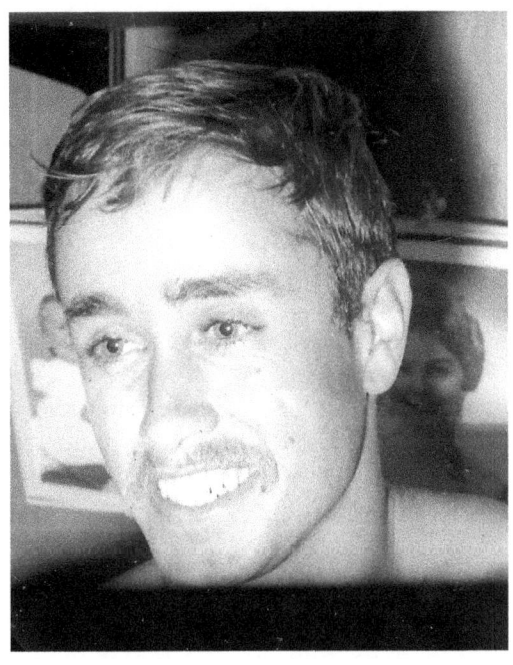

Author in a friend's hooch. Referred to in the letter of August 4th (author's collection).

With respect to my R&R which you asked about, it will be December at the earliest before I can go to Hawaii. As you may well imagine, Hawaii is the most popular R&R site and consequently is inundated with people wanting to go there. Priority on an R&R flight to Hawaii is dependent upon a person's length of time in country, as of course it should be. Right now, Hawaii R&R's are backlogged through November. But I should be able to get there in December if you still want to see me then. I think with the Hawaii trip I will get about six days actually in Hawaii. I am looking forward very much to seeing you there.

Well, I must close this and go join the festivities. These things usually turn into drinking bouts, as stag parties invariably do, and I have to help tend bar.

I'm enclosing a picture of my smiling countenance. The big black strip on the bottom of the picture is a processing error courtesy of the local VC film processors.

Love, Stu

✤ ✤ ✤

August 9, 1968

My Darling Jean,

It's two o'clock of a Friday morning. The night is still and generally quiet. A full silvery moon floods the night with its ghostly half-light. I am on alert tonight which is why I am awake to witness the wonderful stillness of the night. This alert is a tiresome business; 12 hours of sitting, waiting for the call to come that will send us on our way. If you get to fly several missions, it's not so bad. It's the interminable waiting that is so tiresome. I have been on day alert for the past two days and only got one mission. Now I have two nights of alert to look forward to and not much better prospects. I think that we will get a mission later on this morning. It should be beautiful up there tonight.

Things have been very quiet for me recently. The war is quiet—very little activity of any consequence anywhere in the country. The time just seems to drag now.

Much later—

I'm back on alert again. My letter got interrupted by a mission. By the time I was finished with that it was morning and time for us to be relieved. Unfortunately, then I had some administrative duties to take care of back at the squadron. By the time that was settled it was nearly noon and my duty day was extending to nearly 24 hours. My flight commander all but ordered me to go home and get some sleep at that point. Needless to say, I wasn't too hard to convince on the merits of that proposal.

At any rate I was back on alert at 6:00 this evening so you can see that it is very much later. We were scrambled earlier this evening. In fact, I just got back about 20 minutes ago. There is a full moon out tonight to help dispel the darkness. Unfortunately, there are also numerous black clouds lurking about the sky. On top of the clouds, they appear as an immense snowfield stretched out in the eerie twilight of the moon. The thunderstorm buildups look like mountains of white rock piled up to unknown heights. The valleys and canyons formed by the tumbling clouds are ghostly and not quite real. It is really an awesome scene.

I hope that all is going well for you this summer. You should by now have amassed considerable wealth from your summer job. It is hard to believe that we are well into August and that summer will soon be done. For myself, I shall count the summer as a blank spot, an empty succession of days that have no more character or meaning than the passing minutes of a wintery afternoon. I hope that you have fared better with your summer. I longed to share the long summer days with you.

What I want to say, I guess, is that I hope that you are happy ... your happiness is very important to me. I wish that I could insure it in some manner.

Be good now—

Love, Stu

✳ ✳ ✳

Weather

Vietnam is a tropical country spanning from eight degrees latitude in the south to 25 degrees in the north. It is a narrow country over 1,000 miles long. The Demilitarized Zone (DMZ) separating North Vietnam from South Vietnam was placed along the 17th parallel.

Weather in South Vietnam was dominated by the tropical wind cycle. This meant periods of relative fair weather in the spring and early summer. The short southwest monsoon brought heavy rains and low ceilings in midsummer. This lasted for several weeks. Then mid-level clouds and thunderstorms returned until the northeast monsoon season rose to dominate the fall and winter. The fall monsoon season brought weeks, months of low clouds and driving rain and the serious threat of typhoons.

I remember when I first started flying in mid–May, the weather was quite pleasant, if hot. There typically was a scattered to broken cumulous cloud layer at around 10,000 feet, with thunderstorms imbedded, particularly over the low mountainous region between Tuy Hoa and the Saigon area. The F-100 did not have a radar, so as we flew south from Tuy Hoa, we had to pick our way visually between the thunderstorms.

In mid–July, the southwest monsoon turned the weather into low ceilings at about 1,000 feet, with drizzling rain. Fortunately, it only lasted a couple of weeks and did not entail dangerous winds. It mostly meant a chance to practice instrument landing approaches, and to experience the danger of bombing under low ceilings. By early August, the weather returned to the previous pattern, swelteringly hot with mid-level clouds, and thunderstorms.

The thunderstorms were the predominant weather danger in this period. I remember on several occasions returning to Tuy Hoa, low on fuel, only to be told the field was closed because of a thunderstorm, and I had to divert to Phu Cat 80 miles to the north. A little tense but no real problem.

The fall monsoon season was not so benign. Low ceilings and

driving rain lasted for weeks, only to be relieved for short periods by relatively pleasant weather—a chance to work on my tan. During November and again in December, we experienced typhoon alerts that caused flying to stand down and the airplanes prepared for possible evacuation to Thailand. In both cases, the typhoons passed to our south and the evacuation was not necessary. But the rain came in wind-blown sheets which drenched everything. The letter of 26 November provides a vivid description of these conditions.

In early February, the weather returned to the spring/summer pattern.

If weather was a constant threat that lurked in the back of our minds, it was also the source of the impossible savagery and beauty of Nature. Blundering into a thunderstorm not only tossed the airplanes around, but also excited the phenomena of St. Elmo's fire. This happened when electrically charged particles of water turned luminescent in greens and purples. Often it occurred at high pressure points on the aircraft, the base of the windscreen or the end of the refueling probe. The particles at the windscreen would generally break loose and trickle up the wind screen in a flood of green, while a purple fan spread in front of the end of the refueling probe.

The beauty of Nature was also seen in sunrises that captured the spreading orange rise of the sun against black cloud formations that seemed to want to hold the sun back. Seen from 20,000 feet, with the coastline just beginning to emerge from the darkness, was a bit of Nature's artistry that was captivating.

Weather was certainly a constant danger, enroute to/from the target area, in the target area, and on recovery back at Tuy Hoa. But I don't remember ever having a mission canceled because of weather, although we did stand down for the two typhoons. Often it required creative thinking to just get back on the ground. And low fuel was always a complicating factor.

I remember one incident in which I was leading a flight of two. When we returned to Tuy Hoa we found the base with a 1,000-foot ceiling and several flights in front of us waiting for clearance to start an instrument approach to the field. The published instrument approach was a tear drop; that is, we would fly away from the airfield for fifteen miles then make a turn back to line up with the runway, all the while descending from 18,000 feet to 1,500 feet at seven miles from the runway. This point was called the final approach fix from which we would make a precise descent to landing.

My two-ship flight entered a holding pattern to wait our turn with an anxious eye on the fuel gauge. In about 10 minutes we had our turn.

Five—Attacked

Approach Control called, "Saber 21, cleared for TACAN approach, landing opposite direction runway 03, call out of 18,000." TACAN is a radio navigation device that gives direction and distance to the selected station, in this case Tuy Hoa's runway. Approach Control's directions meant we would fly the standard TACAN approach over the water, then transition to a visual approach when we broke out for an opposite direction landing on Runway 03.

"Roger," I replied. "Out of 18, Two take spacing in the penetration turn." This meant for Two to break off from the formation and to fly a wider arc from me as we turned back towards the runway. This would enable Two to gain spacing from my aircraft for his individual landing.

There was a pause, then Two said, "Uh, Lead, my TACAN won't lock on."

Now this was a dilemma. Without his TACAN, Two would have no way of navigating in the weather after he broke formation. Shit, I said to myself. A great time to learn about this problem.

"OK, Two, take spacing after we break out [*get below the clouds*]. I'll keep my speed up."

The approach was normal. I dipped under the published altitude profile and we broke out at 1,000 feet several miles from the runway. I pushed my speed up to 230 knots, the maximum gear down speed and Two slowed to approach speed to gain spacing. I wanted to give Two as much room as I could so he had room for his own landing approach. As I reached the downwind to final turn point, I was still at 230 knots, well above the normal turn speed. I pulled the throttle to idle and started my descending 180 degree turn to final. Halfway around I realized I was too fast to make the turn in a normal fashion. And with not enough fuel to go around—What now? I thought. Well, this is easy. Just make a roll-in on the end of the runway as I would a target. I eased the bank angle, pushed the throttle to Mil and pulled the nose up to level flight. Then I relaxed the G, rolled to about 120 degrees of bank, pulled the nose down to point at the runway, pulled the throttle to idle and rolled wings level in a descending flight path. Not SOP [*standard operating procedure*] for sure, but it worked. I continued to descend with idle power. I landed about 1,500 feet down the runway. It's amazing what you can do with an airplane when you are flying her every day; when you can really feel what she is telling you.

A friend, who was in mobile at the time, told me later he was reaching for the crash phone when he saw me go on my back in the final turn, but then I was suddenly just on landing roll out. Again, I had pushed my F-100 *Jeannie* to the limit, but we were still friends. Maybe I was pushing my other Jeannie to her limit as well. I hoped we were still friends.

Things didn't always turn out so well with weather issues. On one particularly bad weather night in mid-winter, a flight of two from the Wing went missed approach [*couldn't find the runway*] at Tuy Hoa and diverted to Cam Ranh Bay. They never arrived at Cam Ranh.

* * *

August 12, 1968

Dear Mom,

I hope that you have a very happy birthday. Wish that I could be there to help you celebrate it. I hope that you enjoy many more.

I have been frightfully busy lately. Twelve-hour days and more are becoming standard here. The war itself seems to be at an uneasy pause. We are flying more, however. It looks like Charlie is building up for another big offensive and we are trying to hamper his operations as much as possible. Last week I was on alert for four days and it looks like I will have another couple of days of it this week. That means 12 hours a day sitting around waiting for something to happen. Usually you get a scramble or two to break up the monotony.

Today I went down to Ban Me Thuot to visit the Special Forces headquarters there. That is about 100 miles north of Saigon near the Cambodian border. The squadron is responsible for the air support of several Special Forces camps. I was down there gathering some intelligence on one of the camps. It is always interesting, I think, to get out and see more of the rest of this war. Those Special Forces troops have got a tough job. It makes me appreciate my air-conditioned, supersonic office. If you have to fight a war, that's the place to do it from.

I just got a letter from Dad today. He sounded as though the move to Washington has done him good. He said that the farm is as beautiful as ever and that he is well on his way to getting it fixed up.

I've been wondering if you have had any luck selling the house. I certainly hope that you have. I hope this letter gets there before you leave.

Well, that's about all the news I have. And again have a very happy birthday.

Love, Stewart

* * *

August 16, 1968

My Darling,

I'm so glad that you enjoyed the picture and I'm glad that you are happier these days. I will try to get some more pictures in the

Five—Attacked

forthcoming weeks. I have dispatched an emissary to Hong Kong to purchase a Minolta SRT101 [*a high-quality single lens reflex camera*].

I rather suspected that the background of that picture would cause you some consternation. That's why I didn't say anything about it. By way of explanation, let me say that the picture was taken by a classmate from Luke in his hooch. The woman and baby belonged to his now departed roommate, the notorious Captain "Crash" Patterson, intrepid aviator, who during his Vietnam tour, walked away from the wreckage of two F-100 Super Sabres (one flaming, the other just smoldering). Well, as you can readily see the background adds rather than detracts from the overall force of the picture. It adds an aura of romance and adventure as a counterpoint to the benign and innocent smile that is the main theme of the picture. It is even more appropriate since I am currently favored to take over the legacy that Crash left behind.

I am back on alert again this week. I had two days of day alert and now I have two nights of alert to look forward to. I am presently sitting in the sun crew resting.

Not too much exciting has transpired of late. My airplane got hit a couple of times yesterday which didn't make me too happy. I wasn't flying it at the time, but I hate to see patches all over it. I got scrambled off alert to go hit the same target. While we were up there, my leader took a hit. Very unpropitious day, I should say. Neither one was very serious, fortunately. It's the first time I've even had anybody in my flight get shot. It just goes to show you that Charlie is down there blazing away whether you know it or not.

Today at 5 o'clock I must go to Wing headquarters to be presented with a medal. This is for being alive and breathing in Vietnam while taking part in numerous hazardous aerial flights over enemy territory. With that and a dime I can get a cup of coffee.

My mother will be leaving California on the 19th of this month. I understand that my father is already deeply enmeshed in his new job back in Virginia. I guess that I can no longer count California as my home.

Did you really offer not to date anyone for a year? That was foolish. My magnanimity won't permit me to hold you to that, of course. As you say, that would be most ungallant of me.

Just be good—

Love, Stu

✢ ✢ ✢

Note: In her letter of August 8, Jean reminded me that she had promised not to date for the year I was gone, and I had not rejected the idea. This letter above released her from that promise. I could hardly do otherwise given my recent interlude with Sara in Manila, which I had pointedly not mentioned to Jean in my July 25 letter.*

※ ※ ※

August 21, 1968

Dearest Jean,

The days are slipping by quickly and at the same time with terrible slowness. It's hard to believe that August is nearly done already.

The war is stagnant, almost as if without motion. If it were not for the few hours I spend flying every day, I think that I would go out of my mind. But then you have always considered me slightly crazy anyway.

It is interesting how such a thing as war can become routine after a while. I was just about to say that nothing particularly exciting has been happening to me. Yet several days ago my Lead on an alert scramble flight got hit with small arms fire. It was nothing serious, just punched a hole in the wing. Then I had a couple of night missions off alert into the southern part of North Vietnam. That is an active SAM environment and really had my attention, I can assure you. To make the mission even more interesting, both nights were dark and stormy. We were in thunderstorms and weather a good bit of the time. I hardly think it is sporting to have a thunderstorm sitting atop your home base when you return from a mission like that. During the let down to landing, I could barely keep sight of Lead's wingtip light which was a scant 8 to 10 feet away. The turbulence was tossing us about so that I had to alternately fight to keep from hitting Lead and then from losing sight of him. All the while the radar operators manning the approach control radars droned on in their well-rehearsed monologue as they directed us right into the heart of the thunderstorm. Finally they said, "Litter 05, understand the wingman is on the right." To which Lead replied rather dryly, "He is now, but he may not be for long."

Somehow, I'm forced to think that all of this must be a bit more exciting than the usual nine-to-five job.

I am still reading *The Idiot*. It'll probably keep me occupied for quite some time to come also. I don't think I'm prepared to comment on it as yet. In fact, I may never be.

You haven't told me a thing about what you are doing these days. I assume that you are still working in the hardware store, amassing a sizable fortune. I should also hope that you are spending lazy days at

---

*Tuomy, *Is Love Enough?*, 82.

the beach or in the mountains or perhaps just lying about a pool somewhere. You must remember that you have to live the good life enough for both of us. I guess that school will be starting again soon enough. That should keep you out of trouble. I think that my sister will be returning to California about the 1st of September in preparation for her first big day at college. Under the evil influences of UCSB [*University of California, Santa Barbara*] she will probably end up a hippie.

Time will shortly be upon me when I must forecast for an assignment after I leave Vietnam. After you have been in-country for four months you are allowed to enter your choices for the next assignment. This doesn't mean of course that your choice will be honored, but you have a better than an even chance. I find myself at a complete loss as to what to ask for. If I'm to stay in the F-100, then my choices are fairly limited. There is either Luke, Cannon Air Force Base, New Mexico, Myrtle Beach Air Force Base, South Carolina, or Europe. The first three would be instructing jobs and you know how I feel about that. Any other fighter would more than likely mean Europe also. Plus that, to change airplanes would mean an additional commitment to the Air Force. I guess that boils down to a question of whether or not I want to stay in the Air Force. I would also like to go back to school but there is little chance of that with the so-called pilot shortage. It is a very troublesome decision. So much may depend on it for the future. Then again it may all come to nothing.

Love, Stu

✣ ✣ ✣

Note: In a letter in mid–August, Jean mentioned that she had met an attractive guy from the city government at a party she and her mother had given for the leadership of the city. His name was Richard. Hence her coy reminder of her promise not to date in her August 8 letter.

✣ ✣ ✣

August 27, 1968

Dearest Jean,

Your remarks regarding the <u>attractive</u> city guy both pleased and saddened me.... And what a hypocrite I must appear. I chastise you for not drinking fully of life's offerings. But at the same time, I convey to you my wish that you shut yourself off from all contact with life....

Now perhaps you are wondering what I've been up to of late.

Actually, it is not much. The war has been somewhat more active this past week and I have been on alert quite a lot. In fact, the base is nightly alerted to the possibility of another attack and mobilizes every night to defend against it. So far Charlie has been dissuaded.

We have been flying a lot of missions of late in support of the little Special Forces camp at Duc Lap. It lies right on the Cambodian border and has lately been the object of a concerted offensive by the VC. They were under continual siege, but the continued and concentrated air support has finally broken the enemy offensive. One of the lads from the New York National Guard outfit here at Tuy Hoa got shot down over there early in the siege. He ejected successfully from his flaming aircraft but landed only a few hundred feet from the enemy lines—in the no man's land of the battle zone actually. He hunkered down in the tall grass till the Green Berets could get a rescue party to him. Then they had to fight their way back to the Special Forces camp. It was quite a harrowing experience for him, but he made it through unscathed.

Right now, I am in the mobile control unit at the end of the runway. I'm supposed to monitor the airplanes as they take off and land and render assistance, as necessary. It was quite hectic earlier but now we are at the end of the flying day and things are quiet. I'm only awaiting a few wayward birds to come home now. This is one of my additional duties.

Well, I must close for now. Remember, be good—

Love, Stu

✤ ✤ ✤

Note: On August 31, Jean wrote:

You may be curious about my date with Richard. By the way I may as well tell you he's an assistant manager, not a city manager. And it's only our local city. Forgive me for trying to make him sound a little more attractive than he actually is, that was <u>very</u> wrong of me. We went to a place called the FEZ on Sunset and Vermont. It was fully equipped with Turkish food, musicians and belly dancers. It was a very enjoyable evening, and it was interesting to get a new perspective on some of the same old topics.*

✤ ✤ ✤

Hmmm, this dating thing didn't take long—trouble ahead?

✤ ✤ ✤

---

*Tuomy, *Is Love Enough?*, 99.

Five—Attacked

August 29, 1968

Dear Mom & Dad,

I'm amazed that the month of August is nearly finished already. Time just seems to slip by unnoticed. I have been standing alert quite regularly of late. It is a 12 hour on 12 hour off proposition and really gets to be a rat race. It seems you don't do anything but sleep and eat and wait for the next scramble. Right now I'm on the night cycle so I hardly see the light of day. And there is nothing like a little night gunnery to really get your attention.

The tempo of the war has picked up considerably this past week. The VC launched a massive attack last week against Duc Lap, a little Special Forces camp on the Cambodian border. It [*the battle*] was, I should think, an awesome display of the might of tactical air power. There was a flight or two of fighters on station over the camp continually. In the half dozen or so flights I made over there the fighter flights were stacked up four deep waiting to get on the target.

I got to do a little air refueling about a week ago. That was fun for a change, but 2½ hours at a time is just too long to sit in that little cockpit. I was pleased to find that I could still get on the tanker without undue difficulty.

Have you all heard anything from George lately? I was interested in hearing what he thought of the survival schools. I'd also like his address at Cannon [*Air Force Base*]. I tried to send him a letter at Reese [*Air Force Base*] but it got returned marked addressee unknown.

Well, I guess I'd better close for now. It is basketball season at Tuy Hoa and I have to go lend my feeble support to the squadron basketball team this afternoon.

Love, Stewart

✤ ✤ ✤

Air Refueling

The ability to refuel aircraft in the air had become an important part of the Air Force's (and Navy's) capabilities following World War II. The Army Air Corps had experimented with the concept of aerial refueling as early as 1929. In an experiment in January, an Air Corps airplane was kept aloft for over 150 hours by 42 refuelings. Both the receiver and the refueling aircraft were open cockpit, so the refueling could be accomplished by manually passing hoses between the two aircraft. The closed cockpit aircraft of WW II and after preclude that approach.

As the Cold War emerged in the early '50s, long-range bombers were the mainstay of the U.S.'s retaliatory nuclear strike capability. In order to achieve adequate range for missions over the North Pole, in-flight refueling was a necessity, and specialized refueling aircraft and transfer equipment were developed to meet this need. Initially, long hoses with drogues [*cone shaped webbing that looked like a basket*] at their ends were deployed from the refueling aircraft. The receiver intercepted the drogue with a special refueling probe.

With the advent of jet aircraft, the B-47 and B-52, refueling capability was built into the design, and the refueling aircraft were modified to be compatible with the receiving aircrafts' systems. This basic design approach is still used today.

The standard system today involves specialized refueling aircraft, called tankers, the KC-135 and KC-46. The "K" in front of the basic "C" or cargo designation, indicates refueling capability in Air Force designation terminology. These aircraft are equipped with a 28-foot refueling tube, called a "Boom," that contains an inner tube that can extend the Boom's reach another 20 feet. The Boom is installed

Two F-100s air refueling. The far aircraft is on the boom, taking on fuel (author's collection).

underneath the tail section of the refueling aircraft. The Boom is fitted with winglets and is maneuverable within a limited area. A boom operator (or "Boomer") controls the Boom. All modern Air Force jet aircraft (fighter, bomber and cargo) are fitted with a receiver capability consisting of a receptacle, or port, a set of jaws that lock on to the end of the Boom and plumbing that allows fuel to pass from the refueling aircraft to the receiver's fuel tanks.

In operation today, the receiver pilot positions her aircraft under the tail of the tanker, guided by a set of lights on the bottom of the tanker's fuselage. The Boomer then "flies" the boom to align with the receiver refueling port and extends the inner boom to connect with the receiver. Fuel is then transferred at up to 1,000 gallons per minute. This process is very effective, even for large receiver aircraft such as the C-17. The receiver role is static and the Boomer has the delicate job of aligning and inserting the Boom into the receiver.

The F-100 was a transitional aircraft and was not designed with an inflight refueling capability. However, as the Cold War heated up in the mid '50s, F-100s deployed in Europe took on a nuclear strike mission. The need for aerial refueling was obvious, both for the transatlantic deployment and for the deep strike nuclear mission. This was provided in the C/D/F models introduced in the mid-'50s. But rather than a receiver port, the F-100s were equipped with a refueling probe, a long, S-shaped pipe that extended from the leading edge of the right wing up to a position adjacent to the canopy. To refuel, this probe was connected to the drogue, or "basket," that trailed off the end of the Boom. Thus the Tanker had the static, female role, and the F-100 had the male role. This could be a tenuous task for the pilot of a heavily laden F-100 as described in Chapter Eleven.

Refueling capability played a significant role in Vietnam, especially for forces attacking the Hanoi area. Even getting to South East Asia (SEA) required refueling multiple times for fighters to cross the vast Pacific. During the Linebacker II operation against the Hanoi area in December 1972, 160 tankers flew 1,312 sorties with 4,500 air refuelings. The tankers were credited with over 500 "saves" of attack aircraft that otherwise would not have made it home.*

For us at Tuy Hoa, air refueling made it possible to reach targets in the far reaches of the Mekong delta. Then as missions to the Ho Chi Minh Trail in Laos increased, regular tanker orbits were set up over northern South Vietnam. This availability of refueling greatly

---

*James Pfaff, "The KC-135," *Friends Journal* of the Air Force Museum Foundation 47, no. 2 (Spring 2024): 10–12.

improved time on target and our effectiveness against targets along the Trail.

✢ ✢ ✢

September 2, 1968

Dearest Jean,

Happy Labor Day! I hope that you thoroughly enjoyed the holiday. I should think that a long weekend, a chance to go to the seacoast or mountains and to relax in the quietue of nature would be a glorious respite from the rigors of daily life. I went flying every day during the holiday myself. It was great fun—you know bombing, strafing, getting shot at, etcetera.

My maid just accused me of being lazy and not working. She said all I do is sleep. Well, the fact that I'm on night alert on a nearly continual basis now helps to explain that. But so it must seem to her. And indeed, I have been so tired of late that all I seem to do is sleep and fly.

As for my medal, I thought that I had explained all of that though perhaps a little cryptically. You get one of these trinkets for every 20 combat missions you fly. I guess because they figure you came close enough to busting your ass for flag, country and motherhood on at least one of those missions. Besides, you deserve something for putting up with all of the rubbish the Air Force hands out in the interim and still getting your job done.

But let me quote for you the citation and you may draw your own conclusions:

"By direction of the President, each of the following is awarded the Air Medal for meritorious achievement while participating in aerial flight. During the period indicated, outstanding airmanship and courage were exhibited in the successful accomplishment of important missions under extremely hazardous conditions. The highly professional efforts of each individual cited contributed materially to the mission of the United States Air Force in Southeast Asia."

Thereafter follows a list of the recipients. As you say, 23% fewer cavities.

So, you are perplexed by my thoughts on my next assignment? But then why shouldn't you be? ... How can you understand my anguish when I'm not sure that I understand it myself? But it doesn't matter. There is nothing for it anyway.

I'm still trying to struggle through *The Idiot*. I've mixed emotions about the book. Its ideas are powerful and thought-provoking, but the characters seem stilted and foolish and the plot nearly incomprehensible. At times I think that Dostoyevsky would have been better off to have written an essay. But then I'm in no position to judge a work of art.

I hope that everything is going well for you. It won't be long now, I guess, before you are back in school. At least you should find some solace in the fact that this is your last year.

I must close for now and go back to work. It is a black and stormy night with the rain pouring down in torrential sheets. It should be fun.

Be good now—

Love, Stu

✦ ✦ ✦

September 10, 1968

My Dearest Jean,

Time does seem to be racing quickly by. You'll be going off to school by the time you receive this, and I will be over ⅓ finished with my tour here. It is all so strange how even the most alien of environments eventually become accepted as the natural way of things. To fly combat missions has become a part of my way of life now. The placid beauty of the country and the awesome destructiveness of the bombs, the joy of life and the emptiness of death are a part of my reality.

No, perhaps that is not entirely true either. Another good friend of mine was killed last Friday. I find it hard to reconcile his death. He was a C-130 pilot and was killed trying to fly a load of rice into an isolated village in bad weather conditions. It seems so insane. He needn't have been there at all. He had been due to go back to the States in August but had extended for six months over here. But then, that's not the point either. I'm not sure what is.

For me, things are going well enough. I'm starting to lead flights now rather than flying the wing position all of the time. Most of the senior guys in the squadron are going home in the next couple of months. That will leave us young lieutenants (the objects of so much derision) as the most combat experienced pilots in the squadron. That will be an interesting turn of events.

By a stroke of good fortune, I have been afforded the opportunity to go to Hong Kong for several days. I leave tomorrow on this adventure. I am really looking forward to this trip. I plan to spend a small fortune on stereo equipment, clothes, etc. They say it is a shopper's paradise. By the way, I didn't get that camera yet; the guy who was going to buy it for me ran out of money before he got around to the camera.

I hope that you weren't finding the task of packing for school too strenuous. At any rate, don't study too hard. I must close for now and do some packing myself for my trip to Hong Kong. Remember I miss you terribly.

Be good now—

Love, Stu

❋ ❋ ❋

September 18, 1968

Dearest Jean,

I just got back from Hong Kong about 11:30 last night. I have spent most of today sorting through all of the varied and interesting things I bought up there. Right now, I'm listening to some of my new stereo equipment which I just assembled. You would simply love Hong Kong. It is a shopper's paradise with endless bargains on things you "simply must have." Most people go quite broke saving money on the good deals.

As I wrote you rather hurriedly last week, we were to leave here last Wednesday and go down to Saigon. We got down there a little before noon and we're promptly taken in tow by Bill, a friend of Jack's. He is an attorney in the legal office at Tan Son Nhut. He took us down to his penthouse apartment in Saigon where we spent the night. His place is a bit rundown to be sure, having suffered a bit from the war, but still, it isn't a bad way to fight the war. He took us to dinner at the International House, an embassy club, for a brief look at Saigon's underground nightlife. It was interesting, but the evening was cut short by the 10 o'clock curfew.

Next morning Bill saw that we got on our plane safely and we were off for Hong Kong. This was a regular R&R flight, Pan Am charter and quite nice. I don't know how Bill managed to get us on it.

By the time we got to Hong Kong and suffered through the interminable briefings and finally got checked in at the hotel (the Peninsula), it was nearly ten o'clock. We wandered up to the restaurant on top of the hotel for dinner. The view of the city was magnificent, and the food was excellent, and I began to feel like I was alive again.

We got up early the next morning to get started on our shopping spree. First a stop by our friendly Hong Kong tailor to order a wardrobe. I think perhaps I went overboard here, but I'm very happy with the clothes I got. It is interesting the way they do business. When you give them an idea of what you want, they begin pulling down bolt after bolt of material until you finally select what you like. I know virtually nothing about material so that meant little to me. I just picked out the color I liked.

Anyway, after that I had to have some trousers (5) and some shirts (10) and finally some shoes. I trust I won't look quite so disheveled the next time I see you.

After we were finished with our selecting and measuring, the tailor drove us to Hong Kong Island (we were staying in Kowloon on the mainland) where we shopped for stereo equipment. I bought a tape recorder and two Sansui speaker systems. I wanted to get a Sansui tuner but was unable to find one. Getting all of that and getting it shipped and looking at it in awe and wonder killed most of the afternoon. I was exhausted by the time we got back to the hotel. Still, we couldn't miss happy hour and the magnificent view of the sunset from the bar atop the hotel. And after that, a cautious sampling of Hong Kong's abundant nightlife.

The next two days were more of the same, albeit a bit more leisurely. It seemed to be a constant round of tailor fittings, another shop to go to, another bargain to search out. On Sunday afternoon we were in the tailor shop for another fitting. I was watching as Jack tried on his clothing and happened to remark that I really liked the brown Glen Plaid suit he had ordered. The tailor overheard this remark and hurried to persuade me to get one of the same. Well, I really did like it and it was only $54, so why not? All the clothes turned out quite nicely. They fit beautifully and since I have a difficult time getting many things to fit well, I didn't mind spending a little money at the tailor shop.

By Monday evening all of our money was gone, my clothes were finished, and I was nearly exhausted. We left about 9:00 Tuesday morning and headed back for the war zone. Tan Son Nhut was in its usual state of chaos, and it took us nearly 10 hours to find an airplane back to Tuy Hoa. For some reason, the people in Saigon seem strangely reluctant to help anyone out at all. I'm glad I'm not stationed down there. Tomorrow, I start flying again.

The trip to Hong Kong was really great. It is a fascinating city. How much more fascinating it would be to see it with you. I think that you would really enjoy it also. A particularly beautiful sunset can also be particularly lonely because, I guess, I want so much to share it with you.

I must close for now and get some sleep. After one of these brief "vacations," I really need about three days of rest and quiet before I'm ready to face the war again.

Love, Stu

⚓ ⚓ ⚓

September 20, 1968

Dear Mom & Dad,

I just got back from a week's trip to Hong Kong.

We got to Hong Kong Thursday evening.... Perhaps you remember my senior English teacher from Cocoa high school. She is now married and owns a fashion shop in Hong Kong. I chatted with her briefly. She was anxiously awaiting the imminent arrival of Paul Cardin and I dare say didn't have much time for one of her old students.

We left Hong Kong early Tuesday morning.... Getting back to Tuy Hoa was a bit of an adventure also. It took us nearly 14 hours to get here from Tan Son Nhut and on the way we visited Bien Hoa and Qui Nhon. We finally talked the C-130 crew into ops stopping at Tuy Hoa and literally depositing us on the end of the runway.

The war has been fairly normal for the past month or so. The whole thing has settled into a bit of a routine. That, of course, can be somewhat dangerous so I think my little vacation was a good thing. I can't say I've had any particularly exciting missions of late. I have recently received a couple of letters of appreciation from ground commanders for work we did in support of them last month. Contrary to the popular press, B-52's are not the only combat aircraft airborne over South Vietnam. It is commonly felt by the Army that tactical air support saved Duc Lap and many other camps like it.

I've just been checked out as an element lead which means I can lead two-ship flights. That takes much more thought than just flying the wing position.

Well, wish I could be there to see the leaves change. I'm really going to miss football season—perhaps next year.

               Love, Stewart

✢ ✢ ✢

September 25, 1968

My Darling Jean,

How are you finding your first few days at school? A welcome change from the home life you endured all summer I should imagine. I can't say that that I envy you your particular hermitage. I'm sure that someplace like UCLA or USC would be an even more welcome change. But then, I would be apprehensive about that. I hope that you don't have to work too hard this year. One's senior year was meant to be spent with a minimum of effort and a maximum of fun and games.

I've been back from my Hong Kong adventure for a week now.... In reflection, I now see that that trip was not only welcome, but it was also medicinal. Before, life had become so stagnant, so routine that I often found myself doing very foolish things with my airplane. I all too frequently would needlessly, heedlessly press the target to the last possible split second. Then I found myself almost idly wondering if my beloved F-100 could possibly recover from that position again. It was all very serious.

I must also pause to wonder if one could ever react much differently to this situation. How long could one daily play for the ultimate stakes? Not long I don't think. Either the stakes must change, or your thinking must be developed somehow. And, of course, the latter is the only option that is really available to me. At any rate, the brief pause gave me time to reflect and to reassess the value of life itself. At least I find that I'm a bit more prudent now.

I've started to lead flights now on occasion. That is a big step forward for a young and eager fighter pilot like me. But it means also that I can no longer be a carefree, irresponsible wingman. Now, as an element lead, I must accept the responsibility for the conduct of the flight and for the accomplishment of the mission on the flights I lead.

When I try to tell you of my experiences the words seem somehow perfunctory and have an empty ring. When I attempt to plum the meaning from the experiences, the words seem even more hollow to me. How can you possibly understand what I see and experience and yet I cannot understand? It is very important to me that you do understand, but still, I despair at the futility of such an undertaking. Often, I suppose you are disturbed and disquieted by what I relate. But more often my hand is stayed from revealing what I see and feel because I know that this or that would surely be painful to you, that you would not be able to empathize and thus would misinterpret what I put so poorly anyway.

I will close because I've said too much, too poorly, already, and revealed too little.

Love, Stu

✤ ✤ ✤

October 1, 1968

My Dearest Jean,

How strange it is that another month has slipped quietly away. The long months blend together into the endless stream of interminable days. I wonder now why we even have such things as days or weeks or months. I guess we must have some way of marking off our sentence.

Although they are too numerous to count, each one's passing does bring me a little closer to you.

The weather here at Tuy Hoa has turned foul with the coming of the northeast monsoon season. The clouds hang low and menacing, forming a dull gray ceiling at about 1,000 feet. It rains intermittently all day and night. By afternoon, the wind blows fiercely from the sea and the waves crash upon the beach in an endless procession of thundering breakers. The sea itself is dark and foreboding. I understand that this sort of weather will last for the better part of the fall and winter. I guess that I will lose my beautiful tan. In fact, it has already started to fade noticeably. That's a real shame. I wanted to meet you in Hawaii bronzed and beautiful.

The weather also makes flying doubly interesting. When you take off amid the rain and gloom you must climb up through the clouds until suddenly you break out on top to a beautiful blue sky. The undercast forms a cottony white field that sparkles in the sunlight. It's really quite a change. Of course, trying to fly formation in the clouds is another interesting matter. And attempting to bomb below a low ceiling gets pretty exciting at times. You have to be very careful that your own bombs don't shoot you down with shrapnel when they go off. It makes Charlie's job a little easier too since you have to stay fairly low to keep the target in sight. So far, my luck is holding. I haven't taken a hit yet. During the first part of September the VC seemed to really be making an effort towards me. I got shot at on every mission. That is, I know I was getting shot at. Normally you don't see it, so it doesn't bother you.

The war is pretty quiet now. I did have a pretty hot target over by Duc Lap the other day. The VC were blazing away at us on every pass. We shot it out with them for a while, but I think the battle was a draw. We didn't take any hits and the FAC wasn't about to go over the target area to see what we did to Charlie. For the most part, however, the missions now are very routine.

You know, I guess I'm very lucky just to have you to ... be my connection with the real world.

I must close and go fly. Study hard—it will keep you out of trouble. Be good now—

Love, Stu

✣ ✣ ✣

October 3, 1968

Dear Mom & Dad,

I finally got a letter from George in which he vividly described his adventures across the country. He was real pleased at having had to take the long course at Fairchild [*survival school*]. I guess he knows what it is like to be hungry now. He seemed quite enthusiastic about Cannon and the "100." He asked me to do what I can about getting him assigned to Tuy Hoa. With my shiny silver bars [*1st lieutenant insignia*] I'm sure I can do a lot.

I have 125 combat missions now and nearly 200 combat hours. The war itself has been very quiet of late. Most of our missions are of the harassment variety, although we occasionally get to help out some guys on the ground that have gotten in trouble. I had one like that about a week ago northwest of Saigon. Charlie had a long-range patrol pinned down and cut off from their helicopter pickup zone. We were bombing and strafing within 125 yards of the friendlies. It was all pretty routine, but when we left, the ground commander relayed the message that "we had gotten them out of a world of hurt."

The weather has gotten kind of foul with the coming of the northeast monsoon. We expect to get a lot of instrument practice for the rest of the winter. Sometimes it gets pretty gamey trying to deliver ordnance under the low ceilings that prevail in this season. The worst part is taking off and landing in the rain: everything gets wet on preflight; the cockpit fills with water; and, of course, everything gets damp and doesn't work. Give me the blazing hot summer any day. By the way, the temperature seldom gets over 90° now.

We are presently in the midst of building ourselves an officer's club, so much of my spare time is taken up on forced labor details. I never was much of a carpenter, but I can wield a hammer as well as the next one, I guess. It should be nice when it's finished. It's right on the beach.

You asked about Christmas. Well, frankly I'm in favor of declaring a moratorium this year. It seems a trifle absurd to me to mail packages back and forth. Besides, my shopping opportunities at Tuy Hoa are limited. I'm sure that in my travels throughout the year I will be able to find some really nice gifts. However, I doubt that will be by Christmas. I bought Janet some cashmere sweaters in Hong Kong which I must mail one of these days. If there is anything you all want that I can pick up over here, please let me know. Many things are very, very cheap.

Take care now—

Love, Stewart

Six

Just a Routine Combat Sky Spot Mission

The mission described below reflects the hazards of the weather over South Vietnam during the Northeast Monsoon season. It also provides a glimpse into the physiological dangers of flying in significantly reduced visibility conditions. Again, the dialogue in this story has been reconstructed to give the reader a sense of being in the cockpit with me.

Tuy Hoa AB
Republic of South Vietnam.
October 1968

The night was warm, sultry, with low clouds and intermittent rain.

"Your mission tonight will be a sky spot," the Intel Officer said by way of opening the flight briefing.

COMBAT SKY SPOT was a weapons delivery method that relied on an MSQ-77 radar to direct the attacking aircraft to a weapons release point in the sky. The release point was offset from the target by the calculated ballistic trajectory of the weapons. In practice, the method was similar to a ground radar-controlled landing approach. COMBAT SKY SPOT was implemented in Vietnam in 1966 to improve night and all-weather weapons delivery accuracy.

The Intel Officer continued, "Your target is an NVA [*North Vietnamese Army*] supply depot just south of the DMZ. Frag'd Time over Target is zero one thirty hours. Contact Sky Spot Control on 267.8. Are there any questions?"

Note: "Frag'd" referred to a portion or fragment of the daily Air Tasking Order or ATO sent out by 7th Air Force Headquarters. It specified and authorized all strike missions in the Southeast Asia Theater

Six—Just a Routine Combat Sky Spot Mission

of Operations. In our case, we were designated a flight of two F-100Ds from the 31st Tactical Fighter Wing, call sign Saber Four One. Our weapons load was four Mk 117 bombs each. We were directed to operate under Sky Spot Control for the strike portion of the mission.

Flight Lead asked, "Any threats?"

"There are no known threats at the altitude you will run in at," the Intel officer replied. "There is a report of a 23mm battery near Khe San, but you should be well above its effective altitude. Anything else?"

The Flight Lead looked at me. He was senior captain, highly experienced with over 2000 hours in the F-100. He had spent two tours in Europe before coming to Vietnam and was now approaching the end of his one-year tour here. I'd flown with him on numerous missions and had total confidence in his airmanship. I was his wingman on this mission. At this point, I was 4 months into my tour in Southeast Asia (SEA), and now had nearly 200 combat flying hours, but only just over 300 hours overall in the F-100. As these things go, I was still relatively inexperienced in the F-100.

I shook my head.

The Intel Officer looked quizzically at us for a moment. "If there are no more questions, have a good mission," he said.

Next, was the weather briefing.

"Currently, Tuy Hoa is 1200 overcast in light rain," the briefer began. "Temperature is 73 degrees, wind from the southeast at eight knots." He paused, consulting his weather map and then continued, "There is a frontal boundary lying just north of Quang Ngai with stratus clouds between ten and thirty thousand feet. You can expect imbedded thunderstorms from the vicinity of Da Nang to the DMZ with tops up to thirty-five thousand."

He paused and looked at us for questions. When there were none, he continued, "Weather here at Tuy when you return, 0200 to 0300, is forecast to be 1,000-foot overcast, clear underneath with seven miles visibility. Clouds will be layered up to 20 to 25 thousand feet. Winds remain southeast at 10 knots. Are there any questions?"

Again Flight Lead looked at me. "None for me," I said.

"No questions," Lead said to the weather briefer. "Thank you."

Turning to me, he said, "Looks like a routine sky spot mission."

Looking at the flight briefing guide, Lead ran his finger down the items quickly and said to me, "All the briefing items are squadron standard. Take 10 second spacing on takeoff. It will be a right turn after takeoff. to head up the coast. I'll stay under the weather at 300 knots until you come aboard. Questions?"

"Nope, no questions," I said. "Like you said, pretty routine."

As we started to rise from the briefing table, Lead said, "Suggest you set up your comm and weapons panels before taxi. Weather might be a little dicey up there."

I nodded. Good idea, I thought.

Lead looked at his watch. "It's eleven forty-five now," he said. "Let's check in at twelve twenty for a twelve thirty takeoff."

Twenty minutes later, external preflight done, I climbed into the cockpit and strapped in. Then it was a quick run through the cockpit and engine start checks. Everything looked good.

A few minutes later, with the engine started and after start checks complete, I waited for Lead's check-in call.

The radio crackled. "Saber Four One check," Lead called.

"Two's on," I replied.

"Tuy Hoa Ground, Saber Four One taxi two takeoff," Lead said.

"Roger, Four One, taxi runway two one, altimeter 29.96, wind one five zero at four," Ground Control responded.

Ten minutes later we were through Last Chance and Arming, the final safety inspection and removal of weapons safety pins at the end of the runway. The rain had given way to a mist, and the cloud bases were clearly visible in the reflected light from the Last Chance apron and perimeter lighting. The air was warm and close.

Lead's canopy closed and I gave a thumbs-up sign as my canopy came down. He responded with three fingers held up indicating radio change to Channel 3.

Moments later, "Four One check."

"Two," I replied.

Then, "Tower, Saber Four One, ready for takeoff," Lead said.

"Roger," the tower replied. "Cleared for takeoff. Wind one five zero at six. Contact departure control on 234.8."

As he advanced power to taxi onto the runway, Lead held up four fingers for Ch 4, the radio preset for Departure Control.

"Check," Lead called.

"Two," I replied.

Lead taxied onto the far half of the runway, leaving room for me to take formation position on the near half. With a quick glance as I took position on Lead's left wing, I saw him twirl his left index finger indicating engine run-up. I pushed the throttle full forward to MIL power and pressed hard on the brakes. The airplane surged against the brakes, the nose strut compressing slightly under the thrust from the accelerating engine. I watched the engine instruments settle to their normal full power setting, and then gave a thumbs-up to Lead. He immediately

Six—Just a Routine Combat Sky Spot Mission

gave an exaggerated head nod and released brakes. I punched the second hand on the clock and watched Lead's afterburner light and then recede rapidly into the distance.

Ten ticks of the clock later, I released brakes and pushed the throttle outboard to light the afterburner. The bump from the suddenly increased thrust was reassuring, but with over 39,000 lbs. for the engine to push, the acceleration, while smooth, was hardly exhilarating. Takeoff roll at this weight was typically over 8000 feet. Just past the 3,000-foot remaining marker, I pulled back on the control stick to rotate the airplane to nose up, takeoff attitude. I felt the bump as the main tires rolled over the departure end barrier cable, 1,500 feet from the end of the runway. Normal takeoff, I mused, and moments later I was airborne.

My attention now shifted to Lead as I raised the landing gear and flaps. As the airspeed increased, I banked hard to cut off Lead who was now in a 30-degree banked right hand turn just under the cloud base.

"Departure, Saber Four One airborne in a right turn," Lead called.

Departure Control responded with the standard, "Roger, continue turn to three five zero, climb to ten thousand at your discretion."

To join up with Lead, I pointed my airplane ahead of his such that he appeared about 45 degrees off my nose, in front of my left wing. This established the rejoin angle so that the airplanes converged to a single point in space. Then it was a matter of judging the cut-off angle and rate of closure to get to the rejoin point as quickly as possible without overshooting. I liked this part of flying, the fine judgment and delicate control to precisely manage the rate of closure. A minute or so later I slid into position, three feet from Lead's right wingtip.

I keyed the mike and said, "Twos in." I was pleased with myself for the expeditious rejoin.

Lead glanced over and smoothly increased power to just below full MIL. That gave me a little excess power to play with to stay on Lead's wing. As our airspeed approached 400 knots we started a climb into the clouds. The clouds thickened around us, and I focused intently on the green navigation light on Lead's wingtip.

For the wingman, things are never static in formation flying. Ripples in the surrounding air cause the two airplanes to move independently which changes the relative motion between the two aircraft. This must be corrected, or the wingman could collide with Lead or, in weather, lose sight of Lead entirely. Like all fighters, the F-100 was highly responsive to control inputs. To maintain position, precise, usually very small, adjustments of the stick and throttle were continually required—large enough to control the disturbance, but never too large or too late. In the thick clouds we were in, the margin of error was very small. I concentrated on keeping Lead's green wingtip light in a small area on the left side of my canopy. Little did I know that light was going to become my only link to the "real" world.

After a few minutes, Departure Control said, "Saber Four One, continue climb and maintain Flight Level two zero zero, contact Peacock on 236.6."

"Roger, Saber, Ch 6, go," Lead replied.

Peacock was the air traffic control center or ATCC for the northern half of South Vietnam. Unlike an ATCC in the States that dictated flight paths and altitudes, Peacock functioned more as a flight following and coordinating agency. In Vietnam, the pilots determined where to go and at what altitude.

After checking in with Peacock, we continued our climb. We were in and out of clouds and reflections off Lead's blinking navigation lights became distracting. Lead's white navigation light just behind the cockpit was also out, and so I had no sense of depth when we were in the thicker clouds and Lead's fuselage was obscured. It was like watching a singular green light in a gray fog.

Presently, I keyed my mike and said, "Lead, go dim steady and turn on your formation lights." Formation lights were spotlights embedded in the upper wing surface and oriented to shine on the fuselage to give depth perspective to the wingman.

After a pause, the green light stopped blinking and became a steady, dim green point in the gray fog.

"Formation lights are on," Lead said.

Actually, they're not, I thought to myself. This is going to be a long night if we stay in this weather. I tightened my focus on the green light and hung on.

After we leveled off at 20,000 feet, Lead called, "Saber, fuel check. Lead's eight thousand, tanks dry."

I glanced quickly at the fuel gauge, located on the bottom center of the instrument panel. The needle seemed to be near the five o'clock position or just below the 8000 mark. As I remained concentrated on the green light, I dared not fumble for the switch that would confirm the drop tanks had fed out.

I replied, "Two is seven eight hundred, tanks dry."

We settled in for the remainder of the flight to our target area. At least the air was relatively smooth until we reached the frontal boundary south of Da Nang. The turbulence was mild at first, little bumps that rocked the airplane. These bumps progressed to sharp, jarring motions and the green light bobbed and weaved as I struggled to keep it centered on the side of the canopy. "Easy," I said to myself, "Don't over control." My concentration became intense—and as the turbulence increased, I slowly began to lose my sense of orientation in the real, three-dimensional world.

From my physiological training I knew that spatial disorientation occurred when the various sensors in the body, particularly the semi-circular canals in the ear, are confused by banking and climbing/diving motions of an aircraft. Visual cues normally override these false sensations, but in the absence of a clear visual horizon, the other bodily senses prevail. The result is an inability to accurately tell your orientation to the physical world. In extreme cases, a tumbling sensation can result. Spatial disorientation is typically a major factor in fatal, loss of control aviation accidents. This knowledge was not comforting. But it did emphasize the urgency of keeping sight of the limited visual cue I did have, Lead's green wingtip light.

The tension now became palpable. Sweat beads formed on my forehead and I could feel dampness under my flight suit. The F-100 had no weather radar, so we basically had no choice but to plunge ahead into the gloom. Occasionally, flashes of lightning would illuminate the entirety of Lead's airplane, but against the grey background of clouds they did not provide the visual cue I needed to fight my worsening spatial disorientation. A powerful feeling crept in that we were no longer flying straight and level. Even though I knew we were basically wings level, I felt we were in a steep bank so that I was looking up at Lead's airplane. The wingtip light was my only visual reference to counter this illusion. I ignored this sensation as best I could and concentrated desperately on holding the green light—my connection to reality—in place on the canopy. As long as I could do that—and believe in Lead—I knew, at least intellectually, that we were OK.

The minutes now dragged on. Out of the corner of my eye, I could see St. Elmo's fire form at the base of the wind screen as little luminescent green balls that trickled up the wind screen. From time to time, turbulence would sharply jar my airplane and the green wingtip light would dance erratically. Moments of near panic would then set in as I struggled to regain control of that light. Somehow I fought back the disoriented sensation and held on to my green light. I had to consciously remind myself to relax the ever-tightening grip that I had on the stick and throttle. Sweat continued to build inside my mask.

In due time, Peacock came on the radio, "Saber Four One, turn left to two eight zero, maintain, twenty thousand, contact Sky Spot Control on 267.8."

Lead replied, "Roger, left to two eight zero, twenty thousand, Saber go Manual."

This last was a command to change the radio to the briefed Sky Spot frequency. Fortunately, at Lead's suggestion, I had preset that frequency in the manual setting on the radio control. I quickly let go of the throttle and flipped the radio control to manual. Meanwhile, Lead's left turn to 280 was so smooth that I didn't even recognize we were banking. But when we rolled out on heading I now felt we were flying knife edge, that is in 90 degrees of bank, and that I was looking straight up at Lead. It was a bizarre sensation.

Lead said, "Sky Spot, Saber Four One, check."

I keyed the mike, "Two's on."

The Sky Spot controller responded, "Roger Saber Four One, squawk six five. You are two minutes from the IP, turn left to two seven five, maintain twenty thousand feet altitude, set altimeter to three zero zero one."

The IP or Initial Point was a point in the sky from which the final approach to the weapons release point was made. With only a few minutes to go, I knew I only had to hold on a little longer to at least complete the bombing run.

Lead replied, "Two seven five, twenty thousand, altimeter three zero zero one."

The altimeter setting was the local atmospheric pressure reading and ensured our height above the terrain matched the calculated ballistic profile of the Mk 117 bombs we were carrying. Fortunately, only Lead needed to adjust his altimeter.

As we continued the run in, the clouds thinned enough that I had nearly a full view of Lead's airplane. This was reassuring except that I still felt we were in 90 degrees of right bank. In this disoriented state I had this peculiar feeling that, since I was directly below Lead, when his bombs released, they would fall down on me.

A minute or so later Sky Spot said, "Saber Four One, come right to two eight zero, you are on track, do not acknowledge further transmissions."

Next Sky Spot, "Saber, left to two seven eight, you are thirty seconds from release, arm weapons."

I reached up and flipped the weapons arm switch on the left instrument subpanel.

Next followed a running commentary of small heading changes until, "Saber, release on my mark."

A pause, then "Three, two, one, mark."

At mark, I pressed the pickle [*weapons release*] button on the control stick and felt the airplane jump as 3,000 pounds of ordnance was suddenly released. Simultaneously, I saw the explosive ejection cartridges on Lead's airplane flash and was mesmerized to see the four

Six—Just a Routine Combat Sky Spot Mission

750-pound bombs move smoothly away on what appeared to be a horizontal plane. It took a moment for me to accept this was just an illusion, albeit a powerful one.

After a few more moments, Sky Spot said, "Good run Saber, turn left to one eight zero, contact Peacock on 236.6. Good night."

Lead replied, "Nice run, Sky Spot, Saber arm safe, go Ch 6." He started a gentle left turn to head home.

I switched my radio back to preset and waited.

Presently, Lead called, "Saber check."

I replied, "Two."

Then Lead, "Peacock, Saber Four One, twenty thousand, RTB [*Return to Base*] Tuy Hoa."

Peacock, "Roger Saber Four One. Tuy Hoa is bearing one five zero for two hundred miles, squawk five seven, flash." [*This highlighted our position on Peacock's radar screen.*]

Lead, "Roger one five zero for two hundred, flash."

A pause, then, "Saber fuel check. Lead is four five hundred."

Again a quick glance at the fuel gauge which sat just at 12 o'clock on the dial. "Two is four thousand," I said.

When we passed the frontal boundary heading southeast, the air again became relatively smooth. We were flying basically straight and level, but we were in and out of the clouds. While I still didn't have a visual reference other than Lead's wingtip light, my disorientation slowly began to recede. I began to relax a little.

About 30 minutes later Peacock called, "Saber Four One, Tuy Hoa bears one six zero for twenty-five miles, contact Tuy Hoa Approach on 233.2. Good night."

Lead replied, "Roger, Saber Ch 5 go."

I glanced at my TACAN readout. I had not changed the TACAN frequency since takeoff so it was still tuned to Tuy Hoa. The needle pointed just right of 12 o'clock. For the first time since join up, I had a sense of where I was in the physical world. I switched the radio to Ch 5.

Lead, "Saber, check."

"Two," I replied.

Lead, "Tuy Hoa Approach, Saber Four One."

Approach Control, "Roger Saber Four One, turn left to one four zero, descend to ten thousand, altimeter two niner niner six."

Lead, "Roger, left to one four zero, ten thousand. Approach, bring Two in first. He's a little low on fuel."

"Roger," Approach Control said. "Saber Four Two roll out heading one four zero, descend to five thousand. Saber Four One continue your turn to one zero zero, maintain ten thousand."

This direction from Approach Control was to separate the flight and gain spacing between the two airplanes for individual approaches.

Lead replied, "Roger, Two you're cleared off."

I keyed the mike, "Roger."

I moved the stick gently to the right to roll out of the turn we were in and watched the gap between us quickly widen. Lead disappeared into the grey clouds. The green light was gone. As I turned my head to look at my instruments, suddenly, I had a violent sensation of tumbling. I was in a dark, gray haze with no visual reference to the physical world. I had no idea what was up or down and what to do to control the airplane. I froze. I stared helplessly at the instrument panel and tried to fight back the rising panicky feeling. Seconds passed.

Then a small voice in the back of my mind said, "Trust the attitude indicator. Trust the attitude indicator." It was the voice of my primary instructor from pilot training. As I had struggled to right the training airplane on my spatial disorientation training flight, my instructor had calmly said, "Focus on the attitude indicator. Trust the attitude indicator; it's your only friend until the disorientation passes."

I looked hard at the attitude indicator in the center of the instrument panel. It's a ball, half gray and half black, with a symbol representing the airplane's wings in the center. The ball rotates behind the wing symbol to show a climb or dive, bank left or right. Mine now showed the airplane in slight climb and right bank. "Level the wings," I said to myself. "Keep the gray part up and the black part down. Now hold it there." The panic receded. The feeling of tumbling subsided, but the feeling of total disorientation persisted. I could not sense up or down.

I concentrated fully on the attitude indicator and held it there, wings level, no climb, no dive. I shut out the outside world. After about 30 seconds, I began to feel a sense of up and down. I slowly gained confidence that I could divert my attention to things other than the attitude indicator and not lose control of the airplane. I began to relax. My thoughts turned to the upcoming approach and landing.

Presently, Approach Control said, "Saber Four Two turn right to two one zero. Continue your descent to one thousand five hundred. You are fifteen miles from touchdown."

"Roger," I said, "two one zero, fifteen hundred."

The disorientation was gone, but now I had a new problem. I should be at 1,500 feet and 175 knots airspeed, but instead I was at 20,000 feet and 280 knots. I had 15 miles and about five minutes to get down and slow down. I could do a 360 degree turn to gain time and distance, but that would interfere with Lead's approach and we were both low on fuel.

I snatched the throttle to idle and opened the speed brakes. The airplane slowed. As soon as safe gear down speed, 230 knots, was reached, I threw down the gear and flaps and pushed the nose over to a 20-degree dive.

"This should work," I said to myself, "but it will be interesting."

The rate of descent increased to 8000 feet per minute, but shortly I had to raise the nose to avoid over-speeding the landing gear. The descent rate dropped to 6000 feet per minute. The seconds passed as I watched my decreasing altitude and distance from the runway. Would they converge? I wondered. I was still in the weather and had no visual reference to judge by.

At seven miles from touchdown, I was still at 8000 feet, when I should be at 1,500 feet for a normal approach glide path. But I was beginning to feel more comfortable.

The radio crackled. "Saber Four Two, this is your final controller. Do not acknowledge further transmission. You are on centerline, begin descent."

A few seconds later, the final controller said in his steady monotone, "Four Two, check gear down, turn left to two zero eight, you will be entering the glide path from above."

I smiled to myself. I love it. Here I am in the weather, still at 6000 feet less than six miles from touchdown, idle power, every drag device I have out, falling like a rock and the controller calmly says I'll be entering the glide path from above like this is just normal, normal. You gotta love these guys.

Then followed the usual running commentary from the final approach controller with small heading changes, but always, "still above glide path," always unperturbed.

At 3,000 feet, I eased back on the stick to begin to slow the airplane and the rate of descent.

Thirty seconds or so later, "Four Two turn right to two one zero, on centerline, two miles from touchdown, still above glide path."

Suddenly, I popped out of the base of the clouds. The runway stretched out as a long ribbon of lights in front of me. Off to my left, I could see the lights of the base spread out to the horizon. I raised the nose to slow my descent and watched the airspeed bleed down toward normal final approach speed. As I crossed the runway overrun, I raised the nose a bit more to break my descent. Then I was over the runway threshold. I raised the nose up a touch more to landing attitude. I waited as the airplane settled toward the runway surface. The main tires touched with a bump and then its nose gear down abruptly to the runway and drag chute out.

As I rolled out to the end of the runway, all the built-up tension in the cockpit evaporated. I turned off the runway into the de-arming area and opened the canopy. The warm night air washed over me.

I switched the radio to Ch 2. "Ground, Saber Four Two taxi to parking."

Fifteen minutes later, I was in the chocks, engine shut down and my post flight walk around complete.

"The bird is good, Chief," I said to the crew chief. "No write-ups."

I took the aircraft flight forms and walked to the squadron step van for the short ride to maintenance debriefing. As I climbed into the van, the driver said, "I need to swing by delta row and pick up Saber Four One. He was right behind you." I nodded and sat down, the adrenaline finally draining away, leaving me feeling limp. Shortly, the van stopped and Lead climbed aboard.

"Like I said, a routine sky spot mission," Lead laughed, as he sat down, placing his helmet bag on the floor.

"Yeah," I said.

"Anything for me?" he asked.

"Yeah," I said, "your nav and formation lights are inop and need to be written up."

As I sat there I thought back on the flight just completed. This time I had brought *Jeannie* to the brink of disaster because of my human limitations. It would not be the last time.

Seven

Bombing Halt
(or "Who the hell is Richard?")

On October 31, 1968, President Lyndon Johnson would announce a complete bombing halt of North Vietnam, an unqualified extension of his March 31 bombing pause above the 20th parallel. This bombing halt would be imposed as a gesture to entice the North Vietnamese to negotiate in good faith in the peace talks in Paris. These "good faith" peace talks would go on for over three more years, until President Nixon unleashed renewed bombing of the Hanoi area, and a peace accord was finally reached.

During these times there were increasing protests against the war back in the States, especially on college campuses. We were aware of the protests, of course. The "young sports" in particular had all been on various college campuses two years ago when the protests had been in full flower. But, the protests were not a concern to us. We were too caught up in prosecuting the war the protestors were against.

We also were aware that the war in Vietnam was a major factor in the 1968 presidential campaigns and we had certainly been aware of the turmoil at the Democratic Convention in August. I vaguely remember the Democrats were sympathetic to the protests and favored a bombing halt, while the Republicans favored continuing support for South Vietnam. But, I don't remember ever discussing the protests or the upcoming election with my fellow pilots. What the new bombing halt meant to us in the 308th was that we would no longer face the particular dangers of occasional missions into North Vietnam.

Interestingly, I don't remember any emphasis on voting or even information about the availability of absentee ballots from the Wing or other Air Force authorities. Our major sources of outside information were the *Stars and Stripes* newspaper and letters from home. The *Stars and Stripes* newspaper was the official newspaper of the Department of

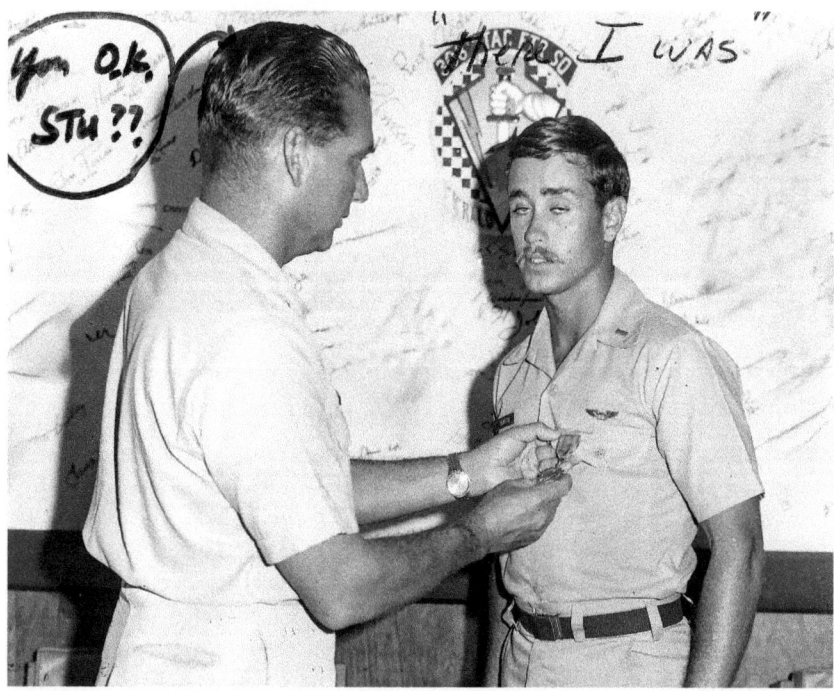

A weary fighter pilot receiving an Air Medal for attacking a heavily defended target. This mission is described in Chapter Eleven (U.S. Air Force Det 8 600th Photo AAVS [MAC]).

Defense for personnel stationed overseas. It was strictly apolitical. My letters from home never spoke of the protests or the elections.

The bombing halt likely saved many lives of the Air Force and Navy pilots that otherwise would have carried the brunt of the attacks against North Vietnam. But the bombing halt had little impact on us in South Vietnam except it seemed to increase the anti-aircraft artillery fire we faced, particularly in Laos. We continued with a heavy flying schedule against increasingly heavily defended targets.

※ ※ ※

October 9, 1968

My Darling Jeannie,

It is a quiet evening here, still and cloudless and serene. The weather has cleared the past few days so that it is now once again hot and bright under a sky of such intense blue that it almost seems to live. The sea laps placidly at the sandy shore. It is a welcome change from the

Seven—Bombing Halt (or "Who the hell is Richard?")

misty gloom of a week ago when the wet and dampness crept into everything until your very soul became soggy and limp.

I am flying nights once again so that I have plenty of time during the day to sit beneath the burning breath of the sun. Perhaps my tan will yet endure. Last night was an exquisite night. The moon was full and, in the cloudless night sky, was shimmering silvery bright. The earth far below lay dark and shadowy while patches of low clouds shone like the placid mirrored surface of a lake in the early morning.

We returned from our last target just at sunrise. As we glided south along the coast, the dawn spread orange and fiery along the eastern horizon. It lay partially hidden by black pillars of clouds that grew in a grotesque forest far to the east but nearer than the dawn. It looked like a primeval, volcanic world caught up in the throes of its own birth pangs. The blazing band of orange crept slowly, falteringly under the crushing weight of the purple-black sky above.

By contrast, to the west the world was quiet, motionless under the icy glare of the full moon. The earth was shadowy, formless save for the glacier-like clouds that filled the low valleys and oozed through the mountain passes. It was a dead world grown cold and lifeless and without substance.

It was strange as if nature had contrived the awesome spectacle for my private viewing and wonder. Surely no mortal artist could have conceived so marked a contrast nor created it so deftly. To the left lay the burning, chaotic, uncertain song of life. To the right, the quiet, icy serenity of lifelessness. Between the two our planes slipped swiftly, silently; two black silhouettes hurrying heedlessly toward the full, pallid lights that were our goal.

Again, I have whiled away another evening trying to piece together the intricate puzzle of our interrelationship. And again, I must close and pursue more mundane tasks, namely flying.

As for Hawaii, I have little say about when I will get to go. I can only put in my request for a month. I can't even guarantee that I'll be able to go in December. It is bound to be a popular month and I have little seniority. I will know about a month beforehand; however, in Hawaii I absolutely will not be staying at any sort of military installation. I rather think the Royal Hawaiian would be nice.

Be good now—

Love, Stu

P.S. It seems I entirely forgot to ask you how school is this year. You certainly have a lot of courage getting up at 7 o'clock for any class let alone for a social encyclical.

P.P.S. Who the hell is Richard??

✤ ✤ ✤

Note: Jean's letter of September 24 (received about October 1) casually mentioned that she was thinking of dropping Richard. I had forgotten about him with my trip to Hong Kong. This mention was more worrisome than I could have imagined, and it added to the melancholy I had expressed in my letter on September 25. I had not expected Jean's "dating" would lead to a steady date partner, perhaps even a steady "boyfriend" with all those implications. I was not prepared for that, but then I hadn't exactly been upfront with Jean about Sara in Manila, or a girl I met in Hong Kong. That was just one evening in the rooftop bar and dining room of the Peninsula Hotel. She was a stewardess with Flying Tigers Airline on layover in Hong Kong. We shared a pleasant evening talking over drinks and dinner. After dinner, she had to get her crew rest for her return flight to San Francisco the next morning. We parted with a hug. She did give me her phone number in San Francisco in case I might get there on my return to the States.

The simple revelation from Jean about Richard turned my mood to a darker side. Due to the clumsy communication caused by having only letters to speak through, the situation with Richard would take the next month and a half to play out. It was not helped by the erratic mail service.

Richard would figure prominently for me in the coming months.

✤ ✤ ✤

October 13, 1968

Darling Jean,

I got your letter of the 5th today (outstanding service, this US Mail) and I was so happy to hear from you again. The time between your letters seems interminable. I was intrigued by the mention of your new nightgown. I trust it is of such quality that one can read a newspaper through two thicknesses of it.

In case you are wondering what prompted this letter, it is prompted by the fact that I am stuck on night mobile tonight—loathsome, dreary and lonely duty—and I need to feel the nearness of you if only in a letter.

In case I've never told you, mobile is a little mobile (hence the name) control tower situated near the end of the runway and provided with a wondrous array of radio, lights, flares and gadgets whereby the mobile officer (me) monitors the airplanes as they take off and land, provides timely assistance to emergency aircraft, controls the flow of traffic, and makes appropriate and cryptic remarks like "nice save" or

Seven—Bombing Halt (or "Who the hell is Richard?")

"oh, Christ" on the form provided. (If nothing else, that's a hell of a sentence.) Beyond that, the mobile officer is a ready-made witness and/or scapegoat (if needed) in case of an accident.

At any rate, the job is bad enough during the day when there is at least a flurry of activity to amuse and engage you. At night, it is insufferable. We only launch about 10 flights throughout the night so there is little to do. Worse yet, this shift is 12 hours long and the unit is small—would you believe a five-by-five box crammed full of the necessary equipment. And finally, this hardly defensible position sits directly astride the logical infiltration route for any enterprising VC. So here I sit with my trusty .38, ready to flee at the slightest alarm. And that is my tall tale of woe for the week, and also the motivation for this letter.

I was delighted to hear that you will be delivering a series of talks on sex (one of my favorite topics). If I send you a stamped, self-addressed envelope, will you send a copy of your address? Or perhaps I could engage your services for a private lecture tour, say in Hawaii (which reminds me, I can't help but wonder how your parents view this misadventure. They must be scandalized). I don't think I need to tell you that, in the event you need some consultation in the preparation of your talks, you are welcome, of course, to draw on my devilishly vast experience. Would that I could give you some personal assistance in the matter.

But how is school treating you these days? I hope that it isn't proving to be too rigorous. I gather your sex talks are a part of your social encyclical. Perhaps it is worth getting up at 7 o'clock for some classes after all. Does the delight at being free of parental scrutiny once more still overcome the innate dreariness of school?

For my part, I must continue to protest that my life is dull and routine. I flew a combat mission early this morning. I must admit it was a bit gamey taking off because of a driving rainstorm, but after that there was nothing more exciting than diving into the blazing guns of the VC to drop my bombs. No, that was yesterday. Today I only had to skim along the treetop levels to deliver the ordnance. The ceilings (bottoms of the cloud) were quite low, and we were working along the Cambodian border west of Tay Ninh City and that's guaranteed to make your life insurance agent not too happy. But altogether it was a very routine flight. Of course, it was lent a certain element of charm by virtue of the fact that I was flying with Happy Jack. He's my squadron commander and so named because no one has ever seen him smile. It's always a pleasure to fly with him first thing in the morning.

It occurs to me that I haven't replied to your repeated inquiries concerning my maid (who by the way, I do require since I'm such a wretched housekeeper). I didn't mean to ignore you, it's just that I keep forgetting to forward the details. At any rate, she is but a shy, simple peasant girl, a winsome lass of hardly eight and ten years with a quick and gracious smile that hides the horror and tragedies she has known in her few years. Her name is Aiya and as she speaks virtually no English; I know nothing else about her. Our conversations to date have consisted of my inquiring, "Hello, how are you this morning?" to which she invariably replies, "I'm fine. And you?" After that she might politely ask, "You no work today?" (It must seem I never do of late.) The question is purely ceremonial anyway because she doesn't understand whatever reply I might make. Having thus dispensed with this amenity, she is free to get on with her work.

Well, I'm afraid that duty beckons to me, and I must close. I must watch with steadfast eye the approach and alighting of the swift air machines upon the ground. Then with fearless determination I must record the fact on the two duly appointed forms. Only then will our intrepid night flyers be officially home.

If all the foregoing seems so much gibberish and nonsense to you, don't be concerned. Quite likely, that's all it is.

Love, Stu

* * *

October 17, 1968

Dear Mom & Dad,

Hello again from beautiful Southeast Asia where all is gray and damp and drizzly. I'm afraid the monsoon is here to stay this time so we're in for a couple of months of nearly continuous downpours. It kind of reminds me of the rainy season at Wheelus [*Air Force Base, Tripoli, Libya*]—cool in comparison to the summer but not really cool, a continual dampness and low ugly gray clouds that periodically discharge a deluge of water. I hope that all of my belongings don't start to mildew. So far I haven't found any.

I'm getting lots of experience in weather flying. The past two days I have logged nearly four hours of weather. Today we took off into a 1,500-foot ceiling, air-refueled between cloud layers, drove to and from the target in the soup and made a ground control approach and landing out of a 1,000-foot ceiling in rain showers. In the target area we were dodging around a broken deck just at release altitude. That can be helpful since the clouds mask your run-in and pull-off as well as obscuring the target from you. If the VC starts shooting, you can go hide behind a cloud.

Seven—Bombing Halt (or "Who the hell is Richard?")

Other than the change in the weather, my routine is about the same—daily missions with little to break the monotony. The weather has kind of rained out the basketball league and definitely dampened the progress of the new club. I guess I'll have to start planning for another trip. I think that I will try to go to Taipei or Tokyo the next time. I still need to get some more stereo equipment.

I haven't heard anything from George for well over a month. I've been rather curious to know how he likes the F-100 now that he has had a chance to fly it. It shouldn't be too much longer before he starts actual gunnery training.

Say, what was your cryptic remark concerning my picture in the Whittier hometown rag sheet all about? What in the world did I do to warrant that?

I certainly envy you your authentic fall with the multi colored leaves, morning frost, the crisp afternoons, and a fire in the fireplace in the evening. I can't believe you don't have any horses or cows yet—what kind of a farm is that? Next you will tell me you buy your milk at the store rather than sampling the homie pleasure of fresh milk—and milking!

I must close for now. Take care—

Stewart

※ ※ ※

October 17, 1968

My Dear Jeannie,

We have been given a new bit of excitement to brighten our day and add adventure to our life. A typhoon is going to narrowly miss dear old Tuy Hoa—at least we hope that it misses. The weather outside is dark and stormy. The surf is rushing in upon the beach with interminable savagery, the gray waters boiling and churning and sending flicks of white foam scurrying along before the wind. The skeletal remains of a small fishing boat have been deposited on the beach by the arrogant sea. It is slowly being pounded to pieces, the planks splintered and ripped from the ribs as flesh torn from the bones of some poor animal. Already the wind is reaching better than 50 knots and sends sheets of rainwater driving like a waterfall across the base. The clouds scurry along, low and livid and ominous, scarcely seeming to be higher than the tops of the buildings. When the rain stops, sand mixes with the wind-driven mist to sting and pit any exposed flesh.

Actually, this is the eighth straight day of rain and ugly low hanging clouds. Until today flight operations continued as normal. When I landed yesterday about 5:00 in the afternoon the weather was so bad that I didn't even see the runway till I was nearly on top of it. Today all flying has been cancelled and we are standing by to evacuate the airplanes on the field if it looks like the storm will pass dangerously close to Tuy Hoa. Right now, it looks like the storm will pass east and south of us and we will get only the edge of it. It shouldn't get any worse than it is right now. Other than that, things are pretty quiet here. The same old daily routine of combat missions punctuated occasionally by the usual amount of stark terror. Ho Hum.

I was mildly surprised when I went to the post office today and found a letter from your mother. It was a very nice note inquiring into my health and welfare, although I must admit that I opened it with not a little trepidation. She implied that you were very niggardly with information concerning me and therefore she was forced to turn to the source to find out how I'm getting on. You must thank her for me—both for the letter and for her concern. Perhaps the true meat of the letter lay in a cryptic observation that we were planning to meet in Hawaii in December—followed by an inquiry as to whether my parents would be there also—hmmm.

I hope the school is going well for you these days. You really must drop me a note sometime soon and tell me about yourself. I trust that you are finding your studies at least somewhat interesting and that life at the Mount isn't too dull this year. You mustn't forget that your final year is the time to build fond memories of the old alma mater. Or at least the time for fun and games to make up for the endless hours of dreary study behind you.

Well, I haven't much more to tell you.... I suppose that I should find certain solace in the fact that my tour over here is nearly half over now. But that just seems to emphasize how terribly long I have got to go here. The last six months seem at once a moment and a lifetime. The six ahead stretch out interminably. One doesn't think of the end of the tour. It is too distant and too fraught with uncertainty. It's better to say I've been here nearly six months and let it go at that.

As I was saying, I do miss you very much.... I wonder if we will ever be together again.

Love, Stu

✢ ✢ ✢

Note: In her letter dated October 14, Jean answered my October 9 question "Who the hell is Richard?"

Who in the hell is Richard? Don't worry about him either; he's the assistant manager I spoke to you about. As a matter of fact, he proposed marriage to me two nights ago. At any rate, that's a dandy excuse not to see him anymore. I know I said I was going to drop him before, but then he sent me a huge bouquet of flowers so what could I say? You must admit, it's pretty poor to drop someone and thank them for flowers at the same time.

I made some new friends so don't be so smug about me staying out of trouble. If I have to worry about you, you can do a little worrying about me.*

This letter was received somewhere around the 20th, so it was nearly a month since she had casually mentioned Richard in a romantic context (on September 25). I asked who he was on October 9. She replied as noted above. People today, with their instant worldwide communications, have no idea of the frustration engendered by the delayed and erratic mail service. The possibility for misinterpretation was a constant threat in the emotionally charged environment of Vietnam. My concern about Richard was not resolved until early November. This is an important aspect of understanding what being in "Vietnam" meant. Indeed, there was no option to call home.

⚜ ⚜ ⚜

Morale

Despite the long days (and nights), morale in the squadron was high, especially among the pilots. I believe it was also good among the crew chiefs and other enlisted personnel. No one complained. (Well, of course, we junior officers complained about the rules and regulations promulgated by the bureaucracy in the larger Air Force [see the "X" in Chapter Three] but that was to be expected. It was a rite of passage for junior officers to complain about such things.)

Certainly, none of the pilots shirked their duty no matter how egregious the flying schedule might seem. I also don't remember anyone being sick except for the occasional cold. No one stood down just because of these minor annoyances. In those cases our Flight Surgeon would just say, "Take three aspirin and see me when you land." (It was always a three aspirin dose; he would explain, "The trouble with aspirin is people take it when they don't need it, and then when they do need it, they don't take enough.") We were also admonished to take our daily

---

*Tuomy, *Is Love Enough?*, 129.

anti-malaria pill and salt tablets. I don't remember any one mentioning good hydration. Ah, but medical science advances.

Morale was generally kept buoyed by the occasional out-of-country opportunities that were afforded the pilots, the lingering adrenaline rush from a particularly grueling mission, frequent parties (could be a whole squadron affair or as little as two or three guys talking at the bar), and pranks. No one except the squadron commander was immune from pranks. One memorable prank involved a senior officer, a major, that was called back to the States for a family emergency. As he was leaving, a couple of us told him to have a good trip and to not get fat and lazy back home. (He prided himself on how he had stayed in shape here in Vietnam.) As soon as he was out the door, we took up the waist band of his G suit a couple of inches This was like substituting say 34-inch trousers for normal 36-inch trousers, not enough to be obvious, but enough that hooking the waist band would be next to impossible. When he went into the personal equipment room to suit up for his first mission back, we watched discreetly. He wrapped his G suit around his waist and tried to hook it up. But he couldn't close the gap. He tried again. No luck. Dismayed, he felt his waist, looked quizzically at the two parts and tried again. Finally, we burst out laughing and revealed the joke. He was a good sport and took it all in stride.

While morale was generally high amongst the pilots, this didn't mean there weren't mood swings in individuals. But we never talked about such things. The fighter pilot mystique was one of bravado in the face of danger. The thought of a "listening session" would have been met with derisive laughter. Still there was unavoidable emotional strain simply in the context of this situation—the lingering excitement of a close call, news that a friend had been killed, a troubling letter from home that wouldn't be resolved for weeks, the endless tedious days—all wore on you to a certain extent. But once the cockpit canopy closed, all that was set aside.

My mood swings went from that excitement left over from a mission to sadness over the loss of a friend, to boredom, to pessimism about my future, to uncertainty about Jean and me. In mid-fall, that turned to a gloomy despair as reflected in the letters in October and November. Always there was the stark realization that the immediate future held only endless days of constant combat. I felt I was always alone there. Jean was my connection to what might be afterwards, to a distant future. To lose that connection would be devastating.

* * *

Note: The letter below responds to Jean's letter of the 14th (in which she mentioned Richard had proposed marriage to her.) This news was,

Seven—Bombing Halt (or "Who the hell is Richard?")

to say the least, very disturbing to me. My response expresses my disquiet in a long analogy in which I try to fathom the ambivalence in our relationship. This was engendered not only by the various references to "Richard," but it also reflects a dark state in my mood that existed for a number of reasons.

October 25, 1968

Dearest Jean,

    You can be very confusing at times, you know. Your letter of the 14th has caused me not a little consternation…. Then you casually mention that good old Richard has just asked you to marry him. I am perplexed. I searched your letter a dozen times for the hidden message contained in this all-too-casual remark. But I must be blind because I was not able to discern with any certainty just what it was you were trying to tell me.

    If nothing else, the incident made me painfully cognizant of just how precarious my position is. There is an imminent danger that you will slip away from me. And I am powerless to prevent it. Forgive me. I don't mean to doubt you. But the passing remark of yours combined with some local events, has precipitated a tendentiousness about me which has brought all manner of dark possibilities to my mind. I consider all facets of our relationship as objectively as possible and wonder just what it means. I try to empathize with you but of course I cannot. The result is confusing and often painful. I wonder, "Can she really cling steadfastly to a future that is vague and uncertain? Can she really be willing to travel 3,000 miles just to see me?" I feel very much alone in the world right now.

    Like a mountaineering team we find ourselves clinging precariously to a precipice, bound together by the most tenuous of ropes. As we have climbed higher towards the top, we have depended on one another—and often the rope that binds us has kept one or the other from plunging headlong into the valley below. But the way has grown increasingly steeper of late. You must feel that. And now as I seem to swing wide over the yawning chasm, bound to you and the mountain by this slender thread, a nightmarish thought forces its way into my mind. The rope has always held firm and strong, but what if the strain was suddenly more than it could bear? Or what if your grip should fail and you must cut the rope to stay on the mountain? Perhaps the most frightening thing of all is the sudden inviting attraction of that chasm. Like one who stands on the edge of a great height, there is a powerful, mystic urge to cast myself into the void, with one deft stroke to sever the bond and so to seal my fate. It is a strange and hellish urge. There is nothing in the void but darkness and jagged rocks, pain and death, but they are a certainty. Here the wind blows bitter and cold, and the sun is often hidden by the darkest of clouds. You are often hidden by rocks and fog and the rope seems to disappear into nothingness and to be anchored nowhere. The whole scene then has a nightmarish lack of substance. Though we climbed together and are bound together, it is very cold and lonely on our mountain now. The summit is obscured by overhanging rocks, and I despair at finding a ledge where we may rest together and feel the warmth and presence of the other. And always the image of the rope fraying and separating plays across the shadows of my mind.

You must forgive me for my little analogy. But I think it illuminates, though not distinctly, the vague confusion that surrounds me. You once said you hoped I wouldn't change too much during my tour over here. The thought has occurred to me that some change in this environment is a must. To change one must react and if I could not react to the experience of war, then I would be emotionally and intellectually dead. But such reactions are deep seated and uncertain. I don't think I will appear so much a stranger to you as I am a stranger to myself. There is so little I know and so much I don't understand.

Please don't be misled by the foregoing. Perhaps you don't quite realize it, but you have the power ... to plunge me into the deepest despair with the most casual of words.

Love, Stu

✢ ✢ ✢

Note: In her letter of October 29, below, Jean responded to my letter of the 25th, but I didn't receive her letter until sometime after November 3. By that time I had written an additional letter to her on the 3rd. With this erratic mail service, it was hard to carry on a conversation.

My Darling Stewart,

Your last letter was very revealing and perhaps a little frightening. It bothers me very much that you feel so alone. It means simply that I have failed you by not being sensitive enough to your needs. I have been a little too playful with our love.

I admit I had hoped to shake you up with Richard's proposal—but I only meant to tease a little bit. I would never seriously consider marrying Richard. I have no intention of slipping away from you. My leaving you would have to be in some way very violent. I just can't imagine a situation in which it would be of my choosing. You are the only guy I'm interested in. I don't want to know anyone else; I don't even like to be with

Seven—Bombing Halt (or "Who the hell is Richard?")

other guys. It only makes me miss you more. Yes, I intend to travel 3,000 miles just to see you. I'd travel to the moon just to see you. Yes, I intend to wait patiently until you can put more faith in the future. I have the utmost faith that everything is going to work out for the best. Every future is vague and uncertain—we kid ourselves when we say it isn't. Stewart, you've got to learn to take the good with the bad again. Your and my future has sublime moments in store for us. You must remember that too.

No, I have not felt that our way has gotten steeper. I have felt a growing assurance in my steps. I see no insurmountable obstacles. I feel no strain. I'm not afraid—in fact, I'm not very worried. Some doubts are perfectly natural.

You are under a great deal of strain and tension. This is reflected continually in your letters. Your perception of the world has changed from seeing it as a warm and friendly place to a hostile, menacing and cruel environment that reaches out towards your life. You used to write me of beauty, lately it has been of cruelty and pain. You are understandably in a state of emotional turmoil which will probably gradually disappear after you have been back in the States for a while. Fighting this turmoil is probably much like fighting a rip tide; never underestimate the power and depth of your emotions. Regardless of what anyone says, they control our lives because they hold the key to perception. The security of logic and clear thinking is almost a special privilege at times.

At any rate, I think our relationship is much more secure than you believe. I am as close to you as you want to see me. I know I have a great deal of difficulty in communicating myself to you in either writing or words. You make me feel very self-conscious. Please remember that I'm always trying to be closer to you. I am making a very serious effort to understand you and your needs. It is my most cherished desire that we become as close to one another as humanly possible. I don't mean to frighten you out of 10 years growth, but can you imagine anything more beautiful than a child who is you and I?

You have been rejecting the future when you should be depending upon it. You refuse to look beyond where you are now because it seems too far away. Can't you see the danger in this? You are letting yourself be seduced by oblivion. Wouldn't it be much better to let yourself be seduced by me? I invite you to think ahead of all the pleasure that awaits you. How can you be fascinated by death when life has so much more in store for you? Be patient.

And for your information, Stewart, do you really think I would ever cut a rope that bound us to save myself? What has life in store for me without you? What reason would I have for getting up every morning? What excuse could I give for breathing? I think dying is more natural to man than living. Yes, death is a kind and understanding mother to those who have nothing to live for. And certainly, I have only you to live for. As for voluntarily jumping off mountain tops—I have a few strong words to say about that. Keep that line of thinking up and I shall have to link a chain between us two. The nerve! (I think this is a case of a man with too much freedom on his hands.)

    I wish I could make you especially happy now. You seem to be more in need of my help now.*

❖ ❖ ❖

    My letter of November 3 below shied away from the entire Richard issue and had a happier tone. Perhaps we were learning to simply accept the lag in a conversation and not worsen things by expounding on things already said without the benefit of the other's response. But it was a strange way to communicate. My letter of November 9, acknowledged hers of October 29, but didn't dwell on the issue. Case closed—or was it? Jean continued to mention Richard from time to time.

November 3, 1968

My Darling Jean,

    Shortly, in a week or so I will know if we will really be permitted to be together for a few moments next month. I won't hazard any guesses as to the prospects. I can only hope it will come to pass.

    This has truly been a memorable week in the conduct of our little war, has it not? Perhaps this new bombing pause will indeed bring us to the portals of settlement to this dreary business. However, realism forces me to recognize the more likely, and unhappy, prospect is that this current interlude will be bought with men's lives. At any rate, the pause has momentarily removed us from the shadow of the prodigious anti-aircraft defenses of North Vietnam. That I suppose is a welcome respite, although our best missions came in that area.

    The war in the South is continuing unabated. Indeed, by way of saluting the looming pause, the VC shelled Bien Hoa, Saigon and An Mia. But then we can't logically expect them to reciprocate, can we? I flew into the A Shau Valley today. It was pretty tame as the A Shau goes. Ground fire was not very intense and was mostly small arms. It was really a beautiful Sunday morning. It was clear and cloudless in the A Shau with a rich blue sky overhead and the lush greenness of the valley below. Of course, the many bomb craters on the valley floor added a discordant note, but

---

*Tuomy, *Is Love Enough?*, 140.

Seven—Bombing Halt (or "Who the hell is Richard?")

one learns to overlook those things. I was reminded of some bright Sunday several years ago when I (we, in fact) ventured into the air to spend a lazy hour or so soaring through the bright sunlight. So, it was today. As we wheeled and dove at the target today, carving lazy, soaring circles in the sky, feeling the rush of the diving aircraft, I was once again aware of the infinite thrill and joy of flying. I'm thankful for that.

Yesterday I was checked out as a flight lead, an important milestone in my short combat career. I now have 151 combat missions and as such I'm considered sufficiently experienced to assume the responsibility of leading flights. In essence this means that I am no longer a carefree, devil may care, hell bent wing man but must now assume the responsibility for leading a flight to the target, coordinating the strike with the FAC, and seeing that the several tons of high explosives involved are delivered on the target. Finally, I must see that the other flight members are shepherded safely home.

That is about the only notable thing that has happened to me of late. In answer to your inquiry, I finished the books you sent me long ago. I enjoyed the diversion immensely. I just finished reading the *Confessions of Nat Turner* by William Styron which I'm sure you are familiar with. If you haven't already done so I can highly recommend that you read it. I thought it was quite well written and I enjoyed it very much.

You also inquired into the health of my family. (And I must confess somewhat sheepishly that I haven't written to them in several weeks.) My mother writes, when she does write, that they are quite happily settled in their place in Virginia. She insists on reminding me, much to my chagrin, of how beautiful the place is as summer blends into fall and the multicolored leaves turn the landscape into an orgy of color. She says that my father is now happy and enthusiastic about his new job. I think that, in a large sense, they have come home at last. I think that we all have always viewed the place in Virginia as home. I think they are happy to be back there. I wish that you could see the place. It is really quite beautiful.

Janet is happily enveloped by the life at UCSB. She seems to have taken quite well to the new adventure of college life. Her enthusiasm for life itself is refreshing.

Finally, George writes that he is beginning his checkout in the F-100 at Cannon. He soloed the bird several weeks ago and seems to be excited about the whole thing. He hopes to get assigned to Tuy Hoa after he leaves Cannon.

And I guess that is about all I have to say for the moment. Perhaps there will be happier, less anguished times for us in the future.

Be good now—

Love, Stu

❖ ❖ ❖

November 9, 1968

My Dear Jeannie,

Here it is another sparkling Saturday in the tropics. An absolutely great day for lying on the beach and getting some rays. It's kind of nice to live in a place that doesn't have a winter of any description. It is a balmy 85 degrees or so. The midmorning sky is richly blue, the clouds are scattered and fluffy white, the sun is pleasantly warm. It could well be an early summer day in some other part of the world.

So much for the weather. The great bombing halt, aside from being a rather astute political move by LBJ, is having little effect on us. In fact, I have been flying more this month than I ever have. Last Monday, I flew three missions off of the alert pad, pretty much covering the country from I Corps to III Corps [*Three of the designated combat zones in South Vietnam; I Corps in the north to IV Corps in the south*]. Then bright and early the next day (0500) we took off to air refuel and strike a target by Binh Thuy in IV Corps. In a 24-hour period, I spent about 10 hours in the cockpit and covered South Vietnam from top to bottom.

Other than missing you, I'm not doing much very important. It's dreadfully dull to be a combat fighter pilot—except of course for those few moments of stark terror that you experience every now and then.

Your letter of October 29 was of course of great interest to me. I was anxious to see if I had accurately explained my feelings in my little analogy [*my letter of October 20*]. I don't think that I was entirely successful, but no matter. You get the idea of what I was trying to tell you. You are right in suggesting I need you more than ever now. If your one comment did not indeed frighten me out of 10 years growth, it certainly did give me cause for reflection.

The list of who goes to Hawaii next month should be out in a couple of days, the 12th, I think. I'll let you know as soon as I know.

Oh yes, about my next assignment. I requested F-104s at Homestead Air Force Base, Miami, FL. Of course, you must realize that my request will probably have very little to do with the assignment I get, so it all has very little meaning. In fact, assignments out of here look very bleak at best. It is becoming increasingly difficult to stay in fighters if you are not flying in the combat zone. I could end up as a copilot in a bomber or a transport. That's indicative of the way the Air Force treats its people. I can assure you my reaction to that would not be pleasant. What this all means of course, is that I haven't the faintest idea where I will be stationed a year from now. It could be very good or could be very bad.

Well, I must close for now. Shortly I must go and take my appointed place at mobile, there to guide the intrepid aviators as they grope once more for the safety of the earth. Before I close, I must tell you ... to take care of yourself and be good.

Love, Stu

* * *

Crew Chiefs

The heart of any flying operation are the maintenance personnel that keep the aircraft primed and ready. They were truly the unsung heroes of the air war in Vietnam. The crew chiefs were assigned to individual aircraft which they were very proud of. But they worked wherever they were needed. A main task was to preflight the bird to be sure it was ready for the upcoming mission. They also assisted the weapons load crews and any maintenance specialists that might be needed. My crew chief met me when I arrived at the aircraft, assisted me with my walk around [*preflight inspection*] and helped me strap into the cockpit. Startup procedures were a well-choreographed routine (head phones were seldom used or needed): fire guard posted, started up hand signal, engine start, flight controls check [*checked the proper movement of ailerons and rudder to stick inputs*], my cockpit checklist done, wheel cocks pulled. He marshalled me out of the revetment and saluted me on my way—in driving rain or blistering heat. When I landed in the middle of the night with rain slashing down and forming pools on the ramp, a crew chief was there to greet me. He guided me into the parking spot, chocked the wheels and helped me unstrap and climb out. At the bottom of the ladder, he greeted me with a cheerful "How's the bird, sir? Any write-ups [*maintenance issues with the aircraft*]?"

It always felt good to be able to say, "Bird's good, Chief. No write-ups." Still, I knew he would be there for another hour at least, rain or not, heat of the day or still of the night. He had his own tasks to do—refueling, inspections, paperwork to fill out—before the aircraft was bedded down, ready for the next mission. An aircraft was never left partially fueled. To do so was to invite an explosion as the remaining fuel absorbed the heat of the airframe and engine and outgassed.

Equally important to combat operations were the weapons personnel, or load crews, as they were known. They were the ones that uploaded the bombs or other munitions on the aircraft. A delicate job to be sure. This involved retrieving the weapons from the bomb dump [*heavily reinforced bunkers well away from the flight line and living areas*], transporting them to the flight line on special trailers, then maneuvering the trailers under the weapons pylons of the aircraft. Obviously, a 750 lb. bomb is not manhandled into place. Instead the weapons trailers had hydraulic lifts that raised and positioned the bombs against the weapons pylons. Then the jaws of the pylon were locked around lugs on the bomb, and sway braces tightened. The job was only half done at this point. The fuse that would set off the bomb was carefully inserted into the fuse well in the bomb's nose and arming wires were strung to a solenoid in the pylon. If this was not done properly, the fuse would not be activated on release. Finally, cartridges were inserted into wells on the pylon that were electrically connected to the weapons control panel in the cockpit. These cartridges would explosively open the jaws and eject the weapon when activated. A complex task that the load crews would perform dozens of times a day across the Wing. Unlike the crew chiefs, the pilots seldom had direct contact with the load crews. We didn't thank them properly for the critical job they performed in the chain of combat operations. (In 300 missions with nearly a thousand weapons releases I only had one hung store. That was a 2.75-inch rocket pod; the rockets fired but the pod would not jettison with the normal system.)

The crew chiefs and other enlisted personnel generally worked 12-hour shifts, six days a week. Their housing was in long, bungalow type buildings, with a center aisle and individual sleeping/living quarters on either side of the aisle. The walls were paneled with plywood part way up with screening above for ventilation—no air conditioning here! Vertically hinged shutters could be lowered to cover the screening in inclement weather. It was spartan, but no one complained.

My crew chief, during most of 1968, was from a rural background and he had set himself a task of making a grand hunting knife to while away his spare time here in Vietnam. It started as a piece of high strength steel bar stock. The occasional times when we were waiting at the airplane to launch, he would pull out the knife and carefully file away at some part of it. I knew it was going to be beautiful.

Around Christmas, two men replaced my previous crew chief. The additional person reflected the improved manning situation at Tuy Hoa as the war settled into a routine across the Air Force. Both guys loved to talk about the missions I flew and the progress of the war. At the end of my tour, they presented me with the plaque shown on the next page. I have received many plagues and other remembrances in my career, but this one holds a special place on my wall of memories.

If crew chiefs are the unsung heroes of flight operations, the enlisted force is the backbone of all Air Force units. There are hundreds of enlisted personnel doing all the routine tasks that keep a deployed fighter wing going—back shop maintenance experts, supply specialists, parachute riggers, medics, weather forecasters, air traffic controllers to guide us down on a stormy night. There are cooks, mailroom attendants, transportation mechanics and drivers, POL [*petroleum, oil, lubricants*] specialists to keep the jets fueled, and civil engineers to keep the runways open. Security forces to man the perimeter defenses and administrative support specialists in a variety of areas. All of these skills are critical to accomplishing the myriad tasks necessary to keep a small city functioning.

A proud possession. Image of a plaque presented to author by his two crew chiefs at the end of his Vietnam tour, May 1969 (author's collection).

I worked closely with an administrative NCO in the squadron in my additional duty as squadron security officer. His expertise saved me in this job. An important part of this duty was insuring that classified information was properly handled. In our squadron, this meant that these documents were properly stored in the squadron safe. I got this duty in early January and we were looking at an inspection later that month. When he and I opened the safe we found a mess. For years, classified documents were simply stuffed into the safe with no rhyme or reason. Most of the documents should have been destroyed long ago and the rest properly recorded and stored. We went to work; he provided the knowledge and expertise; we both provided the labor to straighten the mess out—and hopefully pass the inspection (benignly called a "Staff Assistance Visit"). He was great to work with—sometimes into the late evening. This job took him away from his normal duties but there was no complaint even as I was called away to fly. Thanks to him, we passed the "Assistance Visit" with flying colors. The inspection report read in part:

> Overall security was excellent.... Both the Unit Security Officer and his administrative NCO appeared highly motivated and were aware of pertinent security directives. Discrepancies were insignificant in nature and not worthy of comment.*

We got a nice cover endorsement to the report from the squadron commander for our work.

✦ ✦ ✦

November 12, 1968

My Darling Jean,

    Not knowing how to relay the following I suppose it is best to just attack the problem directly. I was not chosen to take my R and R in December. I won't speculate too long on the reasons, therefore. It would seem that many people are partial to the idea of spending Christmas near a loved one. And not everyone could go. Selections are made on the length of time you have in-country by the way.

    Of course, the Christmas season has immediately lost much of its cheer. I'm terribly sorry that, after so many long months, this has come to pass. Of course, I will apply for January, and we may hope that I get an early date in January. I only hope that this disappointment is not too bitter for you. I know it was for me.

    I often fear that in my aloneness I have grown cold and sour. This is what I have been trying to tell you, to warn you of in my last few letters. I can sense an icy, cynical bitterness clouding my view of the world.... I hope you understand this. I'm certain that I don't.

    I will be getting a bit of a break from the routine of flying the next few days. I'm going to Taiwan to pick up an airplane and fly it back here. It is always good for a couple of days of relaxing in the real world of Taiwan and Clark in the Philippines. It suddenly occurs to me that it has been nearly two months since I have been away from Tuy Hoa. It seems that I have been here all of my life. Even the trip to Hong Kong seems a vague, uncertain figment of my imagination. At least I will get a chance to wear some of the clothes I got in Hong Kong.

    Not much exciting has been happening around old Tuy Hoa. The weather's turned again so that makes things a little more exciting when we fly. I have been flying quite a bit so far this month, so I don't have that

---

*John Welch, "Report of Administrative Security Staff Assistance Visit," Tuy Hoa Air Base, Republic of South Vietnam: Unpublished, 1969.

Seven—Bombing Halt (or "Who the hell is Richard?")

much time to be bored. I've also been blessed with afternoon flights, so I've become very lazy sleeping in till mid-morning and just generally leading a life of leisure. Now I must catch a plane at two o'clock in the morning to go to Taiwan.

I hope that you are having a lovely time back there in exciting Los Angeles. I trust that your host of suitors is not interfering too much with your studies. I mean, after all, you know how important school is(?)

I must close for now and pack. Sorry, this is so short. I just wanted to let you know about Hawaii as soon as possible. I'm sorry the news had to be bad.

Be good now—

Love, Stu

◈ ◈ ◈

November 20, 1968

Dearest Jean,

I have a more cheerful outlook on life now that I have been away from the God forsaken war for a while. My trip to Taiwan was uneventful but relaxing. I left here at 2:45 in the morning last Wednesday and arrived at Taichung [*Taiwan*] about dawn. The crew of the C-130 I rode up there on took me in hand and showed me all of the important sights in Taichung.

On Thursday I caught a train for Tainan. It took 2½ hours and was a rather pleasant ride through the countryside of Taiwan. I was impressed by the friendliness and industriousness of the people in Taiwan. I wish that I had had a chance to go to Taipei. I understand that is outstanding. I spent another night carousing about Tainan, taking in the points of cultural interest, and on Friday went to the Air Asia facility to take delivery of my airplane. That place is really intriguing. The entire facility is inside a great stone wall topped with broken glass. Once you have gained admittance through the several gates, you are met with a curious scene. There spread before you in a jumbled disarray is a large number of F-4s, F-105s, and F-100s, all in battle dress and all in various states of disassembly. Also sprinkled about is a smattering of old DC-3s, C-46s, etc., bearing such cryptic names as Air America, Air Vietnam, China Airlines, etc. And swarming over each airplane are a dozen or so mechanics, all dressed in blue Air Asia uniforms. The whole scene looks right out of a Hollywood spy movie. To add to the aura of intrigue, a large solid metal gate blocks the taxiway leading out of the compound to the runway. When you sign the necessary papers for your airplane, you are given a gate pass good for 15 minutes either side of your proposed takeoff time. This must be presented to the guard at the gate during the allotted time or you can't get out. It's all very mysterious.

On Friday, I flew to Clark Air Base in the Philippines where I spent the weekend. Clark is another interesting place. It is a veritable crossroads of the Air Force. If you sit in the Officers' Club long enough, you will see everyone in the Air Force. It's also the last outpost of civilization before the war zone. All of the pilot types on the way to Vietnam pass through there. As you might imagine, it has a rather festive atmosphere and is always a welcome taste of the good life after being at war for a while. A mediocre level of pulchritude is provided by schoolteachers and stewardesses at Clark. At any rate, I have a couple of old friends from pilot training at Clark, one who was a partner in the boat I had in Laredo. I hadn't seen him for over a year. I was somewhat surprised when he introduced his wife. I didn't even know he was married.

After a couple of days of relaxing about the pool at Clark, it was time to head back home. I flew back on Monday in a five-ship flight comprised of an F-4, an F-101, and three F-100s. That was quite a sight and I wished that I had had a camera to capture that formation.

Note: It was Air Force policy that a fighter could not fly single ship from Clark to Vietnam. Rather, you had to be accompanied by other fighters and an SA-16 (amphibious aircraft) had to be on station midway. This requirement could cause several days' delay in getting back to Vietnam. Ironically, you could fly single ship for the 500 miles from Taiwan to Clark with an airplane just out of heavy maintenance, but you needed companions for the 750-mile flight from Clark to Vietnam.

As soon as I got back, the squadron put me on night alert. That was very nice of them. I had flown so little in the past week that I nearly crashed on takeoff. Nothing like a pitch-dark night to get your attention.

I received your letter of the 13th today and was very happy to hear from you. You didn't seem very happy, however, and as I read over your letter, I began to think how strange, and strained, our relationship has become.... I guess that I haven't been too sweet of late, have I? I'm very sorry for that. But loneliness is a powerful, unceasing force.

I hope that you will be able to forgive my bitterness.

Be good now—

                                        Love, Stu

P.S. Happy Turkey Day

Seven—Bombing Halt (or "Who the hell is Richard?")

* * *

November 23, 1968

Dear Mom & Dad,

You will be happy to learn that I survived my trip to Tainan with no ill effects. I left here on the 13th to go to Tainan and retrieve an airplane from our IRAN [*Inspect and Repair as Necessary*] facility there.

My train trip from Taichung to Tainan through the countryside was quite an experience. It is interesting to be thrust into the peculiar situation of being totally illiterate. I had no idea which train went where in the station at Taichung. Of course the signs were just so many hieroglyphs. I finally found a porter who spoke pidgin English and he put me on the right train for a modest fee.

The IRAN facility is really fascinating.... The entire place is surrounded by a glass topped stone wall a la Wheelus. The whole thing looks rather clandestine.

I left Tainan on Friday afternoon and arrived at Clark just after dark. As luck would have it, I lost my radio enroute. I ended up spending the weekend at Clark. Friday night I ran into a friend from pilot training at the O Club. He is married (a surprise to me) and stationed at Clark flying F-4's. I also ran into one of George's roommates at Reese, there at Clark. He is on his way to Phu Cat in C-7's. At any rate, it seems to be old home week at Clark.

As soon as I got back, I went on night alert. We are now sitting idle in anticipation of the coming of another typhoon. The weather is increasingly stormy and all flight operations are suspended. We may have to evacuate the airplanes to Thailand.

The war is progressing as usual, I guess. I haven't seen that the bombing halt has had much effect except to give Charlie a chance to regroup. That's evidenced by the ground fire we are taking now. I have not had any particularly exciting or momentous missions of late. It's all pretty much routine, it seems.

I hope all is well with you all these days. From your letters I judge that you are all keeping busy and are enjoying the life of a Virginia gentleman and family.

Take care now—

Love, Stewart

* * *

November 23, 1968

My Darling Jeannie,

I received your package today and I was surprised and delighted with its contents. Thank you very much. What are you trying to do, add a touch of culture and refinement to my drinking? Now instead of drinking my Beefeaters straight I'll have to get some vermouth and olives and mix a proper martini. Or maybe I will start mixing Manhattans.

I have determined not to send you a Christmas gift at all. Rather I am going to give them to you personally when I see you in January. The 25th of December has little enough meaning to me (another mission or two or three?). Besides, I want the pleasure of seeing you receive my humble gifts. (I'm assuming you receive them well and like them.) I hope you won't think badly of me for my lack of Christmas spirit, whatever that is.

Your question of the future troubled me. Certainly, it is a question that has often occurred to me. But so far, I have successfully avoided confronting the problem. What will become of us?

We are presently sitting idle in anticipation of the impending impact of another typhoon. As in the last one, the surf is gray and boiling, rain falls in endless wind driven sheets. So far, the wind has been rather mild, but its intensity has started to mount during the past few hours. Shortly the low, uneven moan will begin to grow in ever increasing crescendos until it becomes a shriek that fills the world and threatens all living things through its very ferocity. As the storm mounts, the sea will dash ever higher on the beach, leaving deep masses of foam high on the beach to be whisked away by the wind. The wind will tug mercilessly at every projection; it will drive the rain with such force that any crack or small hole will admit a torrent of water. If we receive the full brunt of the storm, everything not securely fastened down will be whisked away to join the jumbled mass of debris even now being swept away to oblivion by the wind. But by then, we will have received the order to evacuate the aircraft and will have launched ourselves into the teeth of the rising gale in hopes of finding, eventually, a safe haven. But so much for possibilities. More than likely the storm will miss us, and we will have only lost a day of flying.

Well, I have nothing else to do, I guess that I had better write my parents a letter for a change. No doubt they will be wondering what has become of me.

Be good now—

Love, Stu

P.S. Thanks again for the shaker. It is really beautiful.

Seven—Bombing Halt (or "Who the hell is Richard?")

✳ ✳ ✳

Note: Jean had sent a silver cocktail shaker with my initials on it. She commented on how infatuated I had been in the silver shop we visited in Santa Monica.

Eight

Anticipation

My R&R in Hawaii would finally be confirmed on December 9 to start on January 9. That gave us roughly a month to make room reservations and travel plans for Jean. This promised to be an expensive holiday—hotel rates at the Hilton Hawaiian Village were $17 to $19 a night—very expensive in 1969! Since communications were nearly impossible from Vietnam, I asked Jean to make the hotel reservation and to advise me of her flight schedule. Since the R&R was now officially pushed into the new year, Christmas loomed as just another day in the war zone for me. I suggested to both Jean and my family that we not try to exchange gifts for the holiday. This suggestion was only partially accepted.

As had become customary, the Air Force in South Vietnam marked Christmas with a unilateral shut down of flying. Although we were all on semi-alert status, the pilots in the squadron took advantage of the stand down to throw a party for the enlisted troops—steaks and 35 cases of beer!

Mail service during December seemed to suffer from the holiday season. I did not receive a letter from Jean for about three weeks. At least one of her letters was lost in the mail. I began to be concerned that she had changed her mind about the rendezvous in Hawaii, or even that Richard had crept back into the picture. That added some gloom to my Christmas. My anxiety was finally relieved on January 1 when I received her letter written December 25.

✤ ✤ ✤

December 2, 1968

Dearest Jean,

Happy finals. That's a bit of a cruel thing to say I know since finals are never, never happy. But consider that the long and difficult hours of

Eight—Anticipation

study are good character builders, intellectual stimulus sharpens your wit, and the physical privations ruin your health. Isn't that wonderful? Sometimes I think that our education system is second only to the Inquisition for gross cruelty and inhumanity.

I received your care package several days ago and was amazed at the quantity and variety of things that you sent. Though I will probably never be able to consume it all, I'm enjoying the varied and assorted delicacies. When I opened the fruitcake, I wondered if perhaps you weren't trying to make an alcoholic of me. That thing was embalmed. Caution dictated that I post no smoking signs all around it. Due to regulations against alcohol consumption, I can't eat any of it 12 hours before I fly. Actually, I am saving it for Christmas Day itself. I trust that it will be delicious. At the very least, it will add immensely to the Christmas spirit.

I also received your little packet of books a few days ago. I immediately fell to reading the volume on stress-seeking. It does have some interesting ideas and views on the subject of why man must continually be foolhardy. I don't know whether it provided you with any insight into my irrational behavior or not. I think for one not inclined to such stress seeking that the entire concept must be nearly impossible to grasp.

I was amused that you also included several volumes on art. Are you perhaps trying to instill some culture in me? A most ambitious undertaking to be sure. But of course, it's true that I haven't even a rudimentary knowledge of art, so your efforts are well directed. Hesse's book looks interesting as always, but I don't know about the *Pillars of Fire*. I do thank you for your thoughtfulness as much as for the many things you have sent me. How can I ever repay you? Everything is going well enough for me here except of course that I miss you. If Christmas holds little promise or attraction for me, the new year holds every promise and attraction. I am anxiously awaiting the arrival of January.

Actually, life here has become quite stale. At the same time, my complacency with regard to the missions I fly has become frightening. As Marshall implied, any situation will become routine after a while and so has this for me. I have an almost callous disregard for the danger (intellectually, I must assume they still exist) inherent in this occupation. It would seem that I have adopted an attitude of resignation to fate. No, that's not right either. More like a deliberate and somewhat reckless challenging of fate, almost as if I were defying my luck to desert me. It's all very curious. Such is the capriciousness of life and fate. Often the most meticulous planning and prudent execution is to no avail, while the seemingly foolhardy and reckless attacks are just as often successful.

Well, that's quite enough of my melancholia. I wish that for

Christmas I could give you happiness. But it is a fleeting, elusive thing and it's not mine to give. Perhaps if it could be easily captured and savored it would not be so attractive.

I hope the finals don't treat you too badly.

Love, Stu

✤ ✤ ✤

December 9, 1968

Dearest Jean,

Would you believe the 9th of January? That seems to be the magic date now. Actually, there is some confusion in the R&R Center because they have been swamped by requests for January. They told me that since I have been here so long that I can just about depend on the 9th even though they haven't published the list officially. I hope that this is satisfactory with you. You said anytime in January, so I thought the earlier the better.

This means that I will be leaving Vietnam on the 9th and thanks to the international dateline will be arriving in Hawaii probably during the morning of the ninth. I don't know exactly what time. On this R&R we get five days and six nights so I would be leaving again on the morning of the 15th. Since connections from Vietnam to the outside world are next to impossible, I am going to ask you to make the hotel reservations for us. I rather imagine that we will want to stay in Waikiki. I don't know much about the hotels there, but I understand that the Princess Kaiulani, the Moana and the Surfrider are all nice and fairly reasonable. Single rates run from about $12 to $17 a night at these hotels. Of course, there is a Royal Hawaiian and the Outrigger, but they run $22 to $25 for a single. Hilton Hawaiian Village falls in between in price. But I will leave all of this up to you. I'm sure that your friendly local travel bureau will be more knowledgeable and helpful than me.

At least now we have something a little more definite to look forward to. I'm sure the days 'til then will fly by. I'm afraid that Christmas promises to be a rather dreary affair, but the new year is already looking much, much brighter.

I trust that finals went well for you, and that you are now thoroughly enjoying your release from the strain of academic pleasures—at least for a few weeks. When I think of Christmas, my thoughts are invariably turned back to last Christmas and the time we spent together. Your last letter recalled to my mind our little shopping excursion. Well do I remember the silver shop. It was fascinating.

I must close for now and go to work. I do want to get this mailed as quickly as possible. I hope that the news brightens your day. It did mine. Everything is well with me.

Until I see you remember to be good.

Love, Stu

✢ ✢ ✢

December 17, 1968

My Darling Jeannie,

The 9th of January is confirmed. I will be arriving in Hawaii fairly early on the 9th apparently and should be finished with their silly briefings and processing by mid-morning. I am anxiously awaiting the coming of the new year now.

This is the first day in many that I have a little time off. This past week I have either been on night alert or have been flying several times a day, or both so that it seems I hardly had time to sink into bed before I had to get up again. It's just as well that I stay busy like that. The days pass swiftly by at such times.

Today is a beautiful day. I am presently lounging in the sun attempting to cultivate a golden tan. It's one of the few good days we have had recently. Mostly the weather has been dreary and damp, the sky perpetually hidden behind a dark layer of clouds. My spirits are much brightened with the sun shining gaily overhead.

I was happy to hear that you are passing all of your courses this semester. I was afraid that the social whirl around Los Angeles would be cutting into your studies too much. (That wasn't very kind, was it?) I wish that I could have been there this fall to totally disrupt your academic career. Maybe it is a good thing I've been away for your senior year.

You know, it's exceedingly difficult to get very much in the Christmas spirit while lounging beneath the bright tropical sun. My roommate did a little house cleaning about a week ago, and what should he discover in a dust filled corner but an artificial Christmas tree. He dutifully put it together and decorated it, and we placed our few meager packages beneath it so that we may have a proper Christmas in the old tradition, Christmas morn. I've put your gift to work so it shan't be languishing beneath the silly tree. Now I must lay in a stock of Christmas cheer (the liquid kind—perhaps I can just wring out your fruitcake).

I hope that you all are enjoying a very Merry Christmas. Have a happy New Year and say hello to your parents and family for me.

Love, Stu

December 18, 1968

Dear Mom and Dad,

   Just a short note to wish you all a very Merry Christmas and a Happy New Year. This card and letter will probably get there late, however, I wanted to thank both mother and Janet for their respective packages. Your thoughtfulness is greatly appreciated—and it was nice to have a taste of Home.

   Everything is going quite normally for me. We even have a little artificial tree in our quarters. It must have been a relic from last year, but it is still serviceable and it has been trimmed. Otherwise it will be a pretty bleak Christmas.

   Our flight operations are continuing as normal. I don't know if anything will come of the Christmas truce or not. It will probably just give the VC a respite from our bombing and a chance to resupply.

   As I said before, I wish that you all have a white and happy Christmas. I also wish that I could be there.

   The very best to all of you in the New Year.

                                      Love, Stewart

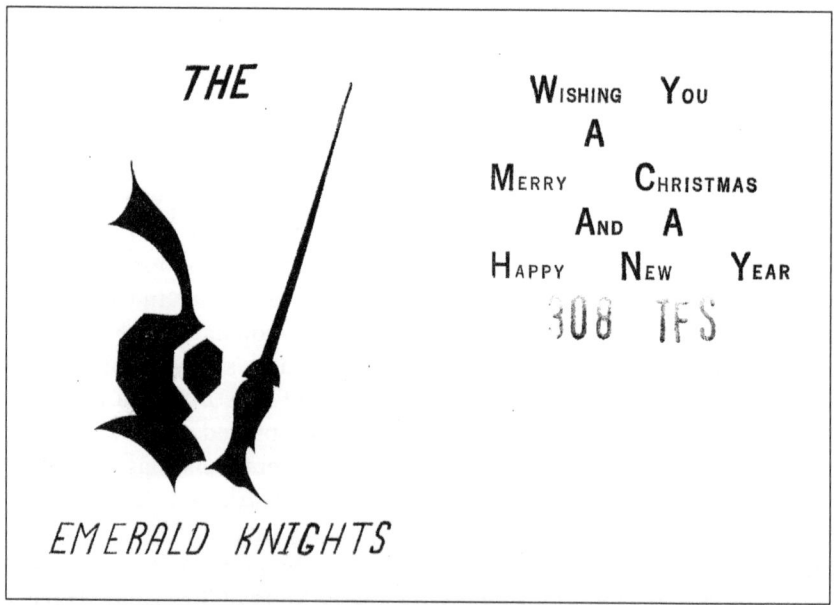

Image of Emerald Knights Christmas greetings, December 1968 (author's collection).

Eight—Anticipation

December 25, 1968

My Darling,

As you might expect, Christmas Day here is somewhat dreary. We aren't flying today and even though the whole squadron is on varying stages of alert, it is essentially a day of rest. It gives me time to reflect, and that is not necessarily good. I keep remembering last Christmas and the one before that ... when we were able to be together. It was a beautiful time.

Last night we had a party for the squadron. The pilots got together and bought 35 cases of beer, plus steaks, etcetera for the crew chiefs and other enlisted personnel in the squadron. I didn't think it was possible, but those guys quite rapidly drank all 35 cases and then some. Of course, I drank my share also. It was really a pretty good party considering the circumstances. It was a little show of appreciation to the enlisted troops for the long and thankless hours that they put in keeping our airplanes air worthy. And they don't have the thrill and excitement of flying to relieve the endless boredom of succeeding days.

I will be arriving in Honolulu about 7:30 in the morning of the 9th. From the airport we will be taken to Fort DeRussy, a small Army installation in downtown Honolulu, for a briefing (the military feels they must brief everything) before we are turned loose on the poor natives of Hawaii. I will return to Vietnam on the 15th, rather early in the morning, I think. By the way, were you able to get any hotel reservation? You must tell me where, and also what time you will be arriving in Hawaii so that I can meet you, or you meet me or whatever.

I hope that you and your family had a Merry Christmas. Please thank your mother for me for the pictures of you that she sent. I enjoyed them very much. I wish that I had more recent ones of you. But then, I'm not very good about sending pictures along either, am I?

Everything has been going along quite normally of late. I haven't been working very hard I must confess. I seem to be finding ample time of late to lounge in the sun and work on my tan. That is one advantage of Christmas in the tropics. Now I suppose that the sun will hide for the next two weeks, and my tan will fade into nothing. War is full of pitfalls and dangers.

I hope the next two weeks pass quickly.
Until then, be good.

Love, Stu

Note: I had not received a letter from Jean since December 5, received around December 10. I think her letter telling me of her travel plans must have been lost in the mails. At any rate, I'd grown quite anxious at not hearing from her.

✤ ✤ ✤

January 1, 1969

My Darling Jean,

Happy New Year to you! I was very happy to receive your letter of the 25th today; that is after I opened it. I don't think that the mail has been getting through with the certainty advertised by the postal department. This is the first letter I have received from you in over three weeks. Needless to say, the intervening weeks have been anxious ones for me.... I had begun to reconcile myself to the possibility that you had perhaps forsaken me. Worse, I even imagined that something dreadful had befallen you. And always I hoped that nothing was amiss, that it was only some monumental postal error that was causing my anxious concern.

At any rate, it was with considerable apprehension that I viewed your unopened letter today.... Was this missive to be a harbinger of joy or of tragedy? Would it contain the simple words of plans for our forthcoming adventure—or would it rather be that infamous terse announcement, the ever-tasteless obituary of the inexplicable death of love. I tore open the letter with hope, and of course that hope was vindicated. Now I feel bad for my doubts of you. I can tell you, however, that a salutation was never more beautiful than the one on that letter.

I was happy to hear that you were able to get us some room reservations though I was prepared to sleep on the beach if necessary. You do have expensive tastes though, don't you? I don't quite know how to react to the promised luxury of the Hawaiian Village, but I'm looking forward to you. (By the way, the promise of a few days with you raises some very pleasant reactions in me.)

You mentioned that you will be arriving via Pan Am at the time you mentioned earlier. Well, that didn't mean a great deal to me since apparently the earlier letter has been lost in the postal shuffle. I'm assuming that you will arrive on the 9th. If necessary, I shall meet every arriving Pan Am flight until I find you—that is if you don't beat me here.

I most heartily second your thought that it will be good to be done with this damn letter writing for a while. There seems to be so much I want to say to you that never comes out quite right when written. But even if we can't communicate any better at close range, at least the effort will be fun.

I am looking forward to seeing you very much.... If we have become strangers through the passage of time, then I hope that we will no longer be strangers when we part again.

Until I see you,

Love, Stu

✢ ✢ ✢

January 4, 1969

Dearest Jean,

Just a short note to tell you how eagerly I am awaiting the next few days to pass. I don't even know if this letter will have time to get to you before you are on your way. It is scarcely believable that we will really be together so soon.

The weather here is very dreary with continually falling rain and dark, ugly clouds. But somehow my spirits refuse to be dampened by these minor irritations.

But then there are times when my spirit is dark, and it seems that I have spent my entire life in this godforsaken wilderness. My whole past life seems then to be a curious dream and I must wonder if anything as wonderful as you could truly have happened to me. At such times, I think how embarrassing it would be if we did not even recognize one another. (You can always look for my mustache, but I shall have to search the crowds for a mysterious and alluring blond.)

Can I even begin to tell you how I have missed you these past eight months? But if the separation has been insufferable, then the promise of our reunion is the agony of too much happiness.

Until I see you, be good—

Love, Stu

Nine

Hawaii

My R & R flight arrived in Hawaii pretty much on time around 7:30 in the morning. We were bused to Fort DeRussy in downtown Honolulu for a briefing—basically told to behave ourselves and be back at the airport on time for the return flight to Vietnam.

From the briefing I made the short walk to the Hilton Hawaiian Village and checked in. They gave me a very nice room for my $17 a night. Since Jean's letter giving me her arrival information had apparently been lost in the mails, I changed clothes and went directly to the Honolulu Airport and waited for the arrival of any Pan Am flights from Los Angeles. I got there a little before noon to discover that the only Pan Am flight from LA was late and would arrive about two o'clock.

I went to the bar to have lunch and wait. I was chatting with an attractive young lady in the bar when the PA system announced the impending arrival of the flight from LA. I excused myself, paid my check and proceeded to the arrival gate. As I got there the passengers were already deplaning. Looking around, I was afraid I wouldn't recognize Jean in the crowd. Then I saw her looking bewildered as she surveyed the arrival area. I walked towards her and she saw me. In a moment, we were locked in a tight embrace.

We were inseparable as we claimed her luggage and walked to the taxi stand. I think the driver and taxi attendant were slightly embarrassed by the intensity of our hold on each other as they ushered us into the cab. Her room at the Hawaiian Village (at $19 a night) was not as nice as mine, but no matter, she didn't spend much time there.

The next five days were a whirl: we explored downtown Honolulu, shopped at the tourist places, dined at lovely (and expensive) restaurants, took long walks along the beach. She was alluring in her bikini. On the third day, we rented a car, a red convertible, and drove around the island. At North Beach, the scene of monstrous waves and surfing competitions, the ocean lapped softly on the shore. No matter, the only thing that existed for us was each other.

One evening we strolled along the streets of downtown Honolulu, window shopping and enjoying the pleasant night air. We speculated on other couples we passed; were they happy with each other? We stopped to buy ice cream at a street vendor and as I fumbled for the right change, I absently handed my wallet to Jean to hold. She flipped the wallet open revealing several pictures of old girl friends I'd forgotten were there. Jean was not amused. "How could you?!" she exclaimed, obviously upset. I tried to shrug it off, but she would not be mollified. She had a possessive streak, I knew, but her reaction also reflected an uncertainty about me, and us.

On our last full day, we simply shared each other—lounged on the beach, enjoyed the sun, took short walks. Jean was quiet, pensive. She sat beside me as I lay on a beach towel watching the breakers roll in across the reef that protects the Waikiki lagoon.

I knew she expected some commitment from this brief sojourn in Hawaii—either engagement or engaged to be engaged. Finally, she said, "What's going to become of us, Stewart? Is there a future for us? Tomorrow, are we just going to go back to letters and long separation? Are we ever going to just be together? Are we going to marry?"*

I did not respond for a long while. Her questions were not unexpected nor were they inappropriate. I too wondered what was going to become of us.

Finally, I said, "I don't know, Jean. I simply don't know what to say. We both want to be together. I can't imagine a life without you. I do dream that you will marry me someday. But now—but now I'm so uncertain about my own future. I'm stuck in this God-forsaken war. I don't know from day-to-day what's going to happen to me. I don't know where I'm going, or even who I am. I just can't commit to something long term when I don't even know if I'll be alive a month or four months from now. I think it would be unfair to you to promise a future when I don't know if I can keep that promise."

"And what about you?" I asked. "You have not really had a chance to experience life. You've been cloistered in the arms of your family and the Mount. You have not had the satisfaction of facing life in all its complexity and knowing that you, by yourself, can conquer it. You have not had the chance to really know yourself and understand your strength and worth."

"I'm so sorry." I said, "I hope you can understand."

---

*Tuomy, *Is Love Enough?*, 189.

She in turn was silent for a long while. Then she stood up, looking at the lagoon and the breaking waves far off. Turning to me she said, "I think I'll take a walk."

I started to get up, saying, "I'll go with you."

But she held her hand out to stop me and said, "No, I need to be by myself for a while. I need to think."

I watched her as she turned and walked away, down the beach towards Diamond Head. I watched her slim form recede, finally disappearing in the sparse crowd of sunbathers and strolling couples and children searching for seashells. My heart was filled with anguish for the pain I was causing her.

How could I expect her to understand the ambivalence I felt at this moment? I have not experienced a normal life in nearly a year now. The war and its uncertainty and dangers had filled my being since even before I got to Vietnam. I was now immersed in a hellish world where the future simply didn't exist; where fate was the determining force, where you as an individual had little control beyond your meager skills. I needed to have a chance to reconnect with a normal reality before I could know what she and I were ultimately to be to each other. I felt deeply the great pain I knew I was causing her, but I simply could not do otherwise at this crucial point.

I lay back down and closed my eyes. In time, she returned, kneeled beside me, smiled at me and touched my cheek.

"I don't understand," she said. "I can't know what you are feeling, but I can't turn away from you. I will wait until you find yourself—and I know myself."*

We both departed Hawaii early the following day—I went west back to the War, Jean east to Los Angeles and her studies. As the R&R airplane winged its way across the vast Pacific I could only hope that the gulf I had created between us did not become an ocean in the coming months.

※ ※ ※

Note: Two days later, on January 17, Jean wrote:

In spite of the deafening silence, in spite of the emptiness, there is a warmth in me.... I felt my very soul was being torn when I realized the arms around me would soon be gone, but I would gladly feel that again and again. I am pleased with our adventure; my greatest fears have been silenced, perhaps once and for all. I will not lose my love for you; you have not lost your love for me. I felt closer to you in our last few hours together

---

*Tuomy, *Is Love Enough?*, 190.

than I have ever felt before. If some of the confidences originally caused me pain, they now are the source of a deep satisfaction.... I know it was difficult for you to share some of these confidences especially after I didn't write you, Richard, etc. I wonder if it's possible to appreciate you enough. You are far better to me than I am to you.

You are probably still worried about having hurt me. If I didn't tell you before, let me tell you now, I respect your decision and I respect you for making it. I'm willing to wait until hell freezes over—as long as you love me. You were right about my still being a child.

I don't really know if I am happy or not. My sublime memories are offset by a great longing to hold you once more. Each moment's memory causes both joy and pain—and the result is not a cancelling out of each other.*

---

*Tuomy, *Is Love Enough?*, 192.

Ten

Battle Damage

In a mission on January 20, I finally took battle damage to my airplane. This occurred when I strafed a heavily defended NVA position in the Mekong Delta south of Saigon. It started as a routine bombing mission against suspected NVA supply points. But the FAC took heavy weapons fire from a covered bridge near our primary target. I happened to be in good position to roll in on this new target, and I engaged the bridge with my 20 mm cannons. I destroyed it, but in return, I received battle damage to my airplane.

The ground fire we faced in South Vietnam was mostly small arms and heavy machine guns. Most were of Soviet bloc origin. The largest and most dangerous was a 14.75mm heavy machine gun, called a ZPU.

The millimeter designation refers to the diameter of the bullet. Most U.S. weapons at that time were designated in calibers, or fractions of an inch. 14.75 mm is roughly .55 caliber, pretty large for an infantry sized weapon.

Often the ZPU guns were quad mounted, that is, four of the guns were mounted on a single platform that could traverse and elevate rapidly as the gunner tried to lead his target. The ZPU was a crew served weapon [*gunner and loader*], with a high rate of fire. It was quite lethal. The other most encountered heavy machine gun in South Vietnam was slightly smaller with a single barrel. It fired a 12.7mm (.51 caliber) round. Both these weapons were optically aimed. In the engagement described in the following letter, I was diving directly at these weapons so there was little need for the gunner to lead me. It was a Wild West shootout a la the streets of Laredo. We both hit each other.

We didn't normally get into gun duels with known anti-aircraft gun positions for obvious reasons. The ZPU was a deadly weapon, particularly in the hands of an experienced gunner; but in this case, we needed to defend our FAC. I did have the advantage of the heavier weapon, my four M39 20mm cannons with a combined rate of fire of 6,000 rounds

Ten—Battle Damage

per minute. We usually just used one pair for typical strafe passes. However, for this attack I flipped the gun switch to ALL as I rolled in. I opened fire at about 3,000 feet (slant range) and fired a three second burst. That was a long burst and it was enough.

Not all aircraft losses in South Vietnam were caused by ground fire. The potential lethality of weather and terrain has been described in earlier chapters. Our own bombs could also be a danger when delivering bombs under a low ceiling. In those cases there was not enough altitude separation to ensure clearance from the fragments of our own bombs. High drag configuration on the bombs (e.g., Snake Eyes) helped with clearance, but we weren't always loaded with the right ordnance for what turned out to be the actual mission (such as a divert for troops in contact). You just took your chances in those situations.

A final threat was failure of a critical system in the airplane, particularly the engine. As described earlier, a heavily loaded F-100 in full afterburner was marginal for takeoff even on Tuy Hoa's 9500-foot runway. Engine failure on takeoff, or even an afterburner blowout at a critical point, could make it impossible to either take off or stop on the available runway. The barrier system was your only hope in those cases. Although the ejection system was supposed to be capable of ejecting you at ground level, the chances of a successful ejection on the runway were poor at best. I lost a friend, an F-4 pilot, to a crash on takeoff.

Note: 243 F-100s were lost in SEA, 198 in combat. First loss 1964, final loss 1971.*

※ ※ ※

January 20, 1969

My Darling Jeannie,

It's been nearly a week now since we said goodbye. I want to tell you that I enjoyed seeing you very much and to thank you for caring enough to go to the trouble and expense to get to Hawaii to see me. If that sounds coldly polite, it is only because I don't possess the ability to tell you what it meant to me to see you again.

My return trip was rather uneventful. Would you believe that I slept most of the way back to Vietnam? We got into Cam Ranh Bay about 9:30 Thursday morning after a 14½-hour flight. It then took me till 4:30 to travel the next 50 miles back to Tuy Hoa. After being stuck at Cam Ranh for six hours it was good to be home. I hope that you had

---

*Dr. Richard Hallion, former Air Force historian in a note from Mike Dunn, Air Force Association, 2010.

a pleasant trip home. I rather imagine you nearly slept through your classes on Wednesday.

I began flying again on Saturday. They gave me a day to recuperate, which wasn't nearly enough. Today I had a bit of excitement on my mission. It was an aerial refueling mission to the far southern tip of South Vietnam. After we had dropped our bombs, the FAC had a couple of sampans he wanted us to sink with strafe. We shot up a couple of them and he went in to mark a third one. As he pulled off from his marking pass, he said, "Well, we must have really pissed them off because they were really shooting at me that time."

He had spotted the area they were shooting from, and he flew over and dropped a smoke can near the position. He said there were about four automatic weapon sites in that large structure over a canal. I saw the house he was talking about and put a good strafe burst into it, but in doing so I picked up a couple of .50 cal hits in the nose gear well (which is directly below the cockpit in the F-100—uncomfortably close). Those are the first ever hits for me. Neither one did any real damage although one narrowly missed an important hydraulic line. The other shot away some wiring and damaged a nose gear tire so that when I lowered my landing gear back here at Tuy Hoa, the nose gear indicated unsafe. I had to make an emergency landing complete with fire trucks chasing me down the runway. Actually, the nose gear assembly itself was not damaged, so it didn't collapse, and the landing was largely uneventful. I think now I'll have to raise my minimums and stop pressing the target. I've been pretty lucky so far.

Other than that, things have been pretty uneventful. One slips easily into the tedium of the war zone and the outside world quickly

Image of the Distinguished Flying Cross awarded to the author for the mission on 20 January 1969 (author's collection).

recedes into a slightly unreal picture. One lives from day-to-day here. Perhaps that is part of my problem when I relate to the future. It is so difficult to consider the future as being more than an abstract and ethereal quantity.

I did get back just in time for the grand opening of our new Officers' Club. It is quite a nice club, situated right on the beach. It was built through the efforts of the officers stationed here and has been many months in construction. Now we are enjoying it.

Be good now and thank you for being patient with me.

Love, Stu

Note: I was awarded the Distinguished Flying Cross for the mission described above.

❋ ❋ ❋

January 27, 1969

My Darling Jean,

You must forgive me (for not writing more often), and you must remember you are ever on my mind.

Your last letter of the 17th was very meaningful to me. I'm glad that you were pleased with our brief interlude in the magic isles. It was a very happy time for me also—and the knowledge that it pleased you makes the memory somehow richer and fonder.... I'm sorry that my pictures caused you such pain. I had no idea that they would be such a trauma to you. Rest assured that those lovely creatures are nothing to me—particularly when compared to you. Are you so uncertain of me and of your own enchanting beauty that poor mortals such as those could cause you pain?

Don't be.

One final point. If indeed you are terribly expensive—I had no idea what I had spent until I got back here—it is only because rare quality such as yours has always been très chère. If it made you happy then every penny was well invested. Perhaps you are a necessity to me.

Note: Credit cards were not typically available to young people in those days, certainly not to a young officer like me. I lived in a cash economy. I took over $1,000 to Hawaii to pay for the week. The hotel held it for me in a safe deposit box which I drew on as required.

I have been dreadfully busy this past week. The worst part about it is that most of the work has not been flying type. You can imagine how happy that has made me. I have been on night alert most of the week. And the days I've had to devote to getting things in the squadron ready for a security inspection. I have the misfortune of being the squadron security officer, and as such, am responsible for the care and feeding of all the super-secret documents we have in the squadron. As you might imagine, the paperwork associated with this sort of thing far outweighs the value of the secrets themselves. Most of this stuff I had been putting off until after my sojourn with you, so that I would be in a happier mood and could bear to face it. But one can only procrastinate so long, and the papers finally demanded to be shuffled.

Well, today we had our little inspection which went quite well, so I guess I can lay these matters aside and go back to being a carefree, reckless fighter pilot.

And what about you? Have you thrown yourself back into your academic pursuit with great fervor? Are you deeply enmeshed in the thrill of research and accomplishment as you labor over your senior paper? (Have you even started your senior paper?) There are times here when my life seems particularly empty, when my daily regimen of flying and bombing seems especially pointless, that I think that it would be nice to return to school. It is amazing how quickly one's intellect atrophies when removed from the stimulus of an academic or intellectual world. And in those times, I wonder how long I can continue to hide from the responsibilities of life in this strange child's play I'm engaged in now. I think that I shall never fail to be thrilled by the majestic wonder of flying, to be enchanted by the dazzling sense of freedom and sensual stimulation. I hope not anyway. But what purpose does it all serve? Or more pointedly, how long can I continue to deny the possibility of any purpose existing for life? I don't know. I feel restless and the urge to seek life grows within me.

I hope that everything is well with you.

Be good now—

Love, Stu

⚜ ⚜ ⚜

Note: After Hawaii, my attitude brightened considerably as indicated below. Jean and I could even tease once again. In her letter of January 22 Jean wrote:

> *I wanted to point out something you said while we were together. After a walk one evening you pointed out that the couples we passed would have preferred to be paired differently. That's naive and I don't know why I let you say it. They probably thought the same of us. Just because I notice a good-looking young man while I am on your arm, and*

Ten—Battle Damage

just because I may smile at him (when you look away) doesn't mean I would rather be with him. Suppose it occurs to me he might be a fun date, that still doesn't mean I'm about to trade you in. Looking is only an innocent game except when you play it. You can't be sure any of those people we pass traded partners in fantasy (although some of them probably did). And even if they did, what's a fantasy for anyway? It doesn't mean that they really wanted someone other than the person they were with. There's an incongruity involved in wanting a total stranger. So, stop trying to tell me marriage is only a dreary business that involves disillusionment of both parties. I remain firm.*

⁕ ⁕ ⁕

Note: I replied.

January 30, 1969

My Dear, Sweet Jeannie,

    One thing I can't understand is your continued illogical adherence to this double standard regarding girl watching. It's perfectly all right for you to make eyes at attractive gentlemen, but you would deny to me completely the right to survey the passing bits of feminine pulchritude. Ah, what hardship I must endure to maintain your favor. Rest assured it is only with the noblest of scientific purpose and objectivity that I search the local scenery. You see, always I seek to discern how it is that you, amongst all women, should be so particularly lovely. Alas, your beauty has remained an enigma and my eyes must search on. (By the way what are you proposing to do with my pictures—stick pins in them?)

    I hope that your job interviews are going well. I suppose you will shortly be moving into the Casa [*an apartment at Mount St. Mary's that home economics majors lived in for six weeks as part of their curriculum*] for your lessons in the domestic life, and the wonders of maintaining an apartment. It seems to me it could be even more instructive if you had to go through the pleasures of apartment hunting, dealing with unscrupulous managers, as well as the gas and electric company, paying bills with insufficient funds, etc. But I guess that that will all come soon enough.

    I have received no word on my next assignment yet, and I am growing increasingly impatient to know what will become of me. I certainly should know within the next couple of weeks. As for the war itself, it stumbles on in its blind, incomprehensible way. Another friend of mine was killed two days ago, an F-4 driver, crashed on takeoff during an alert

---

*Tuomy, *Is Love Enough?*, 196.

scramble. Fate is indeed capricious. I'm sorry. I guess I shouldn't have told you that.

Be good now,

Love, Stu

✤ ✤ ✤

Note: Excerpt from letter, Jean, January 24, 1969. I had mentioned minimums and pressing the target in my January 20 letter.

What did I tell you about pressing the target? You never listen to me. And how many times have I told you to raise your minimums? If I've told you once, I've told you 1,000 times, Stewart, raise your minimums! Now will you please explain that to me?

It seems to me you only have three problems in life. Raising your minimums, lowering your ego, and listening to me. If you had done all those things, I'm sure your nose gear well (what a stupid name) would still be all right.*

✤ ✤ ✤

February 4, 1969

Dearest Jean,

For your edification on matters pertaining to aviation, let me explain what minimums are. Technically, it refers to the minimum altitude that one may descend to when making an instrument approach to an airfield. If you aren't able to see the runway at the minimum altitude, you are required to break off the approach and go somewhere else. Generally speaking, the lower the minimum altitude, the more dangerous the approach. This is because the close proximity of the ground leaves little room for error. A pilot's own minimums refer to his own personal faith and confidence in his ability to safely go that low. It may be higher or lower than the published minimums, and while it is strictly unofficial, it is practically the point at which the pilot will discontinue an approach. At any rate, we apply the same terminology to a combat strike because the danger rises astronomically the closer one gets to the ground. It is used in a jesting sense, but actually everyone has their own minimums, their own thoughts on how far to press.

Well, I wonder what you are up to these days. Have you begun your tenure in the Casa yet? I can just visualize you as a happy homemaker.

Guess what I'm reading now. *Atlas Shrugged* by your favorite author,

---

*Tuomy, *Is Love Enough?*, 198.

Ten—Battle Damage

Ayn Rand. It has been a long while since I've read any of her works. You will of course be pleased to learn that I still find her ideas interesting and perhaps even valid. Her literary talents leave a little to be desired, but that is really a minor inconvenience. I still think that her ideas offer a refreshing counterpoint to the whining self-pity that has become America's favorite pastime.

The war is quiet for the moment. Everyone is speculating on the outcome of this year's Tet (15 to 19 February). It seems that no one is quite sure if the VC will try an encore of last year or not. The general feeling is that they will. The hope is that we will be better prepared this time. I guess that we can only wait and see.

I guess that I will close for now.

Be good now—

Love, Stu

* * *

February 10, 1969

Dearest Jean,

Happy Valentine's to you, sweetheart! I know that this is a feeble substitute for a dozen long stem roses. I couldn't even obtain a Valentine card to send you.

I am presently idling away a few hours lying in the sun. Yesterday I only put in an 18-hour day, so I figured they owe me a little time to lie in the sun. In fact, yesterday was one of those days that shouldn't be. I started off the day at six o'clock with a three hour turn at mobile. Then I had to take care of some paperwork around the squadron and brief some new guys that just came into the squadron. Finally, at 12:30 I started to brief for my flight. An hour or so later, just as I was finishing the preflight of my airplane, the Command Post cancelled my flight. Seems that one of the other squadrons couldn't get any airplanes of theirs ready for alert, so the alert crew took our airplanes for a scramble. That really pissed me off to lose a flight to another squadron after we had briefed and pre-flighted and all. We did all the work and got none of the fun. So about 2:30 I said to hell with it and went home.

Then after 4:00, the squadron called and said I had to go on alert immediately. So back down to the squadron to pick up my gear, back out to the flight line to preflight and finally back to the alert shack to wait. About eight o'clock last night the Command Post called to tell us that our airplanes had been changed so we went through another baggage drill of pre-flighting and cocking the alert birds. Finally, at 9 o'clock we got launched for a target up by Pleiku. That's a hard way to get a mission, however.

It was a nice night to fly anyway. It was pitch black—but clear—and the stars were so richly profuse and brilliant that they fascinated me. They seem much more brilliant from 20,000 feet, away from the artificial glow of the lights on the ground. By the time we landed, however, I was so tired that my aesthetic appreciation was virtually nil.

Well, what is it that you have been up to these days? It must be keeping you terribly busy whatever it is. How about giving me a break and writing me a short note once in a while?

Be good now—

Love, Stu

Eleven

Ho Chi Minh Trail

The infamous Ho Chi Minh Trail was a 1,000-mile spiderweb of roads, trails, and paths stretching from northern Laos to Cambodia and on into lower South Vietnam. It basically followed the Mekong River valley which originates in northern Laos.

Western Vietnam is separated from Laos by a low mountain range. There are three passes that provide access through the mountains from Vietnam to Laos: Nape Pass in the north, Mu Gia in the middle, and Ban Karai in the south. Supplies headed for the Ho Chi Minh Trail mostly flowed through the two southern most passes. Ban Karai Pass was just above the border from what was South Vietnam in 1969.

With the bombing halt of the North imposed by President Johnson on November 1, 1968, much of the air war shifted to interdicting the Ho Chi Minh Trail supply lines in Laos. Later under President Nixon, the air war would extend into Cambodia. We were not permitted to strike NVA supplies on the North Vietnam side of the passes. Ban Karai was increasingly used by the NVA to amass supplies headed for the Trail. And it was the one of most focus to us at Tuy Hoa.

The air war against the Ho Chi Minh Trail was basically centered on the valley of the Mekong River. In the northern part of Laos, above Tchepone and west of the river valley, the terrain was dominated by karst formations. Tchepone was a relatively small town in southern Laos, but it was often used as a reference point for missions into lower Laos. Karst are created when limestone and other soluble rocks dissolve over time, millions of years, leaving in place impervious rock formations that soar above the river valley floor. In Laos, this resulted in massive pillars rising vertically 1,000 feet above the base terrain. The karst posed a threat to pilots attacking targets along the valley floor. On pulling out from a normal dive bomb pass we often just skimmed across the top of a karst.

South of Tchepone, the terrain was more open with rolling hills covered with dense jungle in most cases. The NVA, of course, made use of the jungle cover to hide their movements.

An added danger of the Ho Chi Minh Trail was the increasingly large and profuse anti-aircraft batteries. I never encountered Surface to Air Missiles or SAMs, but there was plenty of anti-aircraft artillery (AAA) up to 37 mm in size. These could reach up to nearly 20,000 feet. There was also plenty of smaller, rapid-fire AAA, 14 and 23 mm, good to above 10,000 feet.

To reach targets in southern Laos, our aircraft from Tuy Hoa often needed to air refuel in order to have sufficient loiter time in the target area. This added a complexity to mission operations typically not seen in South Vietnam.

Today's mission was a four ship into the southern part of Laos. It was early March and the weather had transitioned into the dry season. That meant mid-level scattered to broken clouds, but not yet the violent thunderstorms of the summer season.

The briefing had been routine. All the members of the flight had been in-country at least four months. Although I was still only a lieutenant, I was flight lead. Experience counted more than rank on combat missions.

The intel officer was also experienced and his briefing was straightforward. "Your FAC will be Nail, on 243.8. Target area is the Ho Chi Minh Trail south of Tchepone about 40 miles. There is increasing triple A including 23 mm in the target area. Your tanker today is Hotel 55, on track Bravo, Frequency 279.3. Are there any questions?"

There were none.

"Looks like this will be a routine mission," I said. "Briefing items are squadron standard. Questions?" I looked around the table. Again there were none and we headed to Personal Equipment to put on our flight gear.

Taxi, takeoff and rejoin were normal, normal. When everyone was joined up and clean and dry checks completed, I kicked the flight out to route, a loose flight formation with increased distance between aircraft that allowed all flight members to look around for traffic. We continued our climb to 20,000 feet.

Peacock, the flight following radar agency for the northern half of South Vietnam, gave us a point out to our tanker. It was a pleasant flight as we proceeded north towards our rendezvous with the tanker. There was a scattered cloud deck at 10 to 12,000 feet that we had climbed through, but it was clear, visibility unlimited, at 20,000. Vietnam below us was lush, green and tranquil, at least to us far above its reality.

After about 30 minutes, Peacock said, "Saber 41, your tanker is bearing 020 degrees at 30 miles, southbound. Contact Hotel 55 on frequency 279.3."

At our closure rate of over 10 miles per minute, we were less than three minutes away from the tanker. I called the flight over to the tanker frequency and checked in with the tanker.

"Hotel 55, Saber 42."

"Roger Saber, Hotel 55, standing by turn."

We were now less than 20 miles from the tanker. He was poised to make a 180 degree left turn away from us. This was standard procedure for a join up with a tanker. If done right, that would put us slightly in trail of the tanker with limited need for maneuvering by my four ship.

"Roger 55," I said. I paused, waiting for the right moment, then, "Tally, 55. You can start your turn."

Now I just watched the evolving picture with the tanker, judging our closure on him and adjusting our closure rate with the continuation of his 180-degree turn. It was like a choreographed dance.

As the tanker began to roll out of his 30-degree bank, he called, "Saber, join right. The previous flight is still on the boom." This meant the previous flight of receivers had not finished refueling yet, and we were to join on the tanker's right wing.

I called, "Roger, Sabers, echelon right and close it up." This instructed the three wingmen to position themselves on my right wing and move to a loose, but close formation. I watched as number two moved from my left wing to my right wing. Aircraft three and four made room for him.

I adjusted power to match the tanker's airspeed and we slid into position on his right wing. I smiled to myself. It was beautiful.

We watched number four of the previous flight plug the refueling basket and start to take on fuel. A tanker period was normally scheduled for 30 minutes for a four ship. We joined a few minutes late and with the previous flight just finishing up, that meant we would be about 10 minutes behind.

As the previous flight finished refueling and turned smoothly away, Hotel 55 called, "Saber you're cleared to pre contact position." This meant each one of us would move sequentially into refueling position, hookup, take-on our scheduled off load, then move to the opposite wing. Normal off load was 1,500 lbs. While the tanker could pump at over 6,000 lbs. per minute, a combat loaded F-100 could take fuel at no more than about 1,500 lbs. a minute. More than that and the fuel pressure would cause a disconnect. With maneuvering and hook up time, the minimum time a four ship F-100 flight could refuel was about 15 minutes.

As I started to move into position, I called, "OK Sabers, let's get Hotel 55 back on schedule."

In a moment I was in position about 15 feet behind the basket with it off set slightly to my right. My refueling probe lined up with it as trailed from the end of the boom. I called, "Leads ready."

"Cleared to contact," the boom operator said.

I advanced the power and slowly closed on the basket. As I pushed the throttle forward, I noted that it was almost against the stop, almost full military power. Not much to play with there, I said to myself. This will be interesting.

A little overtake on the basket developed and I began to slide forward. As the basket neared the engine inlet at the F-100's nose, the basket veered towards the inlet, pulled by the suction of the engine, then slid back in line with the refueling probe as it passed the nose. That was normal. You learned to ignore the veer caused by the inlet. Shortly, the probe entered the rim of the basket, then the basket settled on the nozzle of the probe.

I felt a slight bump and the boomer said, "Contact" as the jaws of the basket closed on the probe. A slight bend appeared in the basket's hose.

"Roger, contact," I replied and pushed the throttle against the stop. Now a delicate dance began. The momentum of my aircraft had allowed the probe to pick up the drag of the basket and put the slight bend in the hose. Standard procedure was to pick up the basket and move it up and left about three feet. That was "the book" fuel transfer position. But with my marginal excess power, I'd be lucky to even stay on the basket. I had to stay ahead of it, let it settle so that the hose was straight, letting the tanker carry the drag of the basket. I eased the throttle back a touch.

"Transferring," the boomer said. I only nodded; I couldn't afford even the slight distraction of keying the mike. I tried to be as gentle with the airplane as I could. Fingertips only on stick and throttle. Fortunately, the air was smooth.

I could feel the weight of the transferring fuel as it refilled tanks and the drag of my aircraft increased to carry the new load. The throttle was now full against the forward stop. The tanker was now towing me a bit—but just by the strength of the locking jaws in the basket. I held on. It seemed like an eternity.

After a minute or so, the boomer said, "Transfer complete. Off load, one thousand five hundred."

I breathed, eased the throttle back, and disconnected from the basket. As I moved up to the left wing of the tanker, I heard the boomer say, "Two, cleared to pre-contact."

Two connected. I noted he had a little more power margin than I had; he could maintain the bend in the refueling hose. The same proved true for Three and Four.

When Four completed his refueling and joined our formation on the left wing of the tanker, I looked at my clock. There were two minutes left in our refueling period. The tanker pilot called, "Nice work, Saber. Total off load today was six thousand pounds."

"Roger, six thousand. Thanks," I said. We turned away, towards our rendezvous with the Nail FAC.

I checked in with Peacock and got vectors to Nail's working area. As we flew west into Laos, I couldn't help thinking it was good work on the tanker. I was pleased. Now we just needed to do good work on our target, stay focused, and not take any foolish chances.

Not like I did two weeks ago, I mused. I had gotten complacent, too confident, too lazy. Maybe I've been here too long. That time, the target was just north of Tchepone, an area of sharp karst formations. The target was a storage area up against the base of a 1,000-foot karst. Everything was normal, routine, as we set up to bomb the target, except that somehow my G suit had become disconnected—or maybe in my complacency I had simply neglected to connect it. The bomb run was a textbook, 30-degree dive, release at 3,000 feet above ground level, 4G pull, bottom out at 1,500 feet. Textbook except the karst rose vertically 1,000 feet immediately in front of us leaving only 500 feet of ground clearance at the bottom of the pullout. A little close but no sweat. On my first pullout, I did not stay ahead of the G forces, lazily depending on my G suit which was not connected. I began to black out. Blackout is a condition where G forces pull blood from the eyes, resulting in temporary loss of vision. It does not imply loss of consciousness. This condition is normally resisted by tightening abdominal and thigh muscles against the pressure from the G suit. Now what? I thought. That no sweat clearance was now a grave concern. I wouldn't be able to see until I relaxed the G's. But if I let off on the G's while still in my dive, I wouldn't clear the karst. With no other choice, I held the G forces until I estimated I was at least in level flight. I eased off the G's. As my vision returned I found myself skimming across the top of the karst. That was too close for sure.

I came back to the present as we entered Laos. I noted the lower cloud deck was beginning to fill in. It looked to be about 10 to 12,000 feet, scattered to broken, just at our normal orbit altitude. The terrain below appeared to be rolling hills covered with thick foliage. A small river ran southeast to northwest toward the Mekong.

We descended to 15,000 feet. Peacock cleared us to the mission frequency. "Nail, Saber 41, at 15 thousand over a small river."

"Roger, Saber, descend below the clouds so I can get a tally," he replied. "I'll be orbiting just west of the river at 3,000 (feet)."

We descended to just below the clouds and entered a left turn west of the river. "Go trail and take spacing," I called to the flight. The three wing men fell into a loose trail as we circled.

"Tally," called Nail, "I'm at your 10 o'clock, low just west of the river."

I saw him about then, an O-2 at what I thought was an unusually low altitude. He was in a tight left-hand orbit just south of a low hill line. The O-2 was a modified Cessna Sky Master. It had twin engines in a pusher-puller configuration. Twin tail booms were a distinctive feature. O-2s were a preferred FAC aircraft in the high threat area that was Laos because their twin engines gave much better performance than the single engine O-1s common in South Vietnam.

I called Tally and passed our line-up to Nail.

"Roger, Copy," he called. "Your target is a triple A battery about three klicks (kilometers) north of that ridgeline to my 10 o'clock. There are four separate gun emplacements, ZSU-4s. Suggest you stay south of the ridgeline until I put in a mark."

Now I understood why Nail was staying well south of the ridgeline.

I tightened our circle to stay south of the ridge and looked intently towards the target area. Nail continued to describe the terrain, and I could see a few distinguishing features.

"I have the area," I called. "Standing by for your mark."

As we talked, I watched Nail climb to about 4500 feet. "Roger," he replied. He rolled out heading towards the area of the target and entered a dive to gain airspeed. As he approached the hills, he pulled the O-2's nose up into a climb and launched a smoke rocket. It arched over the hill and landed with a white puff short and east of the target.

Oh great! I thought, now he's woken them up. Sort of like kicking a hornets' nest. But I now had a pretty clear idea of the target's location.

"Tally, the target," I called and started a climb through the clouds to 12,000 feet. Our Intelligence at Tuy Hoa had never mentioned radar controlled triple A this far south in Laos, and my RHAW gear—Radar Homing and Warning system that detected radar signals in the bands associated with enemy anti-aircraft guns—was not reacting, so I planned to use the cloud deck as cover while we set up our attack orbit.

We circled the target catching glimpses of the gun emplacements through breaks in the clouds. There were four of them, spaced about 100 meters apart in a box configuration. Vegetation had been cleared around the guns to provide an unobstructed view of airspace around the emplacement.

As we circled, I noted a hole through the clouds on the east side towards the river. That would be our attack run-in line, east to west. I briefed the flight on the attack plan. "Use the cloud cover to mask your position as much as possible. Set your pipper depression for a 5,000-foot release and your weapons panel for 'release all.'" This meant all four bombs on each airplane would be released on a single pass. We sure as hell don't need to be making multiple passes on these guys, I thought.

I felt the familiar tightening in my stomach. It will be a miracle if we don't lose somebody today.

As we circled I saw that the flight was equally spaced around the orbit as usual. "Vary your spacing and move it around going in. And jink coming off," I called. And good luck, I thought.

I arrived at the roll in point, and called, "Leads in." I broke out of the base of the clouds at 8,000 feet already in my 30-degree dive. The four separate gun sites were clearly visible, and it was easy to adjust on a particular one. I picked the one on the near right. As I dove towards my target, yellow bits of light, tracer rounds, began to float up towards me. Clearly the gunners had also anticipated our run-in direction. I jinked mildly, coming back to the aiming picture as I neared 5,000 feet, then it was pickle and pull. The airplane lurched as 3,000 lbs. of ordnance was thrust away. I jinked aggressively as I sought the relative safety of the clouds.

After entering the clouds, I started a gentle climbing turn to the right, opposite the orbit direction. I heard two call in. As I exited the clouds at 12,000 feet something caught my eye to my left, where I would have been if I had pulled off straight. It was a flak burst of about a dozen rounds. Too close, I said to myself. I reversed course to the orbit direction and waited for three and four to complete their run.

"Head south for rejoin," I called and rolled out heading back towards Nail's location. In a few minutes, the flight was rejoined and "clean and dry" checks completed. Miraculously, no one had been hit!

I caught sight of the FAC and called, "Nail, Saber 42 Winchester" (meaning we were out of bombs), "ready to copy BDA." I sincerely hope he doesn't want us to strafe that target, I thought.

There was a long pause. Finally Nail said, "I'm not about to putter over there in my little, slow airplane to see what's left. I'll give you two gun emplacements destroyed."

Four then interjected, "Well, there was a lot of smoke around the sites when I went in. I thought my bombs were good."

"OK," Nail said, "three then. Thanks for the work, Saber."

I acknowledged, and we started our climb for home. It had already been a long day and we had 250 miles to go.

※ ※ ※

In early spring, the 308th picked up two missions that were out of the ordinary. One was escorting AC-119 gunships over Laos at night. The other was an operational evaluation of a new weapon, the Wide Area Anti-Personnel Mine (or WAAPoM). It had been developed at the Armament Center at Eglin Air Force Base, Florida, to help suppress foot and light vehicle traffic on the Ho Chi Minh Trail.

Escort of the slow-moving AC-119 at night was demanding because of the speed differential between the two aircraft. The AC-119 flew at about 120 knots, while the F-100 liked to be at 300 knots or more. In addition, the F-100 was not equipped with systems to aid with low altitude navigation at night. The challenge was to keep the AC-119 in sight while avoiding hitting the ground. The WAAPoM tests on the other hand involved evaluating the specialized and rigid weapon delivery protocols required, as well as determining the effectiveness of the weapon. Wisely, our squadron commander decided to dedicate crews to each of these unconventional and demanding missions. I drew the WAAPoM testing.

The WAAPoM consisted of a small grapefruit-sized mine. When it was deployed, several spring-loaded trip wires, about six feet long, were released. These trip wires extended the activation area of the mine and significantly improved its effectiveness in area denial. The mines were packaged in a dispenser, a long aerodynamically-shaped container with an open bottom. Twenty mines were contained in a dispenser. The mines were deployed individually at short intervals when the pickle button was depressed and held. Development testing at Eglin had determined that the optimum dispensing tactic was to deliver them in straight and level flight at 400 knots, 500 feet above the ground. It took about 20 seconds to empty the dispenser. I guess there were no anti-aircraft guns on the Eglin ranges.

For optimum effectiveness, the mines needed to be deployed over relatively open terrain. Our job was to find such terrain along the Ho Chi Minh Trail and then to determine the feasibility of the recommended delivery tactics. The development team at Eglin had also determined that the recommended loadout configuration on our F-100s should be a dispenser on each of the inboard weapons stations with Mk-82 (500 lb.) bombs on the two out-board stations. This would allow a four-ship flight, each loaded as recommended, to mine the largest area while still retaining a flak suppression capability.

So configured, off we went. A FAC had found a likely part of the Trail in the southern part of Laos. We set up to deploy the mines, and then realized we couldn't dispense the mines first because the F-100 weapons control system required the outboard stations to be released in pairs first for aircraft stability reasons. This was because releasing the inboard stations first would cause the center of gravity of the aircraft to shift too far aft and the aircraft would become aerodynamically unstable. We should have thought of that. But if we bombed the target first, that was sure to wake up the defenses.

Anyway, the first trial went without incident, although the delivery tactic was certainly stimulating. But acoustical sensors along the Trail indicated that the effectiveness of the system was not as good as expected, probably because the trip wires became entangled in vegetation along the Trail.

Back to the drawing board. We needed to find a part of the Trail with very limited vegetation, and we needed to reconsider the loadout configuration.

Our intelligence officer pointed out that the exit from Ban Karai Pass had been heavily bombed particularly on the right bank of the small river that ran from the mouth of the pass and turned northwest to connect to the Mekong River. The bombed-out area ran for a number of miles. That area on the right bank was also where the roads and trails were; the left bank still had fairly heavy vegetation. That looked promising.

As for the loadout configuration, we decided to load all the dispensers on two aircraft, Lead and number two in the flight while three and four carried the flak suppression bombs. We also decided that the dispensers should be emptied in a staggered sequence: first the outboard stations would start dispensing, then 10 seconds later the inboard stations would start. With this approach, all four dispensers would empty in about 30 seconds. That configuration was not optimum for area coverage of the mines, but it reduced the exposure of the dispensing aircraft if all four dispensers were emptied on one run rather than in two separate runs. That was the plan for Ban Karai. Lead and two would each make one pass, emptying all four dispensers on their one run. The project officer from Eglin agreed this was OK. The aircraft weapons controllers were modified to initiate this sequence with one push of the pickle button.

Ban Karai Pass was just north of the DMZ. The NVA took advantage of the bombing halt knowing we were no longer allowed to bomb in North Vietnam. They freely amassed supplies in the pass, shortening the distance to South Vietnam and Cambodia in the contested part of the Ho Chi Minh Trail.

With our changes in loadout and tactics, we took off for our rendezvous with the Ban Karai Pass. I was number two; the Lead and I had the dispensers. As we circled to the west of the pass, we could see the target area through the sparse mid-level clouds; it had truly been bombed into oblivion, it looked like a freshly plowed field. It seemed to be a quiet morning there on the ground.

We had agreed to keep radio communications to a minimum to maximize the element of surprise. As we circled, Lead waggled his wings and started his descent to low level, well west of the target area. Presently, he emerged from the background foliage, established himself at the prescribed parameters over the bombed-out area and began his weapons run. It took about four miles to empty all four dispensers with the sequential tactic. He pulled up sharply as he approached the bend in the river and jinked aggressively as he climbed to a safe altitude. There was only erratic triple A fire following him. We had essentially caught them by surprise.

Now it was my turn. As I had watched Lead, I had noted an anti-aircraft site east of a creek that joined the river from the south a mile or so beyond of where Lead had started his pull up. It was probably a ZPU-4 gun position, I thought, semi-concealed in the foliage on a rise above the river. On my setup for my run, I basically followed Lead's path, but I moved my dispensing run more to the north, essentially right at the ZPU site and left of the creek's mouth. I hoped they couldn't depress their guns enough to track me, but I was sure they were eagerly awaiting my pull-up. Established at 400 knots and 500 feet, I pushed the pickle button. I could feel the slight jolts as the outboard dispensers began to step through their intervalometers (a sequential timing device). A few moments later, the inboard dispensers began to empty.

Thirty seconds is more than a lifetime in those conditions, I waited, beyond fear or feeling. I felt the slight jolting stop as the dispensers emptied; knew the

Image of WAAPoM Patch developed by air crews involved in the operational evaluation of the Wide Area Anti-Personnel Mine (author's collection).

ZPU crew was ready for my pull-up. But instead of pulling up, I rolled right and dove for the mouth of the creek. I hoped the gunners could not keep up with the unexpected rapid traverse required; I hoped the intervening foliage would protect me in the creek bed. It did. I stayed in the creek bed for over a mile then pulled up sharply, jinking hard. Soon I was above 10,000 feet, safe from the ZPU.

Three and Four expended their bombs on the gun sites, and we headed for home, feeling lucky to be alive.

This mission was the end of the evaluation. The project officer from Eglin agreed we had done enough. He thanked us for our efforts and headed for Tan Son Nhut and home.

The WAAPoM concept was ultimately adopted into the U.S. Air Force weapons arsenal in the 1980s as part of the Gator air delivered mines program.

To memorialize our very memorial experience with WAAPoM, the test crew adopted a new patch.

Twelve

Times Are Changing

Mid–February, the eve of Tet 1969. We were prepared for a repeat of last year, but things remained relatively quiet. The U.S. imposed a brief 4-hour pause in its operations; the VC/NVA continued business as usual.

The tempo of the war remained as before, but our missions were increasingly directed towards the Ho Chi Minh Trail in Laos, with its increasing anti-aircraft threat. We "young sports" had now been here over nine months. We were the "old heads" now. We had become complacent, bored even, with the dangers of the war. We were also frustrated and cynical as the tenor of the war effort changed, and the Wing moved towards a more routine, stateside feel. Pilot manning had increased so that missions were less frequent; additional duties seemed to be more important.

About this time I received my much-anticipated follow-on assignment: F-106's at Minot Air Force Base, Minot, North Dakota. I had to consult a map to find out exactly where that was. I was not happy with the prospect of spending another year or more in what I imagined was an isolated and desolate part of the world. (Ironically, I was born in South Dakota, not too far from Minot.)

I vented my frustrations unfairly on Jean. She was entering a particularly busy part of her senior year. Not only were her classes demanding, but she also had been put in charge of the school's booth for an upcoming Home Economics Convention involving all of the colleges and universities in Southern California. Her booth would place second in the conference's competition, earning small Mount Saint Mary's College a $300 prize—over $3,000 in today's money. She also began planning for life after school, including job interviews.

The euphoria of Hawaii had worn off and my pessimism about the future had grown thin with her. The time between her letters began to grow. My obtuseness to her situation and feelings was endangering my hold on the Jeannie that mattered most.

Twelve—Times Are Changing

❈ ❈ ❈

February 18, 1969

Dearest Jeannie,

And a happy Tet to you. I hope that you are ringing in the Lunar New Year in glorious fashion as are our Vietnamese friends. So far, they have restricted their celebrations to noisy revelry and have refrained from the interesting pranks that made the last Tet so notorious. Of course, we still expect that the celebrations will take a more customary vicious turn eventually, and we are grimly prepared for that eventuality. I just hope that no mortar rounds land near my hooch and wipe out my stereo equipment. That would really anger me. Actually, everything has been very quiet since the holidays started on Sunday. There was a brief 24-hour truce Sunday night and Monday, and the violations are not too numerous or too noteworthy. It kind of makes you think the bad guys are up to something. Of course, we are on a heightened alert status throughout this period so perhaps Charlie feels it wouldn't be wise to start anything at present. And so, the war goes on, and on, and on, ad infinitum.

Some news of personal importance. I got my assignment this morning: an F-106 at Minot Air Force Base, North Dakota. (I don't really know where that is either.) I am delighted with the airplane, but I am heartsick at the prospect of spending even a brief portion of my life in Minot, ND. You, of course, are free to withdraw your offer to go any place to be with me. (If you don't withdraw it, I may hold you to it.) Whether it is bearable or not will depend upon how the flying is. It has a prospect of being a good squadron with some great flying.

I am going to try to get the assignment changed but the prospect isn't good. You will be happy to learn that they probably won't let me extend my tour over here. It seems there are already too many pilots in Vietnam. I've already lost much of my ardor for staying here anyway and since I couldn't hope to get a better airplane, there seems to be little point in extending.

After I leave here, I will have leave until the 6th of June when I have to go to Perrin Air Force Base, Texas, to check out in the F-102 and attend radar school. I will leave there about the 27th of August and go to F-106 school at Tyndall Air Force Base, Panama City, FL. I should graduate from there about the end of October and then I will finally be forced to go to Minot. My chief hope now is that I can get my assignment changed while I am at Perrin or Tyndall. There is little that can be done while I'm here. At best, however, I can expect to end up somewhere in the cold north.

Other than the really grim location, the assignment should be pretty good. At least I am staying in fighters and that leaves the possibility of getting into test pilot school wide open. I will apply for that as soon as I get to Minot and with a little luck, I might get accepted the following summer. At worst I will have to stay at Minot for 18 months and will then have a good chance of going to Hamilton Air Force Base in San Francisco or Oxnard or some other spot near civilization. If I can't get what I want by then, I'll probably get out of the Air Force.

This at least gives you a glimpse of some of the cheerful prospects offered by the Air Force. Can you even imagine living in Minot, ND? If you find your determination shaken by the very thought of it, I can't blame you. It's a strange and often demanding life whose rewards are often nebulous.

And how are things with you? Do you have any hint of what the future holds for you following graduation? If the squadron at Minot is any good at all, I should be able to take cross country flights almost at will on the weekends.

There was a portion of your last letter that disturbed me. You said it would be better for me to lose you than to lose flying, as if the two were rivals, as if you were competing against my love for flying. Will you never understand this part of me? Flying is a part of me.... Flying is both a thing and a symbol; a thing which is the source of great physical and mental pleasure, and a symbol of all that I hold to be of value in a man's life. To fly is to be free, to be bold, to challenge nature on her own grounds with only the skill and knowledge of your brain for weapons, and only your courage and desire for a mandate. And these are the things that are the essence of a man whatever he does. The soaring freedom of his spirit is what makes a man. His knowledge, skills and courage are the things that give him claim to this freedom. To surrender any of these is to kill that spirit and forfeit his right to any human dignity. If you deny this part of me, then you deny me.

Be good now—

Love, Stu

⁕ ⁕ ⁕

Note: Jean didn't respond to this letter until March 14. Not only was she busy with school and the Convention booth, but in my peevishness, I was asking too much of her. Her frustration was palpable. It's a wonder she didn't tell me to go to hell. In the March 14th letter she wrote:

Twelve—Times Are Changing

Am I supposed to say to you that the best contribution I can make to your life is to get out of it? Your position is set. My position seems to be, "sink or swim." Change my whole value structure, my needs, my love, my desires.... And how long would you love me? As usual, I find myself without the help I need. And if I could change, I would still have to do it on my own.

I can't make that decision. Time must make it for us. I will not put you out of my life. I just wish so badly that we could have a little more time together. We probably won't see each other for two full weeks this year. You won't be here for prom, graduation, Christmas or New Years. If the Air Force wanted you to have a girlfriend, they would have issued you one.*

※ ※ ※

February 20, 1969

Dear Mom & Dad,

How are you all these sparkling winter days? While you are huddled about a fireplace watching the snowfall, I am basking in the sun here in the tropical paradise on the shores of the South China Sea. I can scarcely keep track of the date. That's evident by the fact that I hardly knew it was February and that I completely neglected your birthday, Dad. I hope that it was a pleasant one.

The blind bureaucracy known as the Air Force personnel system has finally succeeded in overmanning Tuy Hoa (with pilots) so that the flying has gone from good to bad to worse in the past few months. We only fly on the average of two out of every three days now. I needn't go into the ramifications of this situation. Combat and flying are rapidly becoming of secondary importance and the additional duties and make-work is leaping to the forefront. And of course as the paper empire becomes pyramided one atop the other, the rules and regulations threatened to completely drown the combat effort. The sad point is that there is a real shooting war going on around here and people are getting killed while our leaders are busy building their petty empires or groping for their stars.

I'm sure you remember Major Cameron from USC's ROTC program. He was flying F-4's out of Cam Ranh Bay. He was killed 3½ weeks ago—crashed on takeoff on an alert scramble. George may have already told you of this.

I suppose the big news for me right now is that of my next

---
*Tuomy, *Is Love Enough?*, 225.

assignment. The Air Force is assigning me to an F-106 in Minot, North Dakota. Actually the airplane is good and ADC [*Air Defense Command*] isn't too bad a command, I understand. But Minot, coming directly upon a year at Tuy Hoa and a year at Laredo, will strain my resiliency to the limit—if not beyond.

Anyway, I will get about four weeks' leave when I return to the States in May. I report for upgrade training at Perrin Air Force Base, Texas, on six June. I'll spend all of the summer and half of the fall in upgrade schools.

I hope that everything is going well for you all. I'm anxious to see the improvements you are making to the house—though I scarcely remember the old house.

Love, Stewart

❖ ❖ ❖

February 28, 1969

Dearest Jean,

Happy birthday. May this day commence the happiest and most fulfilling year of your life.

I'm becoming a bit more reconciled to the prospect of having to spend the winter at Minot. With luck I may be able to get another assignment by the following summer—hopefully to the test pilot school at Edwards [*Air Force Base, CA*]. That is a bit of a dream, of course, but I will have the minimum flying requirements as soon as I leave here, and I will apply at my first opportunity in the States. I won't be eligible to be reassigned from Minot until next May, so at least I shall have to winter over at Minot. What a ghastly thought. Do you have any idea what it is like to be totally snowed in? And not to see the sun for weeks on end? To have blizzards rage so that one risks his very life just by venturing outside? Well, Minot is not quite that bad, but it is pretty grim.

Note: There followed a lengthy discourse on what life in the Service might be like with its frequent moves and isolated places. It was a very pessimistic view reflecting my unhappiness with my assignment to Minot, and my uncertainty about my future in general. In addition, mail service from her had been disrupted for some unknown reason and her letters from early February on were not received until mid-March. This naturally increased my overall anxiety. The following unfairly tries to cast the blame for my ambivalence on her. Was I subconsciously trying to lose the Jeannie back home just as I recklessly pushed the other Jeannie to her limits from time to time?

Twelve—Times Are Changing

What do you think of this immediate future of mine? I notice you were not quick to respond to my cheerless announcement. Perhaps now you will believe me when I tell you that life in the service is often harsh and distasteful. Could you really put up with this sort of thing for the next 20 years or so? ... Could you see your children torn every two or three years from friends and schools to be shunted to some distant and alien part of the globe? Could you bear these things ... with joy and a strength born of determination to live and love life to its fullest, to accept its gifts with gladness and its blows with equanimity? My life is an uncommon one—and I would not have it any other way whether I was in or out of the Service. This is the prospect you would have with me.

This is all very unfair to you. These are questions that swirl through my mind, uncertain and unanswered. Do I have the right to ask such things of you? More important, could I expect—would I deserve—the answer I hope for while my mind shies away from the parallel questions? ... Could I surrender my life as a "nerve ending" for the quiet respectability of a nine to five job and you? And if I did, how long could we last??

How can I expect that you would be able to achieve the opposite of this, to cast off the secure and known, and face with joyful expectation the unknown, the uncertain? ... How can I ask you to do something I am not sure I would be willing to do in return?

This, I think, is the basis of my hesitation. It is what I could not put in words for you in Hawaii. When face to face with the question of marriage, I was speechless because I could not find these words.... What are we to do?

What an unhappy letter this has turned out to be. I probably should not have given voice to these things. I plunged ahead with the hope that understanding might arise between us as a result of my poorly stated questions. Least of all did I intend to question you or to hurt you.

I must close for now. My flying machine beckons to me, and I must go.

Be good now,

Love, Stu

❈ ❈ ❈

Note: Jean wrote on February 17 that she was embittered and depressed. But how could she not be with me being such an ass? She was beginning to have her own doubts. Her next letter would not be written until March 11, received March 19 along with the letter dated March 14.

March 5, 1969

Dear Jeannie,

A quick check of my Playboy calendar has revealed that it is time for me to escape temporarily from this God-forsaken country—lest my sanity leaves me on a permanent basis. So, this morning I'm heading off in the direction of Taiwan to retrieve an airplane from our IRAN facility at Tainan and return it to Tuy Hoa. I hope to be able to spend a few days in Okinawa and Taipei as I endeavor to get to Tainan. Tainan is one of those places you almost can't get to from here. Of course, this trip doesn't carry near the promise that my last one did—nor will it be nearly as much fun.

However, this upcoming adventure will afford me the opportunity to sample a bit of civilization again and probably spend an additional fortune on many good deals. Did I tell you that I have gotten a couple more speakers for my stereo outfit? If nothing else, I will have plenty of good music in Minot.

Everything has been going rather slowly for me these last few weeks. Even though the war has been rather uneventful, I have had a few exciting missions of late. About a week ago I got scrambled off the alert pad to support some friendly troops that had gotten into trouble by Chu Lai. The friendlies had some bad guys trapped in a village with their backs against a river. Some of the friendlies had overextended their position and were pinned down about 500 feet from the village which had turned out to be heavily fortified. We got scrambled right at dusk and it was quite dark by the time we got to the target. Unfortunately, there weren't any flare ships in the area, nor could we afford to wait for one. We went ahead and bombed and strafed the village anyway. The FAC told us that the army was able to pull its pinned-down units back under the cover of our bombs and napalm. It kind of makes you feel good to know that you really helped out some of the guys on the ground. All the time we were attacking the village we were taking intense small arms and automatic weapons fire from some bad guys across the river. Unfortunately, we had been so busy with the situation in the village that we were unable to hit the Charlies that were shooting at us. That kind of pissed me off. I hate to let them get a free shot at me like that.

Fortunately, the long-expected Tet offensive never did amount to much. Tuy Hoa continued to lead its charmed life. We were the only major base in Vietnam that didn't receive any sort of an attack. But that is perfectly all right with me. At the moment, we are all anxious at what the new administration will do with respect to the VC attacks. Nixon has obliquely stated that he will not permit the VC to get away with any offensive without some reaction on our part. That can only mean a renewal of the bombing in the North. Now I wonder if he will stick to that policy. If we start bombing in the North again, this will suddenly get very, very interesting and deadly for the fighter pilots.

I just received my orders to Minot today. That makes it official. My only hope now is that I can get the base changed while I am at Perrin or Tyndall. I'm afraid that there is little hope of that, however. At the moment the only good that I can see in life is the fact that in just two (long) months I shall be back in the States and will be with you again for however briefly.... Now that the end of my tour in Vietnam is in sight, I find that I am anxious to be done with this place. It no longer holds anything for me. Rather it is stale and uncomfortable like an old friendship that has long since grown tedious but cannot be politely terminated.

I must close now and pack for my great adventure.

Be good now—

Love, Stu

⁕ ⁕ ⁕

March 11, 1969

Dearest Jeannie,

Greetings from the magic Isle of Taiwan. My latest China adventure has taken me to the length and breadth of this fabled island. I arrived in Taiwan very early last Thursday morning at Taichung. I have some friends stationed there so I stayed in Taichung for a day and a night. They took me to dinner at the proverbial authentic Chinese restaurant where we dined on boiled sea slugs, eels and other unidentifiable delicacies as well as the more prosaic standbys such as sweet and sour pork, fried shrimp and Peking duck. And, of course, the meal was supplemented by warm rice wine and frequent "Kampia's" (a Japanese toast of sorts).

At noon on Friday, I caught a train north to Taipei and a tour through that world-renowned city. The train ride itself was interesting and afforded me an opportunity to see a portion of the countryside. It is also a real adventure trying to travel in that fashion. You find yourself in the peculiar position of being illiterate since all signs are in Chinese characters, as well as being scarcely able to communicate with the people about you.

I spent three days in Taipei, shopping and sightseeing. Unfortunately, the weather was rather dreary with low-hanging, livid clouds swallowing the surrounding hills and a perpetual mist falling. The city to me seemed very cold. My big purchase in Taipei was a camera. I finally gave up my search for a Minolta SRT and purchased in its stead an Asahi Pentax Spotmatic. It is, as I'm sure you know, a single lens reflex with built-in, through the lens, light meter, interchangeable lenses, etc. Mine has a 50 millimeter, 1.4 lens. It is a fascinating piece of equipment. I haven't the faintest idea of its true capabilities, but it is fun to play with. I guess that I will have to learn something about photography now.

Yesterday I caught the train again to come to Tainan. That was a 5½-hour trip and seriously tried my enthusiasm for the scenic countryside. Again, the weather is miserable, and I am becoming depressed with fabled Formosa. Tainan is a small city without much of cultural interest. It looks like I may be stuck here for several days. We have some rather ridiculous weather minimums here and the grim weather prevented me from taking off for Clark today.

In the meantime, I guess I will just have to relax and enjoy the quiet charm that is the Orient.

Be good now—

Love, Stu

Thirteen

Loss

The weather in Tainan was dreadful. A cold misty rain drifted down from low hung clouds. It had been this way for several days, even before I arrived here. Disgusted with the delay, I went to the bar at the American Club about six, just as the feeble light in the streets turned to gloom.

At the bar there were several guys trapped here as I was by the miserable weather. I joined a group of three that looked congenial—two were an F-4 crew. The other guy was older, didn't look military. CIA I guessed. We had a couple of drinks, told stories—not quite lies, just embellished recollections. All in good humor. After a while, the F-4 crew said it was time for dinner, the weather might lift in the morning and we need to get on with things. We moved to the dining part of the bar, took a table.

After we were settled, the CIA guy suggested we play a dice game for dinner. Whoever lost would buy the dinners for the whole crew. I was apprehensive; I never win in this type of situation. But how could I say No? The dice cup was passed and sure enough, I lost. Everyone else laughed.

Two women at a nearby table had been watching this game play out and they laughed, too. Over dinner a banter developed between the two tables and after dinner the two groups merged. We all were looking for a little merriment to dispel the gloom outside. The two women were American, attractive, trim, smartly dressed in the latest fashions. One had short dark hair and a quick, pretty smile. The other's dusky blond hair fell below her shoulders, framing a delicate face with captivating brown eyes set above high cheek bones. They both were in their late '30s, maybe early '40s, I guessed.

We introduced ourselves. They said they worked for an American company exploring market opportunities and production possibilities in rapidly rising East Asia. That's what had brought them to Tainan for a few days.

We ordered after dinner drinks and fell into easy conversations.

The brown-eyed one, she said her name was Liz, seemed drawn to me. I think she felt bad that I had lost the dice game and wanted to make it up to me somehow. As the evening progressed we talked and teased. We danced a little—she likes to be held, I thought. She doesn't resist when I pull her close. The evening passed in pleasant conversation. Presently it was time to close. Hints were made as expected and were graciously rebuffed. We said good night.

The next morning, she called me at my hotel. She said she was sorry, she didn't know why ... said she could come to my hotel, said we could have breakfast together.

Later at breakfast, we chatted about unimportant things. We talked about the weather. I said I might get a break today, might be able to get on to Clark.

She said she was going on to Manila tomorrow, asked if I could come down to meet her. Or she could come to Clark.

"I don't know," I said. "It depends on Clark, on when the base can put together a formation flight to cross the pond [*the South China Sea*]. I've already been away too long. I need to get back."

She looked at me sharply, "To what?" she asked.

"The War, I guess," I said lamely.

The conversation turned to the war.

"How often do you fly? In combat, I mean," she asked.

"Every day," I replied, "sometimes more."

She asked if I had lost friends in the war.

"Yes," I said. "Seven so far. One I had breakfast with on his last day."

She looked away, "How do you cope with that?" she whispered softly to no one.

I shrugged. "It seems capricious," I said. "You learn to not think about it. You become a fatalist. If you don't have someone somewhere to hold on to, real life simply fades into the background."

She was quiet for a while, solemn, thoughtful.

Presently she said she knew a boy who went to the war nearly two years ago. He would have been 20 years old now, almost 21, almost a man.

I looked at her for a long moment, asked who the boy was.

She didn't answer. She reached for my hand, intertwined her fingers in mine.

A deep sorrow seemed to descend on her. Tears began to well in those beautiful brown eyes. There was a great pain there. She squeezed my hand. I sensed there was a desperate need in her to soothe a boy she knew was on a path to certain peril. As I looked at her a realization settled on me—

Not all casualties of War are in the Combat Zone.

Thirteen—Loss

That afternoon my weather window opened and I was able to get off for Clark. But not so fast. The weather had been good but was deteriorating rapidly when I left. I lost my radio shortly after takeoff, and I was faced with the unhappy prospect of penetrating Taiwan and Philippine airspace and flying the weather approach at Clark without any sort of radio contact since I was flying alone. Tainan was pretty well socked in by this time so there was no point in going back there. Besides, I was anxious to get to Clark, so I pressed on.

As I motored silently through the Taiwan ADIZ [*Air Defense Identification Zone—a designated area in* the *sky that normally required clear identification to enter*], I kept expecting a National Chinese F-104 to intercept me, but no one paid any attention to me. I made it to Clark without incident but found them to have a solid overcast with no holes to let down through.

Normal procedure without radio contact called for simply flying the standard instrument approach without clearance. In such cases, the ground controlling agency is supposed to be aware of your predicament and clear the airspace for you. While I never had much confidence in the alertness of approach control, I had no other choice, so I dropped the speed brakes and descended into the murk. With a great deal of relief, I broke out at 3,000 feet and could see where I was going once again. I soon found that Clark was landing opposite to the way I was approaching, but after a little aggressive maneuvering I was safely and happily on the ground.

A Follow Me truck met me in de-arming [*a space at the end of the runway where safing pins were inserted in the drop tank pylons*] and led me to the transient parking ramp.

"The radio has failed," I said to the crew chief, "but otherwise she should make it to Vietnam."

He nodded. I filled out the "781" [*flight log and maintenance status form*] and walked into Base Operations. I asked the sergeant behind the counter if they had any formations heading to Vietnam. "I'm the pilot of the F-100 that just landed from Tainan," I said.

"We have one leaving tomorrow morning," the sergeant replied. "I can put you in that—unless you want to stay in the real world for a while longer." [*"Real World" was a slang term used by people in Vietnam to refer to any place outside the combat zone.*]

He must have been in-country at some time, I thought.

"No," I said. "Put me in. I need to get back."

What a strange thing for me to say, I thought. Has Tuy Hoa and the War become my real world now?

While I was at Base Ops, I called Approach Control to see if they had tracked me. Not exactly. They said they had cleared the airspace as advertised, but they never picked up my emergency radar beacon and they hadn't monitored my approach at all. In fact, they were carrying me as overdue and missing. With that, I went to the Officers' Club bar.

Early the next morning I launched from Clark in the company of two F-4s and another F-100 for the trip to Vietnam. Again, my radio was acting up, but I wasn't worried, I had plenty of help this time. About 100 miles or so from the coast of Vietnam, I lost my AC generator [*it quit operating*]. Now this may or may not be serious. The AC generator is mounted on the face of the engine compressor. If it is just an electrical issue, there was no real problem; we have backup electrical systems for essential things. At times, however, the generator begins to come apart physically, sending bits and pieces through the engine. At such times it inevitably becomes necessary to jettison the aircraft lest it becomes a coffin. For this reason, our emergency procedures called for landing as soon as possible.

Naturally, the weather in Vietnam was terrible so things were pretty tense for a while. The other F-100 in the flight led me down through the weather for an emergency landing at Phu Cat, the nearest airfield from our position over the South China Sea.

My airplane kept running so there was no big problem. By that time, however, I had had it with that airplane and abandoned it in favor of another Tuy Hoa bird that was stranded at Phu Cat. I took off for Tuy Hoa.

As I slipped south along the coast on the short flight to Tuy Hoa, my thoughts turned to Liz and her loss and anguish. Since then, I've thought about her from time to time, wondered how she is, wondered if she has made peace with her loss. I never saw her again, but even now, memories of her and that morning keep seeping into my mind.

Fourteen

Looking Ahead
(or Slipping Away?)

Despite the rejuvenation I felt from my trip to Taiwan, I was becoming increasingly anxious about my future, including my future with Jean. As explained in Chapter Eleven, there was no want for excitement in the missions we flew, but my mood had become dour. Fortunately, this didn't affect me once I was in the airplane—except I was too reckless at times.

Jean was focusing more and more on the new life she would have after graduation—a job, her own apartment, freedom from the restraints of parents and the school regimen. I was both pleased and wary that she was beginning to realize that she could meet life on her own terms.

At the same time, I was dark and gloomy in my letters to her. I had not helped matters with my pessimism and cheerless ruminations on what life with me might be like. Rather than looking with optimism on the coming end of my time in Vietnam and the end of our separation, I chose to dwell on the worst possible outcomes.

Both Jean and I could feel our relationship slipping away. This was ironic since we were quickly closing in on the end of our separation. But the question loomed—could the relationship be saved? Would we even want to see each other when I returned to the States in May?

Despite my dark mood, I could still appreciate and write about the awe-inspiring beauty and forces of Nature.

⸭ ⸭ ⸭

March 16, 1969

My Dear Jean,

After a few harrowing experiences I finally made it back to Tuy Hoa ... and my latest adventure in the Far East drew to a close.

The trip was a bit of a letdown for me, I think.... In fact, I was anxious to get back to Tuy Hoa just because I felt certain that I would have a letter from you waiting for me here. (Imagine my discomfort at not finding any such.) At any rate, as I said in my previous letter, I found Taiwan to be cold and dreary. It raised a response of foreboding in me. I felt restless there, anxious to leave. I think what it is, is that I am anxious to go home.... Another dreary city with its endless empty wind-swept streets is no longer a lure to me.... I really find it difficult to conceive that soon my year here will be over, and I will be returning to the States. It seems as if I have spent a lifetime here. I guess that in a sense it had always lurked in my mind that I might spend the rest of my life here. Now that the end is indeed in sight, I don't know what to make of it really. Suddenly I must build a future that goes beyond this.

The author by his F-100D. Suited up, ready to climb into the cockpit (author's collection).

Fourteen—Looking Ahead (or Slipping Away?)

How are things with you these days? Are you terribly busy? Let me see, your quarter should be just about drawing to a close now, I should think. I hope that you enjoyed your sojourn at the Casa. Will you be living at the dorm for your last quarter? And finally, what about after graduation? Have you any more definite plans now? I'm anxious to hear.

I must close for now.

Be good now—

Love, Stu

P.S. The picture I've enclosed was taken by my airplane. It's not very good, but I thought you might enjoy it.

✣ ✣ ✣

March 21, 1969

Dearest Jean,

So you have not forsaken me, after all. I can tell you that my life had been pretty dark and despairing during the weeks of your prolonged silence. I had reached the point where I could no longer ignore the fact of your silence. There seemed to be only two possible explanations: either something had happened to you physically or else you had indeed forsaken me. I don't know which possibility troubled me the most. My imagination ran rampant with the latter possibility. But I could not bear to even consider the former. As hurt and angry as I was at your sudden disregard for me, I was more frightened by the prospect that some harm had befallen you. I pray that never happens.

At any rate, the arrival of your two letters (Mar 11 and Mar 14) on the 19th dispelled an incredible gloom from my heart.... You can't imagine the depths of despair to which your silence had plunged me.

I'm sorry that the problems that started between us have caused you so much anguish, as they obviously have by your most recent letter. I did not mean to sound so pessimistic in my letter when I gave voice to these matters. In part, I was very disappointed by my assignment, and by my prospect for the immediate future. I was unkind and wrong to expect you to share the disappointment. I only did so because you are a constant companion of my thoughts, and as such you must be privy to my sadness as well as my joy.

The other reason that I perhaps overstated the adversity that my life holds is because I wanted you to understand fully what life with me might be like.... I wanted you to be fully cognizant of the realities of a life together—and to accept and want it in this full knowledge. It could be immensely joyful so taken.

This letter has been incredibly difficult to write. You would not believe how long I have pondered these few meager lines. And yet they merely touched what I want to say. The things and thoughts I wish to communicate to you dance just out of reach. But it is late, and I am weary, and the damnable war waits as always with the dawn. I should rip these lines asunder and replace them with some happy banalities.

I'm glad that you said you will not give me up.

Love, Stu

✦ ✦ ✦

March 26, 1969

Dearest Jean,

How are you on this bright beautiful spring day? The sun here is so bright and radiant today, so luxuriantly warm and beautiful that I think that you must be happy and smiling, whatever you are doing.... I certainly hope that you are happy.

Right now, I am recuperating from a strenuous night on night alert. That means that I am lounging in the sun on our new mown lawn, trying to return my tan to its former state of bronze beauty. Last night was one of those nights when I had to earn my pay. We were scrambled first in the wee hours of the morning and then again into the gathering light of the new day. The thunderstorm season is just starting here, and it seems that a night mission must invariably carry you into the very heart of one thunderstorm or another. At first there are only the blinding flashes of lightning to warn you that you are approaching a massive thunder boomer. Then suddenly you're in it, the stars are blotted out and the airplane is tossed about as a toy. St. Elmo's fires sprouts in a purple fan from the end of the pitot boom and the refueling probe. Large aquamarine droplets of St. Elmo's fire trickle back along the canopy like large luminescent raindrops. At times, the leading edge of the wings glow with the same ghostly green. All the time, the radio crackles and snaps, the airplane lurches violently and the brilliant flashes of lightning momentarily arrest all movement like a gigantic strobe light. Then the airplane hangs momentarily suspended over the inky abyss of the cloud, released for the briefest instant from its desperate struggle to survive, a brief respite before it is once again plunged with inconceivable violence into the total darkness that follows.

But if the brutal fury of nature is daunting, then the splendor of her artistry is captivating. The dawn this morning—witnessed from high above the earth—was an image of repressed fury. The dawn smoldered in

Fourteen—Looking Ahead (or Slipping Away?)

deep reds and quiet oranges far out over the sea to the east, behind white pillars of clouds. The pillars seemed determined to hold back the fire that raged beneath the horizon. Like the shell of a house that is consumed by an inferno within but maintains its same façade without until, in one terrifying moment, the fire explodes and engulfs it, so too the dawn built the heat of its colors behind its gate of clouds. Its rise slowly consumed the eastern horizon until it could be restrained no longer, and it exploded the day upon us. The massive pillars suddenly became orange-tinged clouds floating lazily above the shimmering blueness of the sea. The explosive transformation of the empty, darkened void below us, into color and form and substance was startling. The universe out of the void as it were.

It is a fringe benefit of my job that occasionally it permits me to view in awed wonder the capricious majesty of nature as she dabbles with her colors and forms solely for my amusement. Of course, these benefits are not always evident, nor is the desirability of the job. I hope to God, however, that I will never lose the ability to look at these incredible canvases and see what has been done there. Nor do I ever want to lose the inner awareness and exhilaration that comes from soaring in effortless, capricious grace high above seas and forest, nor the sheer boundless joy of dashing playfully up the fleecy canyons of an airy, magic world of clouds high above the earth, nor the heart-stopping excitement, the fearful fascination of racing headlong just above the trees, rivers, beaches of the world, scant inches from its physical being but light years away from its reality. It is an elixir, and I guess that I am hopelessly addicted.

Jeannie, how I wish I could make you understand all of this; no, more than that, I would like to make you a part of this facet of my life. I would like you to share as well as understand my exuberance, my excitement, my wonder of the sheer joy of this, my love for flying, if you will.

What is happening to us, Jean? Our yearlong separation is rapidly drawing to a close, and yet now, more than ever, I feel that you are slipping away from me. We were so close for those few days in Hawaii, and now we seem to be separated by a murky abyss that is made of more than miles or minutes. With the promise of being together again nearly fulfilled, you seem somehow to have withdrawn beyond my reach. If I have hurt or offended you in the past few months with too much frankness or too little understanding, then I am deeply sorry. I hope that the damage done will not be irreparable.

Be good now—

Love, Stu

P.S. Did I tell you that brother George is coming to Tuy Hoa? He will get here about the middle of April so we will have nearly a month to fly together. Perhaps in that time I can impart to him some of my invaluable wisdom on how to stay alive in the combat zone. It will be fun to fly with him at any rate.

※ ※ ※

April 1, 1969

Dearest Jean,

I'm happy to find that I have been reinstated on your regular mailing list—and, I hope, returned to a position of some favor with you. Your recent letters, particularly the one of the 25th, have aroused a multitude of confused questions in my mind.

Note: There followed a couple of paragraphs that vastly overstated the impact on my morale by what I viewed as her neglect of me. But I thought it didn't hurt to make her feel a little sorry for me.

I'm glad to know that you have landed a job and one which you can be enthusiastic about. I might also add that I am happy for you that the money was not the final arbiter in your selection of a job. I'm not sure that such consideration falls within the purview of my wisdom any longer.

[Jean had written on March 11 that she would be getting an apartment by herself after school; that none of her girlfriends would be sharing the apartment with her.] I hereby submit for your consideration my application for the vacancy that presently exists in your future apartment/home. Somehow, I don't seem to care if you are an exceptional cook or not. I think that it would be very wonderful to share a bit of your life with you.

Be good now—I will be seeing you very soon. Perhaps then all of this silly business will be swept away by you and I being together.

Love, Stu

※ ※ ※

Note: In her letter of April 4, below, Jean responded to my question, "What is happening to us?" from my letter of March 25. It well describes the effect of trying to reach across a void when the means of communicating is so inadequate and erratic. It confirms the uncertain state of our relationship. I received it on April 9.

What is happening to us? I'm not completely sure, but you were right when you said what we had is slipping away. There is probably a combination of factors working here. One, of course, is the fact that letters are not a very substantial way of loving or receiving love. There have been needs I

Fourteen—Looking Ahead (or Slipping Away?)

feel I have expressed which you have remained insensitive to. But I know I am terribly insensitive to many of your needs also. I can't really blame you for any of the difficulties in our relationship. They spring primarily from the situation. You have been pushing me towards getting a job and establishing myself independently and yet you have been the first to cry. You foresaw neither the trauma nor the inevitable result. Months of panic began to resolve for me when I got a job. Another adjustment was made when I realized none of my girlfriends would be moving into an apartment with me. All right, I've overcome my many fears and now I'm really looking forward to graduation. And now it's your turn to panic. You're beginning to feel now what I felt in Hawaii, with one important exception, and I don't think it is necessary to expound on that. I can't say you rejected me because you didn't. But I did feel that you pulled your support away from me. In addition to that, may I remind you of a couple of the letters you have sent to me since then? One told me in many words that there was no future for us unless I could learn to appreciate you on your own terms, which ultimately would mean I would have to revamp my whole personality structure. The other letter said that our future depended on my ability to learn to love misery. If you ever want to tell anyone about the cruelty in our relationship don't forget to mention those two. But again, and I want you to make a <u>very special note</u> of this, this type of thing is to be expected because an intimate relationship makes very special demands on the people who enter into it, and it is easy to expect too much from each other. I don't think we should blame each other for what we experienced as being cruel. Didn't we always mean the best? I didn't mean to hurt you nor you I. We are changing but our relationship always gets stuck in the past. A once-good way of relating grows stale ("happy banalities") but nothing replaces it. That quality that transcends the paper and ink loses its power slowly until there isn't really any communication at all. Then we grow lonely, and we panic. We feel we've lost each other, and we have. We need so much time together. When are we ever going to have it? I don't want you to feel sorry for yourself. If I refuse to give up, then you have no right to give up either. In spite of everything, I still think we can work something out. And besides, I do happen to love you.—Jean*

❉ ❉ ❉

Note: When I wrote the letter below I hadn't gotten Jean's letter of the 4th. That's why this letter is totally out of context with the state of our relationship. Another example of the inadequacy of our means of communication.

---

*Tuomy, *Is Love Enough?*, 240.

April 7, 1969

My dearest Jeannie,

I am presently engaged in the arduous task of building up my tape library so that I will have endless amounts of good music to comfort me during the long winter months in Minot. Right now, I'm sitting here watching the little reels on the tape recorder going around and round, some fast, others more slowly, like wheels racing to cover some bit of ground, yet going nowhere. It's difficult to believe that the spinning wheels are working in concert. As the tape slowly threads its way past tape guards and heads, as it slowly recedes from the one reel and slowly fills its mate, the plaintive sounds of Peter, Paul and Mary (in this case, I guess I'm regressing) fill my little room. It is all very sad, but I'm sure it will be a great comfort to me in the darkness that lies ahead. Isn't this playing at war terribly strenuous?

Soon I shall have my Big Brother here to look out for me. Or rather, I think it will be my responsibility to watch over him and see to it that he makes it through those first critical 20 or 30 missions without buying the Farm. George should be here in about a week, and I must say I am eagerly anticipating his arrival. We will have about three weeks to fly and drink together before I return to the real world. It's a shame we couldn't be stationed together longer. The entire base seems to think that it is outstanding that he will be coming here, flying the same airplane in the same squadron, etc. etc. I think it is a first ever—for this war anyway.

But let me explain. About a week and a half ago at happy hour one Friday night, I was talking to one of the wheels at Wing headquarters, about the situation and about how great it would be to fly with George for a while. He politely informed me that George and I would never fly together as long as he had anything to say about it (and he has a lot to say about it) because he would not take the responsibility of sending us both out on the same combat mission, endangering both of us at the same time and thereby running the risk that we both might bite the bullet on the same flight. As he said, "How could I write a letter to your mother if that should happen?"

Well, I quickly assured him that my mother understood these things and the inherent dangers, etc., and would not mind. One thing led to another until the colonel conceded that if I had a note from my mother okaying such things, George and I could fly together. All of this was in good fun, but the challenge was given, so I fired off a letter to my mother explaining the situation and asked her to write a note of permission. Well, today I received her reply, and it made me ashamed of myself.

For me, the whole thing was a bit of a joke; she took it all quite seriously. Her letter was excellent. After reading it I began to think there might be some point to this madness, after all. I'm sure that my cynicism will reassert itself shortly, however.

[See the following chapter for a discussion of my mother's letter.]

April 8

I had to interrupt this letter last night. I was so weary that I found it really impossible to remain awake.

Did you have an interesting Easter vacation? I'm afraid that this was one holiday that crept up on me completely unnoticed. I had no idea it was Easter until I went to breakfast early last Sunday. The dining hall had some peculiarly colored hard-boiled eggs which I thought was unusual but attributed it to the early hour and my bleary eyes. I mumbled through my briefing in a sleepy daze and wandered out to my airplane, finally becoming aware of my surroundings. There to greet me was my airplane laden with four gaily decorated bombs that had been cleverly disguised as Easter eggs. It was only then that I became fully aware that it was Easter. I hope that you and your family had a very merry Easter.

Be good—

Love, Stu

✣ ✣ ✣

April 9, 1969

Darling Jean,

I just received your letter of the 4th of April, and I think that I have just been put down bad. I've got to say you really socked it to me this time. But I'm glad to see that you are finally seeing fit to tell it like it is with yourself. If nothing else, that is infinitely preferable to the torturous uncertainty of silence.

There's just one more factor to consider when condemning my insensitivity. It may or may not be relevant. Here in Vietnam, I am engaged in the prosecution of a war. The primary objective in war is to kill people. It is entirely possible that tomorrow I won't have any sensitivity, period. You must forgive me if I am preoccupied at times.

Note: There followed several paragraphs in which I try to justify my insensitivity to the pressures she was under. Mostly, I was too self-absorbed to appreciate what was happening to her in her pending transition from school to life after school. This discussion asks the pertinent question whether we have grown too far apart to recover what we had with each other. The letter concludes as follows:

Although you made no mention of wishing to see me again in your last letter, you did profess to care for me. I will be in Los Angeles around the 12th of next month (I don't know my exact itinerary yet.) for the exact express purpose of seeing you. I hope that you will receive me. I trust that we can recapture what is rightfully ours.

I'm anxiously awaiting your reply.

Love, Stewart

⚜ ⚜ ⚜

Note: Jean received my letter above around the 15th or 16th. In the interim, she had written two more letters, dated April 8 and 12. They were both more conciliatory, but also anguished at our inability to resolve our issues. In her letter of the 12th, she did conclude by saying, "*I wish you would stop by LA. I would like to see you....*" Her next letter (April 17) began,

I went to my mailbox today strongly hoping there would be a letter there from you. I then realized you probably hadn't received my last letter (of the 12th) yet, and so I wouldn't hear from you for several more days.*

In turn, having not heard from her since her letter of the 8th, I wrote on the 18th but couldn't respond to any of her anguish or despair. I could only refer to her letter of the 8th. And so it went. In her following letter on April 21, she again said, *"...no mail today."*

It was maddening. We simply couldn't have a conversation. At a critical, maybe fatal, point in our relationship we could only throw our thoughts blindly into the mails and hope that they were received sometime, somehow, and hopefully with understanding.

Her letter of April 21 was the last letter I would receive from her while I was in Vietnam. I could only write her as cheerfully as I could and hope for the best.

---

*Tuomy, *Is Love Enough?*, 251.

Fifteen

George

George and I were both born during World War II—he in October 1942, I in May 1944. Our father was a pilot during the war. He remained in the Air Force following the war, finally retiring in 1962, just as I graduated from high school.

George and I were inseparable growing up. We were always referred to as a pair—"the boys." He was the big brother, but it hardly seemed to matter. In the dozen or so moves our family made in those growing up years, we were the only constant for each other—companions, fellow adventurers, mischief makers, rivals. We learned to ride horses together, to skin dive, ice skate, water ski, drag race the family car—a stock Plymouth Valiant (We won our class—G stock eliminator)—discover girls. Along with some friends, we bought a boat that had been sunk in a hurricane. Together we made it sea worthy again.

In school, George was two years ahead of me and we lost that everyday togetherness when he graduated from high school. We went to different colleges. George enjoyed college life more than I did. It took him awhile and several different colleges to graduate. I was more diligent. I graduated in four years.

When we graduated, the Vietnam War was in full bloom. We both were in ROTC in college and both wanted to be fighter pilots. But now we had a role reversal. I was the first to go to pilot training and the first in Vietnam. George followed me by a year.

My letters back home over my year in Vietnam make a number of references to George's progress through pilot training. Assignments out of pilot training were based on class standing and we both did well enough to get our first choice—F-100s. We both savored the possibilities of him being assigned to the 308th with me and being able to fly combat missions together. This chapter tells that story.

⚜ ⚜ ⚜

As described in my letter to Jean (April 7), the leadership of the 31st Tactical Fighter Wing was reluctant to permit us to fly together for obvious reasons. "What would your mother say if one or both of you got shot down? We won't take responsibility for that." Ultimately they agreed to allow it if I got permission from our mother. My letter to her asking her permission is provided below.

Friday, March 28, 1969

Dear Mom,

I address this brief letter specifically to you for a very good reason. The news that George will be joining me here at Tuy Hoa in a few short weeks has just been received and noticed by the Wing—and I mean the entire wing. For the most part everyone thinks this situation is just outstanding. Exactly my sentiments. I have already contrived to have George assigned to the 308th and have made arrangements for him to take over my airplane when I leave. The squadron is all for putting me on IP [*Instructor Pilot*] orders temporarily so that I can check George out in the combat zone.

Well, all that is beautiful, but this evening at TGIF I was talking to the assistant DCO [*Deputy Commander Operations*], and he said under no circumstances would he take responsibility for George and me flying together on the same combat mission. After a bit of chiding from me and some of my compatriots, he said he would reconsider if I had a note from my mother saying this was all right with her. Ergo, I respectfully request that you forward, by return post if possible, a note to the effect that it is perfectly all right with you if George and I fly together on combat missions. I'm not really certain if the good colonel was joking or not, but at any rate, such a note from my mother would be highly hilarious, and the source of much amusement to all of us squadron jocks. I assure you there is no danger in this undertaking.

Everything is going well for me these days. We have been flying a great deal these past few weeks. Even with my trip to Taiwan I will probably get nearly 50 hours in the F-100 this month. To say that I have been very busy is an understatement. And now, of course, the end of my year in Vietnam is very much in sight. I find that now I view the end of my tour here with mixed emotions. On the one hand I am anxious to go home, but on the other hand, I am looking forward to George's arrival here and am very sorry that we won't be assigned together here for a longer period. I almost wish that I had extended my tour here in Vietnam for a period so that George and I could have flown a bit more together. I imagine he will find it hard enough to arrive here a "new guy" and find his younger brother is the "old head." I'll try my best to give him the

Fifteen—George

benefit of my experience and accumulated wisdom, and teach him, in a few short weeks, how to stay alive in this silly war.

As I said, everything is fine with me. I will be back in the States on or about the 9th of May. Of course, I think that a brief sojourn in Los Angeles will be in order so I can't say exactly when I will be home. Sometime around the 22nd or so, I should think. I'm looking forward very much to seeing you all on the old homestead.

I hope that everything is going well for everyone back there. Dad, it sounds to me as though you are spending too much effort on your job. I'm glad, however, that you can find it so absorbing. I'm very curious about the changes to the old house, of course.

I must close for now. Be good, everyone—

Love, Stu

P.S. Mother, I'll anxiously be awaiting the arrival of your note of permission.

※ ※ ※

Note: Unfortunately, I don't have a copy of her letter back to me. The gist of it was that she understood the necessity of facing sacrifices in a time of conflict. She, as a young wife in late 1941, had sent her husband, a B-17 pilot, off to his war. She dreaded the possibilities, but she also understood the importance of doing his—and her part—for this great trial her country faced. They had been stationed in Alaska where he was doing cold weather testing on a variety of aircraft. In mid-December, all of the dependents (wives and children) in Alaska were gathered together in Anchorage and transported by ship to Seattle. She went on to her family home in Kansas. The men turned their attention to the Aleutians that Japan would soon invade. The 1,000-mile war as it is known. She said it was hard to let him go, but she knew it must be. So, if it was necessary for two of her sons to face similar perils, to be crew mates in this conflict, she could not object. Some things are more important than personal loss. Her husband, my father, returned to her in late summer 1942, unscathed but not untried.

※ ※ ※

I participated in George's checkout flights and subsequent combat missions (but not in the same airplane). The following letters (Jean, April 18; Mom & Dad, April 22) describe his arrival, the checkout process for him and my final combat flight with him as my wingman. The Wing, in fact the entire base, was enthralled with the prospect of this situation. There was also considerable public affairs coverage of us flying together.

Author and his brother George in the cockpit of a F-100F. George is in the front cockpit. This is a PR photograph, as we were not allowed to actually fly in the same aircraft (U.S. Air Force Det 8 600th Photo AAVS [MAC]).

George went on to have an illustrious tour in Vietnam. In September, he volunteered to join the "Misty" FAC program. Misty FACs were "fast FACs" that flew F-100Fs at low altitude along the more dangerous stretches of the Ho Chi Minh Trail where normal FAC aircraft could not survive. George was "Misty 129"—each Misty pilot had a number, sequentially recognizing their participation in the Misty program. There were a total of 155 "Mistys" through the life of the program. George flew 55 missions between September 1 and December 25, 1969. His tour in Vietnam was curtailed, reflecting the robust pilot manning as the war progressed. He returned to the States in February 1970.

In an interview, George explained that the Misty FACs flew two seat F-100F models. There were two pilots in the airplane, the front seat pilot was responsible for flying the aircraft while the back seat pilot acted as observer, looking for possible targets. Both roles were demanding. Misty pilots were qualified in both roles and would do either as assigned.

For survivability against defenses along the Trail, standard tactics called for staying 4,000 feet above the ground at airspeeds over 400 knots while continually changing altitude, bank angle, and heading. This prevented anti-aircraft guns from tracking them. But with those conditions, it was difficult to spot potential targets in the heavy foliage along most of the Trail, George said. The Misty's only weapons were 2.75 inch smoke rockets and the F model's two 20mm cannons. But, when a target was discovered, the Misty could call in air strikes which the Misty would control. The smoke rockets were used to mark the target.

George noted that the Misty missions were long and tiring, typically five hours or more. The lengthy flight times required multiple air refuelings which provided a bit of relief from the tension and danger of the mission itself. The two pilots alternated these refueling sessions, and a friendly contest always developed as to who was quicker and smoother in their refueling period.*

Note: The Commando Sabre (or Misty) program lost 32 airplanes with 7 pilots killed or missing in action during its existence from June 1967 to May 1970.†

* * *

April 18, 1969

My Darling,

As they say in the jargon of the war zone, I am getting short (i.e., I am ready to go home and will be doing so shortly). This state of being short engenders a change of attitude which I finally find myself indulging in. I just recently realized that in a little more than three weeks (not three lifetimes or years or months) I will be home and in your arms. I can actually consider that as a realistic possibility. Hence, I must raise my minimums and stop doing foolish things in the pursuit of this silly war. The danger ceases to be something to laugh at and defy and becomes something to be taken very seriously, to be calculated and considered. When that happens, one is indeed "short," and it is time to go home. It is time for me to go home. The caution and concern of new guys over here is only outdone by the caution of the guys that are short. And those of us in the latter category have a year of experience to help our cunning schemes to stay alive. I will be home soon.

Speaking of new guys, George arrived at Tuy Hoa last Tuesday evening. He was well introduced to the ineffectiveness of our war after spending two days trying to get from Saigon to Tuy Hoa. It is little

---

*George Cranston, Interview with Stewart Cranston, Unpublished, Clifton, VA, 2024.
†Misty. First Person Stories of the F-100 Misty Fast FACs in the Vietnam War.

trouble coming the 14,000 miles from the States to Saigon, but those last 200 miles are a real chore. It is not a little disconcerting to arrive at Tan Son Nhut, eager to get to war and ready to sacrifice all if necessary and find that nobody there takes even the slightest notice of you. It is up to you to find a ride upcountry to whatever base you are going to. But when George got here, we gave him a cold beer (or a half dozen) and a comfortable bed, and his spirits brightened immensely. Now he is all enthusiastic about plunging into the thick of things. He has his first flight today (just a checkout ride, not a combat mission) and should get his first taste of combat tomorrow. He sat in on one of my briefings on Wednesday, for one of our more dangerous missions, and was a little bit disconcerted, I think, by our informality and apparent lack of concern for the fire expected, etc. As I explained to him later, you have to develop a fatalistic attitude towards these things and not worry about them. Still, I can well remember the temerity with which I faced my first mission, and first enemy fire, and I can sympathize with him. It is the unknown element in all things that makes them frightening. And it is only after you develop enough confidence in your own ability to cope with the situation that it will lose its frightening aspect. Of course, it is difficult if not impossible to have this self-confidence until you have had your baptism in fire and have survived not just once but often enough that you know that it was your knowledge, strength and courage that brought you through, and not blind luck.

It seems to me that life itself must seem a frightening curse to those people who have never had to face it and thus have never discovered the extent of their own will and courage and strength. They have nothing upon which to base any confidence in their own ability. It is strange that these people are the first to cry of the futility of life and to hide from it. They never give themselves a chance to live and to know life. In a way I am grateful to this war for what it has taught me about myself.

Your last letter (of the 8th) was very nice. After months of confusion ... you seem to have a certain peace again. You seemed again to be the wonderful person I know. And for the first time in months your letter conveyed a certain confidence in the existence of a future for us. That makes me very happy.

The other thing I wanted to comment on was your statement that life is an ugly business. Ah Jean, what am I to do with you? You despair too easily. Your probing intellect and great sensitivity divine things from life that others overlook, and you are wounded by what you see. But you are too quick to overlook the beauty in life and too ready to be wounded. You haven't had your reaction to life tempered by hardship, yet.

I wish that I could take you by the hand and show you the endless beauty and wonder that life holds. I wish that I could lead you by the sea at sunset, when the ocean gently caresses the beach, when the breeze plays through your hair and the quiet of twilight descends upon the earth. I wish that you could soar with me up the tumbling slope of a boiling, cottony cloud and on, weightlessly, into the immense blue beyond. I wish that you could walk with me through the cities of the world, to wonder at the manifold accomplishments of man, to grasp the beauty of the toil of minds and bodies that are enshrined in the buildings and streets of those cities. I wish that we could wander aimlessly through high mountain virgin forests to sense and feel the majesty of nature. But I also wish that you could see the storms that rage from time to time upon that same seacoast as the ocean tries to tear the shore, its mate, asunder. I would that you could know the fear, terror even, that is a part of that soaring flight, and the quiet assurance of the skilled hands that have met that fear and conquered it. I wish that you could see the misery, the despair that lies on the periphery of the world's great cities. That too is a product of man's toil, his blind, stupid, blundering toil. And I wish that you could feel the wave of despair that would engulf you as you looked at that forest with the knowledge that you must conquer it, or it would conquer you. And finally, I wish that you could know the understanding that lies in the storm, the human hardship, and nature that has been conquered and bent to the will of man. I wish that you could know the weariness of body and the peace of mind that is your reward for having worked to your limit and beyond to take what is yours from life.

I wish that I could give you some secret to life. I wish that I could give you happiness. But of course, I can't. You are the source of your own happiness. It is your will to happiness that is the final arbiter in the happiness of your life. I shall always be there to help you as I can, but in the final analysis, I cannot give you happiness, nor can I make life beautiful for you.

Well, I guess that I got a little carried away with my commentary. I hope that a little of what I said meant something to you.

I'll be seeing you soon.

Love, Stu

※ ※ ※

April 22, 1969

Dear Mom & Dad,

George arrived here safe and sound a week ago ... he is here and settling down into the routine of things. He has had one combat mission so far, just a back seat "F" [*two seat F-100 model*] ride to take a look at things. The last two days he has been trying to get his first front seat ride but the F model keeps breaking and his IP and I have to press on in "D's" to accomplish the mission. Poor George is left standing on the ground feeling very frustrated, I know. We're going to have another go at it again today.

The base has made a big deal about us being stationed together. Apparently your letter swept aside all objections to our flying together. It was really an excellent letter, Mother. They won't let us fly in the same airplane, which is understandable, but I am being scheduled to lead all of George's checkout missions (if we can get one off of the ground). The squadron commander has been a big help in this respect. He is all for this thing and has lent his influence to see that we are scheduled together.

Apparently, the wing commander's staff's comment to the USAF information office at 7th Air Force has had considerable impact. I understand there is a news team coming up from Saigon tomorrow evening to cover the human-interest aspect of this thing. Look for us in the *Air Force Times*. I'm a little cynical about the publicity side of the Air Force so I'll believe all of this when I see it.

As for myself, I'm getting ready to leave the war in George's capable hands. I have a port call for the 9th of May which means that I will be in the States (McChord Air Force Base, Seattle, WA) on the morning of the 9th of May. I still plan to proceed to LA via San Francisco and from there to Virginia.

Now that the time is drawing near to leave, I find that I am getting more and more anxious to do so. I had rather expected to feel quite the opposite, a bit reluctant to leave this experience. I find it growing a bit stale and I'm looking forward to returning home to new adventures. I think perhaps I'm a little too bitter and cynical about this war business now to gain much further from it.

Both George and I enjoyed your last letter, Dad. Your advice is well taken. But rest assured that when one is "short" as I am, caution far outweighs any youthful exuberance or foolishness (but that's not to say I can't enjoy flying).

Well, I must close for now and go brief this mission with George again. I'm anxious to see you all and the $40,000 remodeling of the house.

Say hello to Ronnie for me.

Love, Stewart

⁕ ⁕ ⁕

Fifteen—George

Below is a transcript of a press release from the 7th Air Force, April 1969:

NEWS RELEASE

United States Air Force
Directorate of Information, Headquarters Seventh Air Force
Tan Son Nhut Air Base, Republic of Vietnam
APO San Francisco 96307
For Immediate Release

APR 1969

Cranston Brothers Make
Life Hot for the Viet Cong

by SSgt Jim White

Tuy Hoa (7AF)—The two Air Force fighter pilots, their sweat-stained flight suits clinging to their bodies, walked into the debriefing room. As they settled into a pair of chairs at a small gray table, an intelligence debriefer entered, sat down and put an air strike report form on the table.

"Who was the Flight Leader?" the debriefer inquired.

"Me," one of the pilots responded, "Lieutenant Cranston."

"And who was your wingman?"

"Lieutenant Cranston" came the reply.

"I already have you, sir," the debriefer said, looking up. "You were the flight lead, right? What was your wingman's name?"

"I was the wingman," the second pilot interjected, "and I'm Lieutenant Cranston, too."

Puzzled, the debriefer looked at the two men. Slowly awareness dawned.

"Why, you must be related," he exclaimed. "You even look alike."

"Right," the first Lieutenant Cranston smiled. "We're brothers."

After completing their post-flight debriefing, the two brothers relaxed in the 308th Tactical Fighter Squadron lounge and, over coffee, discussed their situation.

"Finding brothers together in a war zone is pretty unusual," commented Stewart, 24. "Regulations say that two members of the same immediate family don't have to serve in a combat zone at the same time. We wanted it that way, though."

"Actually, we won't be together that long," added George, 26. "Stu has almost finished his year and I just got here. Our tours overlap just enough for him to break me in as his replacement."

Both men, sons of Colonel (USAF, retired) and Mrs. George E. Cranston of 6700 Newman Rd., Clifton, Va., fly F-100 Super Sabre fighter-bombers with the 31st Tactical Fighter Wing at Tuy Hoa Air Base.

"I volunteered for Vietnam and knew I'd be flying F-100s," George pointed out, "so I asked to be sent to Tuy Hoa, where Stu was stationed. I knew it would probably be the last chance I'd have to see him in quite a while. Besides, I wanted to be able to fly a few combat missions with him."

"And flying together," Stewart added, "provided something of a problem. Believe it or not, we had to get a note from our mother before we could both go up on the same mission. The wing officials didn't like the idea of putting a pair of brothers into a situation in which both of them could get shot down at the same time."

Flying together is nothing new for the Cranstons. When George was 14 and Stewart was 12, both boys became members of the Neurnburg Germany Aero Club. They finally earned their pilots' licenses in college while enrolled in the Air Force Reserve Officers Training Corps program.

"Of course, flying jets in combat is a whole lot different from puttering around in light planes," George said. "I'm glad Stu's been around long enough to give me a few tips on how it's done. On the other hand, there are advantages and disadvantages to being your brother's replacement in a combat unit. You're expected to live up to the reputation he's spent a year building, and it's going to be hard."

"I'm sure George will do as well as I've done, and probably better," Stewart protested.

"I'm going to try," George conceded. "I want to spend a year here putting my bombs on the target and doing my job like a professional. Like the wing motto says, I want to [*Return with Honor*]. But it's still going to be hard to match Stu's record."

"It's been an enjoyable and personally satisfying year," Stewart admitted. "My only regret is that I didn't have more time to fly with George. In fact, I thought about extending my tour, but by the time I found out he was coming here, it was already past the cutoff date for extending."

"I'm sorry we didn't have more time together too," George added, "but the pointers Stu's already given me are going to be a lot of help."

"Speaking of pointers," Stewart said, "there are a couple of things I wanted to mention about that mission today. Let's go eat lunch and talk it over."

"Right," George replied.

Wrapped up in their discussion, the brothers Cranston walked out the door into the sun-splashed Vietnam afternoon.*

※ ※ ※

April 22, 1969

Dear Jean,

As you said in your last letter, we must put an end to this unhappiness. That is precisely what we will do in a few short weeks for a little while anyway.

I will be returning to the States via McChord Air Force Base in Seattle, Washington. Apparently, the Air Force in their infinite wisdom is going to attempt to acclimatize me to the frozen north as quickly as possible. I think, however, that I will spoil their plans by spending as little time as possible in Seattle. In other words, I'm going to take the first available plane to San Francisco and should be in San Francisco on the evening of the 11th. Right now, I plan to spend that night in San Francisco. I have some friends there that I can impose upon for a day or so and they have insisted that I stop by and see them. I plan to jet on to LA on the morning of the 12th. All of this is subject to change of course and I may arrive the evening of the 11th. I will try to give you a little advance notice anyway before I get to Los Angeles.

In addition to getting my personal affairs in order, I've also been flying a pretty heavy schedule. I am trying to get to 300 missions before I leave. Right now, I have about 288, so I am getting close. I've only about 12 days left to fly, however, so I don't know if I'll make it or not. The last few days I have been flying with George on his checkout rides. He's had two combat rides now in the F model or two seat version of the F-100. He should start flying the single seat tomorrow or the next day. He said after his first ride, "That's not as bad as I thought it would be, in fact, it was kind of fun." And so it is—most of the time. I've had my fill of the whole miserable affair, however.

I hope you get caught up on all of your schoolwork before I get there. I plan to take up a great deal of your time while I'm there. You shall be the object of my undivided attention. At least when I'm there

---

*Jim White, "Cranston Brothers Make Things Hot for the Viet Cong," *Official Air Force News Release* (Directorate of Information, Headquarters Seventh Air Force), 1969.

this time I won't have any of my family about demanding part of my time. And yes, I will be most happy to assist you in the darkroom, but I refuse to keep track of the time. I have spent too much effort counting the slow progress of days over here.

I'm terribly sorry that our relationship has been so miserable these past few months.

Well, I must close for now. Be good and don't make any dates for after the 10th of May.

Love, Stu

✢ ✢ ✢

April 27, 1969

My Darling Jeannie,

Today is recovery day from the zoo that we had last night (a "zoo" is a party and is so called because of the animal-like behavior of the participants). The zoo was held in honor of the departure of the "young sports" of which I am one. It was our going away party or go-away party, as the case may be. It was characterized by a few platitudes mouthed about the departing people followed by drunken revelry on everyone's part. These are usually pretty good parties. This one last night ended up with me riding my motorcycle down the hall of the BOQ at three AM. Fortunately, injuries were slight. It was a highly successful party.

The 308th undertook the unfortunate project of completely remodeling our bar about two months ago. Before it was a rather drab, barn-like affair that wasn't too inviting. Well, we undertook to redo it completely, even going so far as to air condition it. This all proved to be a good project while it was going on. It was ambitious enough that it kept all of the drunks busy and out of trouble for a full month and a half. As must happen with all good things, this came to an end on April 6. On the evening of that fateful day, the bar was finished and initiated. Since then, the 308th has been engaged in a marathon zoo. The "Sabre Lounge" as it is affectionately known has become the home away from home for all fighter pilots on the base. We have to assign a zoo-keeper every night to watch over the animals. Between the booze and games like dead bug, half of the squadron is only in a very questionable ready-for-flying state. Actually, the combat missions are tame compared to the dangers of a full combat zoo. I hope that I survive the next two weeks so that I will return home to you unscathed. (By the way, you will be happy to know that George was undaunted being thrust into this trying environment and has adapted himself admirably thereto. Of course, he has had considerable experience in this area.)

Last Friday I went to Udorn, Thailand, for the day to do some last-minute shopping prior to going home. Thailand has some very nice jewelry (very cheap) and of course is famous for the Thai silk and bronze ware. Among other things, I bought a beautiful 100-piece set of bronzeware and of course a complete bar set made of bronze. There is an air base at Udorn, and I was forced to reflect that the people there have a racket as far as fighting the war is concerned. They have such touches as mini-skirted waitresses in the club, etc. How primitive Tuy Hoa seems by comparison. Matt, if you remember him, is stationed there and I enjoyed seeing him again. He is married now, and his wife is in Bangkok.

Your last two letters were very good and enlightening. Some of your statements showed remarkable insight and have been very thought-provoking for me.... This battle you say you have been fighting is one that I can't help you with. You must discover your own mind.... One thing you mustn't do is doubt the strength of your own will.... You ask in your last letter if I were not waiting for you to grow up a little. I think that perhaps I am. I hope that doesn't offend you. I have no doubt of your ability to face our situation maturely.

You know, I'm only slowly beginning to understand the trauma you have been through these past few months. I probably still don't fully appreciate the magnitude of the choice which you see yourself faced with. But at least now we have begun to communicate again. I can now understand the nature of your anguish and the source of your pain, and to feel a great compassion and sympathy for your struggle. I can see now that I have asked far more of you than I had any right to ask. I wonder now that you didn't forsake me for a more likely prospect. I didn't appreciate your struggle before, and I apologize for my lack of insight.

I must close for now. Be good—until I see you again that is.

Love, Stu

Sixteen

Fini and Home

Finally, it was May and my tour in Vietnam was coming to an end. Strangely, I had mixed emotions about leaving. It had been a challenging year, a year of both growth and loss. Growth in my skill as a pilot and maybe even growth in my maturity as an individual. Loss in the friends that would not return with me. I would miss the flying, certainly, and the camaraderie of the squadron. I think what I would miss most was the sense that the mission counted above all else. Whatever it took, get the job done.

But the war was changing and the rule of regulations was settling in. For example, we had battled our way through the most vicious weather Vietnam could throw at us to complete our missions, and now the Air Force wanted us to take an instrument check ride to prove we could fly in weather. Soon flight suits would probably not be permitted in the O'Club.

It was time for me to leave. I was scheduled to have my fini flight with George on Monday the 5th of May. On Sunday, he and I had a good mission up above Qui Nhon, at an abandoned village that was being used by the NVA as a supply depot. It was beautiful skimming back along the coast to Tuy Hoa. But when I checked in with the tower, the mobile officer came up on the radio and said, "Just wanted to let you know this is your fini flight, Stu. You're off the schedule tomorrow." So, that's it, I mused to myself. The brass doesn't want me beating up the airfield as was the tradition.

As I led the flight up initial, I felt a sadness for what I now knew would be my last flight in the F-100. At mid-field, I made a standard pitch-out (180-degree turn) to downwind, lowered the landing gear, turned final and landed. My war was over.

✦ ✦ ✦

Author after traditional "wetting down" to mark the end of his final flight in Vietnam. Homeward bound (U.S. Air Force Det 8 600th Photo AAVS [MAC]).

May 3, 1969

Dearest Jeannie,

I've been trying to get all of my affairs in order over here prior to going home. I'm sifting through my accumulated acquisitions. I am surprised at some of the things I've bought over here. And still, I could easily spend another $500 to $1,000 on things that are too-good-a-bargain to pass up. As well as trying to order my life a bit, I'm also still flying, still trying to get to 300 combat missions. I've just passed the 500-combat hour mark, another one of my little personal goals.

I planned to fly my last combat mission on Monday, the 5th of May. If you don't hear any dreadful news by that date, you'll know that I've cheated death and survived my year. Did I say that I've stopped doing foolish things? I didn't believe myself today as I went after four 37-millimeter anti-aircraft gun sites. Nobody was hit (of course it was under my sterling leadership), but I'm definitely too short to do that sort of thing. We followed up the guns act by strafing a truck that the FAC had suddenly spotted. All of this was in rather unfriendly country (that is, it was decidedly unfriendly). I plead temporary insanity. Although I'm normally mild mannered, the cockpit of my friendly F-100 has an adverse effect on my better judgment.

After I finish flying, I'll have several days around here to get everything packed and shipped, as well as a little time in the tropical sun to ensure that my beautiful bronze tan is up to par. I'm very excited at the thought that in scarcely more than a week I'll be seeing you again. I trust that your hair is now down to your waist and that it is still a golden blonde. (Do I have an idealized vision of you? Of course!) I plan to stay in LA for 10 or 12 days if I don't wear out my welcome sooner. I'm interested in hearing all of the devious plans you mentioned in your last letter.

I was also happy to hear that you've undertaken such energetic pursuits as tennis. I was sorry that you were motivated by such a dreadful thing as an asthma attack. I'm certain that I don't fully appreciate the gift of my own exceptional health. At any rate, your pursuit of a physically demanding sport such as tennis is most encouraging. You'll find yourself loving life for its own sake yet.

Until I see you, then, be good,

Love, Stu

✢ ✢ ✢

May 7, 1969

Dear Jeannie,

Well, I'm about through with this place. I've just finished shipping my hold baggage which was a real chore. I didn't believe all of the junk that I have collected this past year. I'm just a little bit worried about my stereo equipment. I just hope that it makes it back to the States without too much damage. I wasn't too impressed with the way they handled my stuff.

Now I have nothing to do but sit and bask in the sun and wait to leave in a couple of days. I'm leaving Friday and the entire trip will take a day and a half to two days. First, I must go down to Cam Ranh Bay where the planes to the States originate. I'll have to spend the night at Cam Ranh since my flight is scheduled to leave at 12:30 in the afternoon. It's almost a must to go down to Cam Ranh on the day before because of the uncertainty of travel in-country. Anyway, the trip back to the States (which is via Japan) will take about 20 hours. So, I still plan to see you either Sunday evening or Monday morning as I told you before. It will be so good to be with you again.

I had my last mission last Sunday. George and I got to fly together on it, which made it really outstanding. It was a good mission with an extensive NVA supply point to strafe, so I went out with guns blazing so to speak. It was a lot of fun. I miss the flying already. Still I'm looking forward to returning home.... I'm most anxious to see you again.

Well, I hope that you are all caught up on your schoolwork and that you have arranged your social calendar so that I can take up your every waking moment for many days.

Remember.... I will see you soon then you can stop being good.

Love, Stu

✤ ✤ ✤

Home

The return flight from Vietnam was long and tedious, just as the flight to Vietnam was. But this time there was no apprehension of what lay ahead, what dangers lurked in the coming months and year.

I went down to Cam Ranh Bay a day early as was necessary because travel in-country was uncertain. The airplane to the States took off the next afternoon. At liftoff there was muted cheering as we see sometimes in the movies. But for most of us onboard, the feelings were mixed. We had survived our year of peril, made new friends and lost ones, old and new. It was a time of reflection, not of celebration. Was the year worth it?—That was for each of us to answer for ourselves.

The flight was through Yokota in Japan for refueling, then on to Anchorage, Alaska, and finally to McChord AFB, just outside Seattle. We were met by a representative of the United States Government—a Customs and Emigration Officer. He greeted me with:

"Well, Lieutenant, what are you bringing back you aren't supposed to have?"

After clearing customs, a few of us that didn't have someone meeting us wandered into base ops. It was empty. Presently, we asked the sergeant behind the counter, "How do you get to the Seattle airport from here?"

He replied, "Well, there's a bus that comes along every couple of hours, or you can catch a cab at the curb outside."

We opted for the cab.—Welcome home!

The Seattle Airport was very crowded—it seemed to be awash in young people in various stages of "flower child" dress. They glared at us in our rumpled military uniforms. The girls seemed to send the most hateful looks, but thankfully there were no physical encounters.

In those days, the major airlines offered service members in uniform the option of traveling standby at half price. This interjected uncertainty into travel plans, but on a lieutenant's pay, it was too good a deal to pass up. I managed to get to San Francisco that evening, where I had friends from college to take me in. I needed to decompress.

I arrived at LAX mid-morning on May 12. Jean met me as promised. Whatever lingering apprehension that may have existed from our recent letters evaporated in the instant of our first embrace. We were together again—all else was lost in the simple wonder of each other. This began 10 wonderful days in which we were inseparable. We visited our old haunts—the beach, Santa Monica Pier, Griffith Park, her family's mountain cabin. We dined at the Sea Lion again, shopped on Rodeo Drive, lunched at Century Plaza (Jean's soon-to-be place of employment). But mostly we just enjoyed each other's presence.

And we talked. We talked of ourselves, of our pasts and our futures, of our differences and our samenesses, of growth, of longings, of desires, of love. At last, face to face, we were able to explore our understandings of each other unhindered by the intervening miles and delayed mailings that had resulted in so much miscommunication and anguish. She told me she was now excited about her immediate future—her job, her apartment, being her own person. She also told me in no uncertain terms that I could go challenge fate as much as I liked, but that was not her. If we were to have a future I would have to accept her on her terms just as she accepted me on mine. I began to realize that she was beginning to be comfortable with herself. I had pushed her to taste of life and now she was looking forward to just that. Had I pushed too hard? Would she find a different future? Would I lose her? Over our year of separation she had discovered how capable she was, as well as determined. She was beginning to see she could have the future she wanted on her terms. Was I ready for that? We didn't talk of marriage. We both sensed this was not the time. We both needed time to come to peace with these new understandings.

Jean's time was not entirely her own—school beckoned; the demands of her studies could not be entirely ignored. But even in this all was not lost. I was able to spend time with her in the college dark room as she completed tasks for her photography course. On one evening's trip to Mount St. Mary's Photography Dept., I got cut off on the merge between the San Fernando Freeway and the 101. I had to brake sharply, and Jean's ancient VW bug lost momentum. As we struggled up the long hill to the Hollywood Hills crest, barely making 45 mph, cars zoomed past on either side. Soon, a blue flashing light appeared in the rear window, and I managed to pull over to the side.

"You were going too slowly," said the officer. "I'll have to cite you for obstructing traffic."

We chatted as he wrote up the ticket. Yes, I was just back from Vietnam; he was in the National Guard. No matter. Here's your ticket. But the humiliation of it all!—Me, a fighter pilot, cited for going too slow!

Alas, our interlude together had to come to an end. She was in the final weeks of her senior year at Mount St. Mary's College. Finals loomed large in the background for her. I had to begin to get on with my new life in America—visit my own family, buy a car, get ready for my new assignment in the Air Force. On May 22, Jean and I said goodbye at LAX once again, and I boarded a plane to Virginia.

✦ ✦ ✦

Note: Over the next week, Jean wrote a single letter keeping me up to date:

May 22. It is unfortunate you were able to get that flight today. The drive back from the airport this afternoon, the dinner call, unbelievably grim.

May 25. I've developed two pictures of you. They're really cool. In one you are just starting to laugh, and in the other one you are very still and somber. The two of them make a nice contrast together. The somber one is quite dark. It looks like it must have been taken at night, with moonlight instead of sunlight coming in the window. There is a fierce, almost unapproachable quality about it. You look like you are in a very dark mood, and my feelings go out to you because of it. In the brighter picture you look like you are enjoying giving me a bad time. I love it when you tease me, although you do drive me nuts.

May 27. I've turned in my senior paper about two hours ago. What a relief that it is finished.... I've been honored by home economists, by the faculty and pretty soon by the alumni. Good grief. Where were all these people when my classmates and I needed the encouragement? This reminds me of all the supporters I suddenly had when we came in second place at the convention.... You have been right in the decisions you have made about us. It must have been very hard for you at times. It must have been hard when you knew I had been hurt.... I have a good deal of growing up to do before I make anyone a good wife.

May 29. It was sweet of you to write my mother that letter. I hope your parents don't make you work too hard. But remember it's good for your character and it's good for your build.*

---

*Tuomy, *Is Love Enough?*, 270–272.

※ ※ ※

May 26, 1969

My Dearest Jean,

I arrived here in Virginia without incident about 8:15 Thursday evening. My parents had decided not to disown me after all and were there to meet me at the airport. They just moved back into the old house, and it was (and still is) in shambles. Most of what was left of the Thursday evening was spent in a detailed tour of the old house inspecting the changes from top to bottom, from basement to attic. It is really quite nice and I'm sure they'll love it—if they ever get things straightened about.

Friday, I helped my mother unpack all of the junk she had stashed away during the remodeling. Saturday, we straightened the house up, and on Sunday we stored away construction material and hauled away the trash. I plowed a couple of garden plots and mowed hay. This farm work is very nostalgic to me and I'm enjoying it immensely.

I looked at a couple of '67 Corvettes today. One of them was quite nice, but I think the asking price ($3,500) was just a little steep. If I can get it for a few dollars less I may buy it. Somehow, I just can't get too excited about cars right now. (That reminds me, be sure to let me know what I owe your mother for that traffic citation.)

I hope that you have been very, very busy since I left. I'm still hopeful that I'll be able to come to your graduation on the 14th. (You better graduate.) No doubt you have had much better luck with your photography class now that you don't have me to distract you in the dark room.

How wonderfully patient you have been with me. Work hard now and be good. I really enjoyed my stay with you and your family. I think your family is very nice.

Love, Stu

※ ※ ※

Aftermath

In early June 1969, I bought the Corvette and headed to Perrin AFB in Sherman, Texas, 50 miles north of Dallas. This was a temporary assignment for training in the F-102, as a lead-in to the more sophisticated F-106 I was to fly at Minot. Travel from Perrin to Los Angeles was easy, if expensive, and I was able to attend Jean's graduation on June 14. She moved into her new apartment and started her job at Century Plaza on June 23. We were able to spend weekends together a number of times over that summer.

From early October to mid–November, I was at Tyndall, AFB, in Panama City, Florida, where I trained to fly the F-106. Travel to Los Angeles was not practical from Panama City, so we were back to letters. But I was home in Virginia for Thanksgiving, and Jean came east to be with me for that holiday. On December 8, I packed the Corvette and started my travels to Minot. I arrived there on December 10.

If Minot was cold, the reception by my new unit, the 5th Fighter Interceptor Squadron (5 FIS), was warm and welcoming. I settled into the new base, going through the usual processes to become qualified in the squadron's airplanes and missions. I was busy, and the days passed quickly, but Christmas was fast approaching, and Jean and I were once more separated. But at least now we could talk and were not constrained to the uncertain flow of letters.

A few days before Christmas, the squadron operations officer said to me, "Stu, we need to get some flying time on the T-33s before the end of the year. Could you take one of the birds before Christmas and do that for me?"

I said, "Yes, sir. Where do you want me to go, and how much time do you want?"

He said, "Well, go anywhere you want, just try to get us 10 hours of flying time."

A little flight planning showed it was about five hours of flying time to southern California. On December 23, I was on my way. I got to Los Alamitos NAS in the early evening of December 23. Jean met me. We celebrated Christmas with her family.

Mostly we just spent a marvelous five days together, just savoring each other's presence, confirming the bond that had always existed between us. She was comfortable with herself now. She told me she had her job review coming up, and she expected a good raise, maybe even early termination of her training program. She had worked hard for this with intelligence, competence, and determination. She was pleased with herself. If we married I would be asking her to give up all that was familiar to her. Could she do that now, I wondered?

My ambivalence finally resolved itself. You can't know the future. You can only take what life has offered and do the best you can. Differences are not weakness in a relationship; they are strengths if the bond is tight. In marriage, we would be together, not as a mirror of myself, but as a mutually supporting partnership built on our love and understanding of each other. Jean in her wisdom had always understood that. I was the slow learner.

I asked her to marry me. She said, "Yes."

We were married on August 8, 1970, at "the Farm" I had spoken so fondly of in my letters home. It was a bright summer afternoon, not yet the sweltering heat that can mark a Virginia August. The view down the hill from the yard fence where we took our vows was lush with the ripening summer hay swaying in a gentle breeze—just as I remembered from my youth. In many ways, I was "Home."

We settled happily in Minot, North Dakota. The days were bright, and the future was promising. Then, during the spring of 1972, Jean's childhood asthma began to re-emerge. This sickness deepened into the summer, and just six days before our second anniversary my precious Jeannie died. Impossibly, I was the one left behind. I was the one left with the task of facing a life without her. But for her sake, I knew I must begin anew. That was what Jean would want. As she wrote in one of her letters—

One of the greatest sins is to spend the present living in the past. If the present is unlivable, then the proper place for the mind is the Future. Where would we be if we didn't always hope in the Future?—The definition of Hell.

Epilogue

The United States did not have the will to stay the course and prevail in South Vietnam.

Under President Johnson, the U.S. tried to resolve the Vietnam conflict diplomatically, while maintaining military pressure in the South, and interdicting supply and transportation targets in the North. Johnson's bombing halt of November 1968 was meant as a gesture to entice North Vietnam to the negotiating table. It would remain in place until March 1972 when President Nixon renewed limited bombing to increase pressure on the North to negotiate in good faith. It was all to no avail. In December 1972, in a final push to force negotiations, Nixon unleashed heavy bombardment of the Hanoi area. This included mass formations of B-52s. This worked. A peace accord was signed in February 1973.

If the number of combat forces involved is a measure of the progress of a conflict, then the U.S. and South Vietnamese forces were winning the war in the late 1960s and into the early '70s. As the U.S. was able to increasingly turn combat operations over to the ARVN (Army of the Republic of Vietnam) U.S. troop strength dropped from over 536,000 in 1969, to just 24,000 in 1972. This drawdown was foreshadowed in the Air Force with the curtailment of pilot tours starting in 1969, as happened to George. Tuy Hoa AB closed in 1970.

In January 1971, the ARVN invaded the southern part of Laos in an attempt to shut off the continuing flow of war materials to NVA forces operating in the South. The incursion was successful, but the gains were not consolidated. In the spring of 1972 North Vietnam launched a major assault on South Vietnam with tanks and other conventional weapons. After intense fighting, this assault was repulsed by the ARVN supported by U.S. airpower.*

---

*John Shrega, "South East Asia" in *Case Studies in the Development of Close Air Support* (Office of Air Force History, 1990), 467.

Epilogue

In 1974, the U.S. Congress voted to cut off all funding support for South Vietnam. By that time, U.S. military forces in South Vietnam had dwindled to less than 100. In April 1975, the North Vietnamese People's Army of Vietnam launched a conventional invasion of South Vietnam. The invasion quickly turned into a rout.

In the end, the United States did not have the will to win the Vietnam War. We didn't lose in Vietnam so much as we simply quit and abandoned the people of South Vietnam to their fate.

I do not regret my time in Vietnam, nor have I ever felt my small part in that conflict was a waste. I learned much about myself—and life and loss. And we did stem the march of Communism—but inevitably, other forces of tyranny and oppression would rise to take its place.

Strangely, the Americans who bore the brunt of America's war in Vietnam were vilified by their fellow citizens. At least as portrayed in the popular media. Most Americans were simply indifferent to the war and its sacrifices—unless it directly affected them. In 1982, a monument to those killed in the Vietnam War would join the other war memorials on the Mall in Washington, D.C. The memorial is a powerful statement of the human cost of war, inscribing each of the names of those 58,318 who paid the ultimate price for America's war in Vietnam. But the country remained largely ambivalent towards that war and the men and women who fought it on America's behalf. It would not be until the early 21st century, when America herself felt the blow of tyranny on 9/11, that her soldiers, sailors and airmen would once more be held in high regard by the American people.

Military History of Stewart E. Cranston

Stewart Cranston was commissioned a 2nd Lieutenant, United States Air Force, upon graduation from the University of Southern California in June 1966, where he earned a Bachelor of Arts degree in mathematics. He entered active duty on September 6, 1966, to attend Undergraduate Pilot Training (UPT) at Laredo AFB, Texas. He was a Distinguished Graduate of UPT in September 1967 and was then assigned to F-100 upgrade training at Luke AFB, Arizona. In May 1968, he was assigned to the 31st Tactical Fighter Wing, Tuy Hoa Air Base, Republic of Vietnam as an F-100 pilot providing close air support to ground operations and interdicting North Vietnamese supply lines to their forces in South Vietnam. While in Vietnam, he flew 300 combat missions comprising 514 combat flying hours and was awarded the Distinguished Flying Cross and the Air Medal with 15 Oak Leaf Clusters.

Following Vietnam, Capt. Cranston was assigned to the 5th Fighter Interceptor Squadron, Minot AFB, North Dakota, as an F-106 interceptor pilot. While at Minot AFB, he attended the Flying Safety Officers course at USC and was assigned the additional duty of squadron safety officer. In August 1972, he was reassigned to HQ USAF, the Pentagon, Washington, D.C., as a participant in the Air Staff Training (ASTRA) program for promising young officers. In this assignment he helped establish the Sea Launched Ballistic Missile long-range radar system to detect submarine launched missiles, and he served as assistant to the air staff office responsible for the F-15 program.

While at the Air Staff, Capt. Cranston was selected to attend the Air Force Test Pilot School (TPS), his long-standing goal. In November 1973, he was transferred to Edwards AFB, California, to attend TPS. The TPS curriculum involved rigorous aeronautical engineering academics as well as practical exposure to flight test techniques in a variety of aircraft. He was a Distinguished Graduate of TPS and in December 1974 was assigned to the 475th Test Squadron, Tyndall AFB, Florida, where he participated in advanced weapons testing on the F-106. At Tyndall, he was the primary test pilot for an advanced gunsight concept. This project culminated in a demanding, very high angle off gun engagement against a PQM-102 drone in which he successfully shot down the target aircraft. The achievements of this test program were recognized by the Air Force Association with a Citation of Honor.

From August 1978 to June 1979, Maj. Cranston attended Air Command and Staff College at Maxwell AFB, Alabama. He was a Distinguished Graduate from this program as well as earning a Master of Business Administration from Auburn University at Montgomery. Following Air Command and Staff College, he was assigned to HQ USAF in the tactical aircraft requirements division. In this role, he was responsible for developing the requirements and program for the Advanced Tactical Fighter, which later was procured as the F-22.

In June 1982, Lt. Col. Cranston was assigned as Squadron Commander, 3247th Test Squadron, Eglin AFB, Florida. In this assignment, he oversaw all flight activities for a fleet of 41 aircraft of eight different types including F-4, F-15 and F-16. He was an active test pilot and was mission qualified in the F-4 and F-16. In May 1984, he became the Director of Projects for the Advanced Medium Range Air to Air Missile (AMRAAM), which was a breakthrough in air to air missile technology. His primary responsibility in the assignment was ensuring the prime contractor would achieve the first flight milestone of the missile. During this assignment, he continued to be an active test pilot in the F-16.

From August 1985 to June 1986, Col. Cranston attended the Industrial College of the Armed Forces (ICAF) at Ft. McNair, Washington, D.C. ICAF's primary focus is developing the management skills of senior military officers in all aspects of supplying equipment and materiel for combat forces. His dissertation at ICAF, recounting the early development of the ATF/F-22, is an important historical paper for future weapons development programs. After graduating from ICAF, Col. Cranston was assigned as the Commander of the Air Force Systems Command (AFSC) Inspection Center where he led a team of experts in assessing the unit readiness and effectiveness of subordinate units of AFSC.

In July 1987, he became Commander, 3246th Test Wing, Eglin AFB, which was responsible for flight and ground testing, including all support activities, on the Eglin Range complex. The 3246th Test Wing was also responsible for Air Force test activities on the White Sands Missile Range (WSMR), New Mexico, including specialized test capabilities such as the 10-mile-long supersonic rocket test track at WSMR.

Military History of Stewart E. Cranston

From July 1988 until June 1989, he served as Assistant Deputy Chief of Staff for Systems, Headquarters Air Force Systems Command, Andrews AFB, Maryland, overseeing all Air Force weapons systems development programs. From June 1989 until April 1990, he was Director of Special Programs, Office of the Assistant Secretary of the Air Force (Acquisition), Headquarters USAF, Washington, D.C. In this role he was responsible for the budget of highly classified weapons programs. In April 1990, he became Vice Commander, Aeronautical Systems Division, Wright-Patterson AFB, Ohio. He was promoted to Brigadier General on December 1, 1990.

In July 1992, Gen. Cranston was appointed Deputy Chief of Staff, Test and Operations, Headquarters Air Force Materiel Command, Wright-Patterson AFB, Ohio. Then in May 1993, he became Commander, Air Force Development Test Center, Air Force Materiel Command, Eglin AFB, Florida. In this position he conceived of and directed development and demonstration of a concept in aerial weapons that capitalized on precision guidance to reduce the size and explosive weight of bombs. This concept is now incorporated in the Air Force weapons arsenal as the Small Diameter Bomb family.

In December 1997 he was promoted to Lieutenant General and assigned as Vice Commander, Headquarters Air Force Materiel Command, Wright-Patterson AFB, Ohio. He held this position until his retirement from active duty on March 1, 2000, having served his country for 33½ years.

Lieutenant General Cranston's decorations include the Distinguished Service Medal, Legion of Merit, Distinguished Flying Cross, Meritorious Service Medal with four oak leaf clusters, Air Medal with 15 oak leaf clusters, Air Force Commendation Medal with oak leaf cluster, Combat Readiness Medal, Vietnam Service Medal with four service stars, Republic of Vietnam Gallantry Cross with Palm and various unit citations for excellence.

Bibliography

Commando Sabre Operating Instruction 55–1. Department of the Air Force. 1969.

Cranston, George. Interview by Stewart Cranston. June 2024.

Cranston, Stewart. "Just a Routine Combat Sky Spot Mission." *Friends Journal of the Air Force Museum Foundation* 45, no. 4 (Fall 2022): 10–16, 39.

Cranston, Stewart, and Jean Tuomy. *Is Love Enough? Letters from Vietnam*. Amazon KDP, 2023.

Davies, Peter, and David Menard. *F-100 Super Sabre Units of the Vietnam War*. Osprey Publishing, 2011.

Day, Bud, Jim Chestnut, Ray Lee, et al. *Misty. First Person Stories of the F-100 Misty Fast FACs in the Vietnam War*. Edited by Don Sheppard. 1stBooks. 2000, 2002.

Pfaff, James. "The KC-135." *Friends Journal of the Air Force Museum Foundation* 47, no. 2. (Spring 2024): 10–12.

Schandler, Herbert. *Lyndon Johnson and Vietnam: The Unmaking of a President*. Princeton University Press. 1977.

Shrega, John. "South East Asia." In *Case Studies in the Development of Close Air Support*, edited by B. Franklin Cooling, Office of Air Force History, 1990: 411–473.

Welch, John. "Report of Administrative Security Staff Assistance Visit." Headquarters 31st Tactical Fighter Wing (PACAF). Unpublished. 1969.

White, Jim. "Cranston Brothers Make Things Hot for the Viet Cong." *Official Air Force News Release*: Directorate of Information. Seventh Air Force Headquarters. 1969.

Index

Numbers in **_bold italics_** indicate pages with illustrations

A Shau Valley 22, 27, 62, 108
additional duties 22, 32, 72, 113, 152, 155, 199
Air Medal 76, **_96_**, 199, 201
air refuel, air refueling 73, **_74_**, 75, 110, 142–145, 179
aircraft losses 18, 45, 56, 61–62, 72, 77, 133, 179
alert 14, 29, 32, 34, 36–37, 68–69, 70, 72–73, 76, 110, 116–117, 120, 123, 125, 135, 137, 139–140, 155, 158, 168
anti-aircraft artillery (AAA) 26, 29, 96, 108, 142, 150, 180; see also ground (enemy) fire; small arms fire; ZPU; ZSU
arresting gear see barrier
ARVN 197
attack on Tuy Hoa 12, 60–61, 72, 158

Ban Karai 141, 149–150; see also WAAPoM
Ban Me Thout 68
barrier 25, 35, 87, 133
Bien Hoa 6, 7, 14, 16, 35, 80
bombing halt 95–96, 110, 117, 141, 149, 197; see also Johnson, Lyndon
Bullpup training 50

C-130 12, 32, 33, 35, 60–61, 77, 80, 115
Cam Rahn Bay 68, 133, 155, 190, 191
Cannon AFB 13, 46, 71, 73, 83, 109
Charlie 21, 27, 39, 41, 61, 68–69, 72, 82, 83, 117, 153, 158; see also NVA; Viet Cong
Christmas 8, 83, 112, 114, 118, 120–123, **_124_**, 125, 155, 195
Clark (AFB) 11–12, 50–52, 55–56, 114, 116–117, 160, 162–164

Commando Sabre 179, 203
Cranston, Mrs. Frances (aka Mom) 9, 18, 27, 34, 46, 56, 68–69, 73, 80, 82, 100, 109, 117, **_124_**, 155, 172, 176, 181–182, 184, 194
Cranston, George 28, 34, 56, 57, 73, 82, 101, 109, 155, 169, 172, 175–176, 178–186, 188, 190, 197, 203
Cranston, Col. George E. (ret) (aka Dad) 9, 27, 34, 35, 46, 56–57, 68–69, 73, 80, 82, 100, 109, 117, **_124_**, 155, 175, 177, 181–182, 184
Cranston, Janet 56, 83, 109, **_124_**
Cranston, Ron 56, 182
crew chiefs 20, 37, 94, 103, 111–**_113_**, 125, 163

Da Nang 85, 88
Distinguished Flying Cross **_134_**, 135, 199, 201
DMZ (17th parallel) 5, 47, 65, 84–85, 149
Duc Lap 72–73, 80, 82
dumb head injury 27

Easter 173
election, voting 95
Emerald Knights **_14_**, **_124_**; see also 308th Tactical Fighter Squadron
enlisted force 103, 112, **_113_**, 120, 125

F-4 18, 115–117, 133, 137, 155, 161, 164, 200
F-100 6, **_7_**, **_24_**; cockpit 23–**_24_**, 25; flying characteristics 23, 40; slats 23–25; weapons 25, 26
FAC 17, 20–22, 26, 29, 37–39, 41, 82, 109, 132, 134, 142, 145–148, 158, 178, 189
flight/element lead checkout 80, 81, 109

205

Index

G suit, G's 15, 27, 36–37, 104, 145
ground (enemy) fire 16, 18, 22, 26–27, 39, 41, 108, 117, 132–133, 158; *see also* anti-aircraft artillery (AAA); small arms fire; ZPU; ZSU

Hawaii 34, 63, 82, 97, 99, 102, 110, 115, 120, 122–123, 125, 128–130, 133, 135–136, 152, 157, 169, 171
Ho Chi Minh 5
Ho Chi Minh Trail (Trail) 6, 75–76, 141–143, 148, 149, 152, 178–179
Hong Kong 56, 69, 77–80, 83, 98, 114
hooches 13, 61, **63**, 69, 153; *see also* quarters; trailers

interdiction 6, 141, 197, 199
IRAN 117, 158

Johnson, Lyndon 62, 95, 141, 197, 203; *see also* bombing halt

Karst 141, 145

Laos 6, 26, 29, 75, 96, 141–142, 145–146, 148, 152, 197
Laredo AFB 8–9, 116, 132, 156, 199
Liz 162–164
Luke AFB 8, 13, 28, 44, 50, 69, 71, 199

maid 55, 76, 99
mail service 1, 19, 32, 98, 103, 106, 120, 156
Manila 10, 50–53, 55–56
McChord AFB 182, 185, 191
Mekong 7, 33, 75, 132, 141, 145, 149
Minot AFB 152–154, 156, 158–159, 172, 194, 195–196, 199
Misty 178–179
Mobile 67, 72, 98–99, 111, 139, 188
monsoon 65, 82–84, 100
morale 1, 103, 104, 170
Mount St. Mary's College 8, 102, 129, 137, 152, 192–193

napalm 18, 22, 25, 36, 38, 40, 45, 158
Nixon, Richard 95, 141, 158, 197
North Vietnamese People's Army of Vietnam 198
nose wheel steering failure 44, 57–58
NVA 6, 39, 60, 84, 132, 141, 142, 149, 152, 188, 191, 197; *see also* Charlie; Viet Kong (VC)

on flying 30–31, 169

Pagsanjan Falls 52–54
parties, "zoo" 63, 104, 186
Peacock 88, 89, 91, 142, 145
personal flying equipment 15, 16, 142
Phan Thiet 33
Phu Cat 17, 29, 35, 44, 65, 117, 164
pilots killed 18, 29, 44–45, 54, 77, 104, 137, 155, 179
pranks 104
press release 183–185
protests 54, 95–96

quarters 12, 13, 14, 112, 124; *see also* hooches; trailers

R&R 34, 63, 114, 128
real world 8, 82, 88, 114, 163, 172
Reese AFB 56, 73, 117
refueling *see* air refuel, air refueling
relationship, with Jean 8, 43, 48, 105, 107, 116, 120, 128–130, 165, 169–171, 174, 180, 186, 192, 195; *see also* Tuomy, Jean, letters from
Richard 71–72, 95, 97–98, 102–106, 108, 120, 131

Saigon 6, 12, 16–17, 27, 35, 65, 68, 78–79, 83, 108, 132, 179, 180, 182
St. Elmo's Fire 66, 89, 168
SAM 26, 70, 142
San Francisco 9, 10, 54, 98, 154, 182–183, 185, 192
Sara 10, 50–55, 70, 98
Seattle Airport 191
shot down 18, 20, 29, 61, 63, 72, 176, 184, 200
Sky Spot 3, 33, 84–85, 89–91, 94, 203
small arms fire 26, 39, 61, 70, 108, 132, 158; *see also* anti-aircraft artillery (AAA); ground (enemy) fire; ZPU; ZSU
Snake Eyes 25, 38, 133
spatial disorientation 89, 91–92
Special Forces 27, 68, 72–73
Stars and Stripes 95
sunrise, descriptions 66, 97, 168–169
Super Sabre 7, 69, 184, 203
survival training 9, 11–12

Taichung 115, 117, 159
Tainan 115, 117, 158, 160–161, 163
Taiwan 51, 56, 114–116, 158–159, 163, 165–166, 176
Tan Son Nhut 12, 17, 33, 78–80, 151, 180, 183
Tchepone 141–142, 145
Tet 5, 6, 139, 152–153, 158

Index

Thailand 66, 117, 187
31st Tactical Fighter Wing 6–7, 14, 36, 85, 176, 184, 199, 203
308th Tactical Fighter Squadron 6, *14*, 28, 95, 124, 148, l75–176, 183, 186; *see also* Emerald Knights
thunderstorm, descriptions 17, 46–47, 64–66, 70, 85, 168
trailers 13–15, 112; *see also* hooches; quarters
Travis AFB 9–10
troops in contact 17, 35–38, 40, 133
Tuomy, Jean 2, 3, 7–8, *19*, 59, 152, 194–196, 203; letters from 30, 47, 58–59, 69, 71–72, 102–104, 106–108, 126, 130–131, 136–137, 138, 154–155, 157, 170–171, 174, 193; *see also* relationship, with Jean
Tuy Hoa 6, 7, 10, 12–14, 17, 45, 60–62, 72–73, 75, 82–84, 101–102, 112, 133–134, 141–142, 155–156, 158, 176, 179, 183–184, 187, 197, 199
typhoon 65, 66, 101, 117–118

Udorn 187
University of Southern California (USC) 8, 54, 80, 155, 199

Viet Cong (VC) 5, 6, 12, 15, 17, 27, 29, 38–39, 60–63, 72–73, 82, 99, 100, 108, 124, 139, 152, 158, 183, 185, 203; *see also* Charlie; NVA

WAAPoM 148, 150–151, *150*; *see also* Ban Karai
weapons load crews 111–112
weather 26, 46, 57, 65–68, 82–83, 84–85, 87, 89, 93, 100–102, 110, 123, 133, 142

ZPU, ZPU-4 132, 150
ZSU 146

www.ingramcontent.com/pod-product-compliance
Ingram Content Group UK Ltd.
Pitfield, Milton Keynes, MK11 3LW, UK
UKHW042001140426
5217IPUK00015B/926